Inner Alchemy

Energy Work and the Magic of the Body

Inner Alchemy

Energy Work and the Magic of the Body

By Taylor Ellwood

Introduction By Lupa

Megalithica books

Stafford UK

Inner Alchemy: Energy Work and the Magic of the Body
By Taylor Ellwood

Contact Taylor at taylor@spiralnature.com
or email him at http://www.thegreenwolf.com.

Cover by Nemo Boko (http://nemo.org)
Design & Layout by Jo-Ann Byers
Editor: Lupa

Set in Perpetua

First Edition by Megalithica Books, 2007

0 9 8 7 6 5 4 3 2 1

A Megalithica Books Edition
An imprint of Immanion Press
http://www.immanion-press.com
info@immanion-press.com

ISBN 978-1-905713-06-6

Immanion Press
8 Rowley Grove
Stafford ST17 9BJ
UK

Also by Taylor Ellwood

Creating Magickal Entities

(with David Michael Cunningham
and Amanda R. Wagener)

Pop Culture Magick

(available through Immanion Press)

Space/Time Magic

(available through Immanion Press)

Kink Magic

(With Lupa – available through Megalithica Books 2007)

Dedication

To my Lovely Lupa,
for showing me the inner alchemy of love.
And to Jason,
for reminding me of what's really important,
And to the magic,
for keeping me on track with this book.

Acknowledgements

I'd like to thank Storm and the good people at Immanion Press for publishing this book and allowing me to manifest my vision of getting experimental, on-the-edge books on magic published.

To Nemo for coming up with a brilliant cover for this book.

To Maryam for continuing to be my best friend and being so supportive of me.

To Zac Walters, for continually inspiring my own approaches to this subject with his work.

To Susan Davis, your advice helped me through several moments of crisis in 2005.

To Sage Nightstar for stalwart support and high standards.

To Michael Szul and Jason Galt for excellent friendship.

To D. J. Lawrence in the spirit of entrepreneurship.

To Steven Savage for his excellent book recommendations and patience.

To my beautiful wolf woman, Lupa, for the magic, editing, honesty, and love.

My thanks to Jo Byers for doing the Design and Layout for this book.

I am blessed by all of you.

Table of Contents

Introduction

Stasis is only an illusion. We pride ourselves on permanence in American culture. Our buildings are created to last for years; we buy cars that we want to keep running as long as possible; medical science ever seeks the Fountain of Youth (and, therefore, immortality). We strive, at least in theory, for the end to change, so that we may never have to face the sorrow of loss.

Yet our actions belie us. We tear down buildings that are only a few decades old in order to make way for the newest designs. Increasingly vehicles are made cheaply, particularly in the U.S., in an attempt to get people to buy more cars (we see this in a lot of consumer items.). And while we may give lip service to health, we still more or less support habits that shorten the lifespan and lessen the quality of life, such as abuse of drugs (including nicotine and alcohol) and extremely high levels of stress.

Our changes as a culture are erratic and unhealthy. We blindly charge through existence. Our culture is a stampede trampling other cultures, other species, and indeed the very environment before us. Yet unlike herd animals which eventually stop once they've realized the danger is past, we not only continue to run, but in doing so propagate the dangerous signals that continue to trigger our flight instincts, *ad infinitum*.

Post-industrial humanity has forgotten how to flow with change. Observe the weaving of Nature. The cycles may seem to be the same year after year, yet in the long run each season brings a miniscule move forward in the macrocosm. You don't see any other species of animal or plant working to stop this process. Natural beings are comfortable in their environment, drawbacks and all.

Humanity has great potential to consciously evolve as a species. Yet this conscious evolution starts on the individual level. We are not mere slaves to our imprints and habits; to blame our histories, both physiologically and psychologically, is the modern-day equivalent of saying "The Devil made me do it". We too often limit ourselves to what our egos declare: "I AM" and rarely tread outside of those safe boundaries. And we extend the illusion of secure limitations to our external life as well, to the point where, bondage fanatics that we have become, we are mummified in our wishful thinking. Yet every scene must come to an end, no matter how enjoyable, and often we find that we are unable to cope with the rude awakening of being freed. We've been bound for so long that our muscles have atrophied and we no longer know how to use them. Most just give up and lie about like Gary Larson's boneless chickens.

Many, if not all of you, reading this realize that it doesn't have to be this way. There are numerous resources available for those wishing to rebuild weakened muscles, as it were. Some of them, such as the works of Robert Anton Wilson, John C. Lilly, and B.K. Frantzis, are referenced within this book. While these, and other sources that Taylor draws upon may not necessarily be to your liking, there is no dogma within these pages restricting you to his preferences; that would be counterproductive.

Inner Alchemy is about the starting point of conscious evolution—the microcosm. We, and all living beings, can be thought of as the building blocks of the Universal Organism. And, as with the cells in our bodies, we as cells can be healthy or cancerous, affecting the rest of the body in turn. Change begins on the cellular level every time.

Taylor has realized this, and provided the reader with the tools necessary to begin this change in our own cells, that we may become better cells ourselves. Many of these tools are unique, rarely, if ever, discussed previously in a magical sense. As science discovers more and more material that supports what magicians have known all along—biophotonic light, the processes behind the placebo effect, quantum reality—it provides us with new language with which to continue our growth. We are able to take the medieval alchemy, and update it for the 21st century.

Inner Alchemy is a work for today. Some of the ideas are incredibly controversial—but if we don't explore them, we let our stasis and our illusions of safety get the better of us. You may not agree with all of them, but I believe it is important, at the very least, to acknowledge them as the attempt towards conscious evolution that Taylor has brought together in this work. If we do not even try to move, then we are left right where we started, end of story.

Stagnation = Death. Keep moving!

Lupa
22 May, 2006
Seattle, WA

Foreword

Of all my books, *Inner Alchemy* was the hardest one to write so far. It wasn't so much the material or the research, as it was the personal growth that was demanded in the process of writing it. It's fair to say I faced emotional depths within myself that I had never encountered before. And sometimes I dealt with the daunting task of reading a mountain load of books on this subject that seemed to always threaten to bury me in research.

A lot has changed in my life since I started writing this book. I left my graduate program, tired of trying to bash my head through a brick wall of academic stagnancy that wouldn't show flexibility where it was needed. I ended one relationship, and found another with my wife, Lupa. But more than any of the external changes, I've come to find an emotional coherency and clarity that I've lacked for most of my life. The journey for all of this was not easy and involved facing many of my inner demons, and it is an ongoing process. But it is a process wherein one finds a bit more balance, a bit more hope every day, through the journey of refining the inner alchemy of the self.

A few matters to note. I prefer to use the word magic over magick. The bibliography is in APA style, and the internal citations are also in APA. The pronouns used are gender neutral. And I cite the lesser known authors of magic over the popular ones, so as to increase my readers' awareness of these authors and what they have to offer to each of you. I don't agree with all of the people I've cited and I doubt they'd all agree with me, but their writings are worth exploring so check them out! And I've included a lot of non-occult sources as the material in this book goes outside the range of traditional occultism.

Also a disclaimer: The methods in here are devised by me, but neither my publisher nor I are responsible for how any of you use them. If you have a medical condition, make sure consult with your physician and/or therapist before doing any of these exercises.

Finally, as always, the focus of this book is on experimental magic, specifically with a goal to inspire other magicians to continue innovating and pushing magic past where it has been. Be creative and don't be afraid to reinvent the wheel, because you just might come up with a better version!

Chapter One:
Inner Alchemy 101

In the book *Druids*, by Morgan Llewellyn, the protagonist is taught the sanctity of his body by the head druid. He learns to respect this sacredness and to pay attention to the motion of the body and appreciate all of its natural functions. He cultivates not just the five external senses of the body, but also awareness of the processes that occur in it. He doesn't take for granted what he has, a body that allows him to interact with the world around him, to be more substantial than just pure spirit. His body is the key to experiences around and within him. In the same way you can learn to appreciate your body and the magic you can do with it.

Since my teenage years, I've been interested in how the physiology of the body works. Part of this interest comes from my family's genetic heritage. We have a genetic predisposition toward manic depression. When I was younger, I had to deal with this condition. But I knew I didn't want to take medication. I felt there had to be a way to overcome it that didn't rely on drugs. I felt certain that with magic I could do something to change the situation.

These days many more people are getting depressed. Sometimes it's because of situations in their lives that seem out of control, making them feel unable to deal with either the internal reality in their heads or the external realities around them. Other times it's because of genetics. There is a predisposition in some people to be depressed. In both cases, pills are supposed to heal everything. Unfortunately, the pills have side effects and often times do just as much damage as the depression was doing. I can think of at least a couple friends I knew who took anti-depressant drugs. They told that when they were on the drug they felt like zombies. They couldn't feel any emotions. I was told that the issues they needed to deal with were still there, but instead of coping with those issues they numbed them with the drugs.

For the people who are depressed because of their situations, there's usually a way out. The situation can be resolved, perspective can be found, and eventually the depression gives way to other emotions. But for someone who's genetically predisposed to being depressed, it's a different story. It's not a specific situation or even set of situations that has you down. It's the chemicals in your brain, the hormones in your blood. You feel off balance, your head on fire or in a weird soup. Everything is out of whack and there's no obvious way of correcting the problem, short of taking a pill.

Or is there?

When I was twenty I began reading John Lilly's *Programming the Human Biocomputer*. I found his ideas fascinating, especially in regards to the electrochemistry of the brain and how it could be controlled. In combining his concepts with shamanic vision questing and Barbara Brennan's holistic healing approach, I found that I was able to access and work with my brain. I could change the chemistry and alter my moods at will. The day I got rid of my depression was the day I finally felt alive. I could feel emotions again, in full, and I had incentive to live my life, to enjoy it. To feel this way was amazing and I realized I could *continue* to feel that way. I just had to take control of my physiology.

Now at this point I'll include a disclaimer that needs to be made. I am not a professional physician or therapist. If you are taking medicine, you should continue to do so. Don't stop just because you're reading this book. Instead, work with the exercises in this book and see if they work for you, but continue with your medication and consult a trained physician about changing your regimen of pills. If you choose to go off of your medication, realize that it is your choice to do so. Neither I, nor my publisher, are responsible for your choices or how you use this book or the techniques in it. Only you are responsible for how you choose to use the information in this book.

I will admit that I never took medication. I wasn't a severe case, a danger to myself or those around me. I could function, but I wasn't very happy. I felt I didn't need drugs and although I often felt at the mercy of my depression when younger, I eventually did move past it by utilizing the techniques I developed to alter my physiology. Then, even as now, I felt that if medicine could induce changes in the body, there was no reason that those changes couldn't be induced naturally by learning to stimulate and change the electrochemistry of the brain. We do this through a variety of means which include drugs, but are not limited to them. Meditation, herbalism, and experimenting with how sensations effect the body can also be used to change your physiology. This is why holistic medicines and practices are becoming more popular in the West. They offer alternatives to the artificial pharmaceuticals that are pushed by doctors at the behest of the pharmaceutical companies. These companies have sizable economic and political influence, as well as enormous advertising budgets, which leads to our culture being saturated by their products.

Another reason alternative practices are discouraged is because in the U.S. and many other parts of the world people have lost touch with a mindful awareness of the internal realities of their bodies, psyches, and energy. Instead of cultivating such an awareness pills are thrown at the problem which usually only deal with the symptoms, but fail to explore the underlying tension and origin behind the symptoms. This approach to the body and health, on any level, is a result of this very mechanistic approach to the body, which favors an artificial division of the body from emotions, thought, and the spirit.

This viewpoint can be seen in the works of John Lilly and other scientists who try to reduce the biology of a human to the functions of a computer. Such an approach makes the human body a commodity and continues a Western tradition of expendability. Similarly, neuro-linguistic programming (NLP), which acknowledges that the mind and body are interconnected and affect each other, still misses out on other essential elements such as the soul, the emotions, and the role they play in such communication (O'Connor & Seymour 2002). Consider that if you didn't have a body you wouldn't be able to feel, touch, see, hear, or taste. You would have a very vague amorphous perception of reality and no sense of individuality. Your consciousness would exist only as a possibility, instead of as a manifested reality. The body you have gives you a boundary, but also establishes your individuality.

Your Body: A Miracle of Communication

It is very important to realize that when you do work with the body magically you are communicating with it and it will communicate with you as well. You ignore what your body has to say at your own peril. I know of one person who consistently refused to listen to her body and the warnings it gave her about the various situations she was in. Eventually it got to the point where she became consistently sick, vomiting food and getting little sleep. Her body refused to listen to her and acted out by making her sick until she had no choice but to listen to her body. The body will communicate with you to tell you when an imbalance has occurred. How many of you have gone into a situation and felt your stomach churning? Your stomach is reacting to your nervousness and communicating that nervousness to you. Will you ignore what your body is telling you or will you listen? If you listen to your body, you'll go to bed when you're tired, eat when you're hungry, relax when your stressed, in short you'll listen to the signals your body gives you. It is when you learn to listen to your body that you begin to become comfortable with it. We live now in an era where people are mostly uncomfortable with their bodies after two thousand years of repression. The body is perceived as sinful and dirty and how can any of us be comfortable with our own bodies if we are told those bodies are evil?

Inner alchemy, as a system of magic, is a celebration of the body, a recognition of what it can do and how amazing it is. I have only touched the tip of the iceberg in this first chapter on what inner alchemy is. Many magicians may find the focus of this book on the body unusual, but I think that the body is often ignored too readily or taken for granted by magicians. You have only to see the out of shape magician, complete with bad eating habits and other addictions to see that this person is not in touch with hir body. And if you aren't in touch with your body, how you can really be in touch with spirit? Inner alchemy is the appreciation of the body and its processes and how it can be used in magical practices as well as how magic can enhance and improve the body. Perhaps this last point is most significant given the attitude in current times in regards to stem cell research. Right wing radical extreme Christians are against it, because they feel that such research involves playing god with the human body. Never mind that such research does not threaten lives, but could actually help cure many of the diseases and afflictions we have. Such reactions on the part of these radical Christians is a typical response though, concerned as they are not so much with the body, but rather with controlling who can do what to the body. Also in many contemporary cultures there is a fanatic desire to look a certain way. On the covers of magazines we see very skinny women or very buff men and think this is the ideal version of what a woman or man should look like, even though such magazines end up often producing women and men with eating disorders which ultimately hurt them more than anything else. The body is hated for the way it is, without an attempt to appreciate or understand why the body chooses to be that way. Such negative attitudes as the majority of people possess can only be overcome by fostering an appreciation of the body, achieving a sense of not taking it for granted, but also being willing to explore and understand the body, and its connection to the emotions, mind, and spirit.

So we see that it is not just modern prejudices, but also those biases deeply entrenched in religious trappings that prevent us from being aware of our bodies. Puritanism teaches us from an early age that the body is dirty, ugly, and sinful, and either must be covered up or "treated" with cosmetics—and, of course, never, ever smell bad! However, one aspect of inner alchemy that I find really fascinating is using bodily fluids (cum, blood, saliva, and tears), and bodily waste (nails, skin shavings, and hair clippings, but also fecal matter) in magical workings. All of these materials that come from our bodies are, in their own ways, highly effective tools of magic, imbued with our personal energy. I have used the different products of my body for inner alchemical work, particularly DNA magic, which I'll cover in much more depth in one of the coming chapters. The important thing to remember is that you can use your body for a lot of magical workings. It is your best tool in magical practice and as you work with your body it becomes more and more attuned to magic.

Of course the bodily processes are just one aspect of body magic. Through body paints we can intimately connect with our body and with the magic we seek to work. The use of body paints can allow us to connect with entities that we represent through the paints, or can be used to fire sigils. The body merges and melds with the energy of the paint so that the experience becomes one where inner alchemy occurs. This experience can also be achieved through the food we eat and substances we drink. By consecrating what we eat, we put energy into it and consequently that energy merges with the body, affecting the physiology and affecting the alchemy that we create in the body as well as from it. How we choose to perceive our body and what we put into it greatly affects its health. It often surprises me what people put into themselves, not just in terms of physical food, but also mental, emotional, and spiritual food. The reason so many Americans are unhealthy is because they do not have a proper alchemical balance. They eat junk food, don't discuss emotions, or gossip behind someone's back, or have negative attitudes about themselves, or allow themselves to be told they're going to hell if they don't agree with the values of mainstream religions. For any of us to change that, we have to recognize what we put into ourselves, what we accept from other people and then we have to decide if that's what we really want. Inner alchemy is part of the way that a person can question and change what s/he puts into hirself.

What is needed is a cultivation of communication skills--not just with other people, but also with yourself, and with the cells in your body. We need to rethink how we conceive of consciousness, allowing that it can exist on multiple levels and in multiple organisms. We also need to rethink how we communicate and what the purpose of communication is. Gallegos points out the following about communication, "*The function of communication is to lend open expression to one's experience*: words, language, expression, should be available to all aspects of who we are, so that every part can gain vocal expression. Instead we teach the child to fear being wrong, to fear expressing something because that expression has been punished in the past, to speak only that which would be approved, etc. [italics are his]" (1987, p. 163). In living in a culture where communication is not about the expression of the self (below the surface, anyway), it's not surprising to see people repress their emotions and for that matter other forms of expression. This repression inevitably harms the body, the soul, and the emotions of a person. From personal experience I can say that even now I'm still learning to communicate effectively with people because of past conditioning.

If you apply that inability to communicate to communication with yourself, you'll notice how much you don't communicate with your body and what it has to tell you. Yet we are so focused on external communication, via speech, writing, and other forms of multimedia, that as a culture we've forgotten how to communicate energetically and physiologically with our bodies--and with the environment that we live in (Lipton 2005). Inner alchemy involves learning to communicate with your environment, because even as a cell exists in your body, you exist in the body of this Earth and accordingly all of us are cells of the Earth. If this insults your sense of consciousness, just remember you could not live without the Earth, though possibly it could live without you. We need to recognize that we communicate not just with each other, or even internally with our cells, but also with the world and the universe. Every action has consequences in the system of life we live in.

Nothing in *Inner Alchemy* occurs solely on any one level. The major theme of this book is interconnectedness. A lot of my work on the energetic level has happened as a result of work I've done on the physiological and even genetic level, with the goal being to shape the body even as my energy is shaped. By learning to work with your DNA and apply your understanding of DNA to a level beyond just the physical existence of it you can do a lot of inner alchemy. In turn you can achieve an appreciation of not just your own genetic heritage, but how it interacts with everything else. You can fine tune that heritage as well, making changes in your body that allow you to maximize your physical, mental, emotional, and spiritual potentials. You just need to be open to the idea that the body can be controlled on a variety of levels despite what western science and medical health would have you believe. As an example, while the autonomic portion of the brain controls such functions as breathing and the heart beat, you can control these functions and use them to induce altered states of mind. Similarly sex magic practices teach the control of the sexual organs so that a variety of metaphysical experiences can be attained. Sex magic can allow you to enter gnosis or give you a kundalini experience. You can even use the fluids to induce alchemical changes in yourselves or others. Finally, the practice of biofeedback demonstrates that control over the body can be achieved in terms of muscle reaction, blood pressure, brain wave activity and electrical activity on the skin (Keith 2005).

Listening to your body, for example, becomes essential to working true inner alchemy: "What first comes to mind when someone says the word health is the body's ability to overcome illness or recover from injury. Yes, the body's physical health is a major component of health, but is only one component. Beyond the visible health of bodily strength and wellness lies the realm of mental, emotional, and spiritual health" (Perry 2003, p. 22). All of these levels are interconnected, and so the techniques I discuss in this book are also focused on more than just one aspect of the inner alchemy. As an example, my focus on depression wasn't just a change in my body, in terms of the electrochemistry of the brain, but also in terms of the emotions. And while there is certainly some truth that emotions are caused by the hormones in your blood and brain, the emotions do go beyond that. They allow you to connect with people spiritually, mentally, and physically.

If emotions were only physical they wouldn't affect the aura, the energy the person puts out. For example, I can tell if a person has mental disorders or is depressed by the darkness around hir head. It's no coincidence that people who are miserable will attract other miserable people and events that perpetuate the cycle. The emotion infects the energy and even though those people claim they don't want to be miserable, they are addicted to those feelings, to the circumstances that enable them to be miserable. For a good example, listen to any of your co-workers who are miserable. If they constantly complain about situations they get themselves into and yet allow themselves to repeat the cycle, on some level they must want what they are experiencing. Usually this will show in the energy they project around them. Sadly, in this culture, people aren't always aware of energy, or how their emotions affect the health of the body and spirit. If you keep having uncontrollable events happen in your life, try and find the common element in these occurrences. Undoubtedly the root will be your attitude. With inner alchemy you learn to change the lead of emotions into gold that gives you more control of your life.

Continuing with the energy model, there is a lot that can be explored beyond what is currently presented in energy work. While we certainly have standard models that explain how it is done, the number and functions of chakras, and how energy can be used, fresh perspectives on energy work are needed. Often the models of energy work, while touching on how energy interacts with the body, don't thoroughly examine the connection between energy and other aspects of yourself. Also such systems seem to be prescriptive, instead of descriptive, arguing that we can only have seven major chakras or arguing that there is particular way to work with energy. While energy work is not the major theme of this book, it is an important one. I am not out to completely revamp how the model is considered, but instead to advocate an open approach to energy and the energetic body, beyond the existing paradigms used to describe or understand it.

Inner Alchemy is really just another system of magic, much like *Pop Culture Magick* and *Space/Time Magic*. Through it you will learn a lot about your body, your mind, your spirit, your genetics, and the microcosmic quantum level as well. I think all of this is essential to taking magical practice to a different level, one where you can begin to evolve yourself and possibly your descendents. There is no reason not to believe that if we can learn to work with our own genetic code that we can't change certain aspects for future generations. I have weeded out the depression in my genetic code. I have taken that part away and I have done so because I like living a life where I am not depressed all of the time.

But this kind of magic involves some work. It's not enough to read books on energy work or meditation and expect that these techniques alone will aid us in changing our physiology. Inner alchemical practices will help us in our exploration, but we also need to back up what we do with information. I have, over the years, tried to keep up with the latest information on genetics, neural chemistry, and related fields of study. I'm not a scientist, but the concepts are approachable and the more you know about how your body works, the easier it is to visualize and work with it. Some magicians will argue otherwise, saying that you don't need a precise knowledge of the body or physiology: "It [The author's processes of healing] was not difficult and did not require an innate understanding of the physiology and chemical processes of the human body. My process was simple and will focused" (Garbie 2005, p. 31). Certainly the most potent skill of the magician is a directed will, but what hones that ability is sharp awareness and understanding of the target of that will, as well as improving both the psychic and physical senses. I likely do not know as much about the chemical or physiological processes of the body as a trained physician does. But what I have learned has helped me understand what I'm working with, helped me to focus my will even more than if I just had a general, vague knowledge of my body. I certainly do not feel I would be able to work with my physiology as much as I have if it wasn't for reading up on and exploring scientific practices that attempt to understand how the brain and body works. Not all scientific approaches are accurate, and as we have discussed, often leave out nonphysical layers of the self, but just as science changes with the times and new discoveries, so too, ideally, does magical practice change. Part of that change involves exploring and extending magic beyond its current limits through incorporation of a variety of perspectives, including science.

By reading up on and understanding other perspectives on the subject of the physiology you will find it very easy to do the techniques that I'll discuss in this book. These techniques have been very useful for me. They have helped me experience the body, as well as communicate with it, as opposed to understanding it from only an abstract or solely physical perspective. Of course, the ultimate goal of this book is to inspire you to come up with your own approaches and practices for doing inner alchemy.

Inner Alchemy and Traditional Alchemy

It's important to consider the concepts of traditional alchemy as well. Alchemy is usually considered to be a practice where specific substances were mixed together to produce desired effects, from herbal mixtures to metallurgical experiments. However, what makes alchemy so different is that the external changes were not the only ones to occur and not necessarily the most important: "Rather, since the Stone's creation is said to reflect the state of genuine, not imagined, spiritual development of the student, success will only be obtained when the inner process of growth and the outer manipulations in the laboratory have achieved harmony" (Lisiewski 2002, p. 285). In other words, the work that was done to create the various processes and effects externally was a work that had to be mirrored on the inside. The person had to develop an appreciation of not only the external forces s/he was working with, but also the internal forces of hirself that s/he was willing to offer into the creation of the alchemy. One definition of alchemy is: "It is 'The raising of vibrations'" (Albertus 1974, p.14). Albertus goes on to explain that the person who pursues alchemy with the proper attitude will understand what this means. Even in contemporary science, we deal with this concept of vibrations when we consider that physically we are ultimately comprised of vibrating particles. So raising our vibration is something which is not just metaphorical, but occurs on all levels of our existence. The goal is to raise the vibrations, and consequently affect reality.

I am not working with traditional alchemical laboratories, but this principle mentioned above holds true for any magical work, including inner alchemy. The effort you put into magic must also be put into developing yourself. Any person can make an effect happen, but will that person understand the processes as well as what is called for from hirself to make that effect happen? Unfortunately in magic today there is a lot of ignorance about the dynamics of magic.

Other magicians have told me that only the effect matters, that focusing on the process isn't important. But such philosophy is a result of the commodification of society. We want everything now and heavens forbid we should actually have to work for it. Such laziness on the part of a magician is unbecoming and ultimately unfulfilling. The magic is more than just the effect; it is also the process. Inner alchemy relies on a thorough understanding of the processes worked with. You might get an effect you don't want, and if you do and you don't know the process for making this effect happen, it'll be much harder to undo what has been done as well as alter the process to where you do get the desired effect.

In Taoism, inner alchemy has been practiced for a long time. The focus of such alchemy is a refinement of three treasures--vitality, energy and spirit--to the point where a new reality can be manifested:

> The metaphysical practice based on the three treasures is generally seen as a progressive refinement: refining vitality into energy, refining energy into spirit, refining spirit, into space, and finally breaking through space to merge with the reality of the Tao. This is sometimes described as progressive detachment and shifting from awareness of the body to awareness of mind, from awareness of mind to awareness of space to awareness of the Tao, or objective reality. (Cleary 1996, p. 19).

To achieve any sense of objective reality (if that's your goal), it is necessary to start with the body. Understanding the body, the way it affects you, the feelings it brings you, etc., is essential to learning how to work with it and move beyond it, so as to complete the body. In truth, I don't think we ever completely transcend the body, save in death. But we can refine our bodies and in the process we can also refine other aspects of ourselves. However, I want to briefly emphasize that refinement, a very useful process, nonetheless supposedly leaves byproduct behind. I will get into much more depth on this subject, but I argue that the so-called byproduct is a refinement as well and can be used by the person. The product of such refinement is characterized as a gold elixir:

> The gold elixir is the fundamental essence of innate knowledge and innate capacity inherent in people. This essence is intrinsically complete in everyone; it is not more in sages or less in ordinary people. It is not obtained from another, it is inherent in oneself. If you accord with it, you ascend directly into the realm of sages;

> essence is stabilized, life is solidified, never to disintegrate. This fundamental essence of innate knowledge and innate capacity is the great elixir of long life. (Po-Tuan 1996, p. 47)

Such refinement is internal, though inevitably it manifests externally so that the world around you aligns into accordance with your directed intent and manifests reality as you need it to occur. Inner alchemy is ultimately a refinement and challenging of the self, to produce this essence, which is comprised of all your abilities and experiences. But inner alchemy also connects you with what is called the universal mind. For all of this to occur you must first work with the body.

Conclusion

As I mentioned above, in American culture (and those we influence or that have influenced us), we artificially divide the body from the emotions, mind, and spirit. We do this because we have been encouraged to regard the body with the attitude I mentioned above, that it is a dirty thing. But this can be changed. By understanding our physiology and exploring how we can shape it, we can develop and evolve. It's simply a matter of achieving the realization that the body is not separate, but has an impact on the emotions, mind, and spirit and likewise is impacted by those same forces: It's simply a matter of achieving the realization that the body is not separate, but has an impact on the emotions, mind, and spirit and likewise is impacted by those same forces (Proto 1992).

When we understand this relationship then we begin to truly understand inner alchemy, because we have unified what has been kept separate, and in the process have begun to refine it into a substance, a body-emotion-mind-spirit that is not held back by society, but instead seeks to improve the quality and essence of the self, in all of its forms. When we can do this, we leave behind the stale perspectives that have kept us back and we evolve into a new being, still human, but better, because we are not limiting ourselves to societal views on the body, or to artificial divisions, or the vagaries of genetics.

Exercises

1. Get a copy of *Gray's Anatomy*, or borrow one from the library and look it over. Try and get a sense of your anatomy not just from looking over the book, but actually trying to visualize and communicate with the different parts of your body.
2. Describe your own attitude toward your body. Where did you get this attitude from? For example, are you embarrassed if you fart? If so, why, given that it's a perfectly natural function? Even if you aren't, try and determine where your attitude toward your body has come from. Is it a result of your parents, religion, or your own experimentation with it? How does this compare to the prevailing cultural opinions regarding the body and its processes?
3. What's one aspect of your body that you would like to improve or change? How would you do this? Also consider where your attitude toward this need for change comes from. Is it a societal attitude or one from your family or friends? Or is it your own?
4. What is your definition or understanding of alchemy or inner alchemy? What do you think raising vibrations means?

Chapter Two
Body Basics

In this chapter the focus is on the miracle of your body, the alchemical vessel by which you live and breathe. Of course the body is much more than just that. But our perception of it is based on our experience of it, and usually this experience doesn't account for everything that is occurring below the surface. You know this by now because of your experiences with your senses. Consider how you are able to turn these pages or move your eyes over the text. How are your senses involved with these seemingly minor actions?

The next step is to begin working with the body through several different media. Daily exercise is essential, for instance, for training the body. Just recently a fellow magician commented on the fact that in my co-authored book *Creating Magickal Entities*, we mentioned the importance of exercise. My colleague noted that my book was the only one that had mentioned it. Perhaps other books on magic just take for granted that a person exercises and takes care of the body, but I prefer to make it explicit. It is very important to take care of our bodies and here is why: "Keeping the body, this temple, at peak condition is important to any magical endeavor. When the body is in good physical condition there is an abundance of vitality, awareness, and endurance, all of which are important faculties in magical practice" (Seth 2005, p. 8). When the body is in shape there is more life energy to draw on. It's as simple as that.

Exercise has benefits beyond the obvious toning or increasing of physical strength:

> There is a vital spiritual aspect to physical activity. It goes well beyond the well-known 'runner's high' to something much more profound. Regular physical activity can put you in touch with powerfully spiritual aspects of yourself. Exercise wakes up your mind and your spirit, along with your body. Exercise can help you find direction and purpose on your spiritual path. (Perry 2003, p. 60).

Exercise raises the energy in your body. You achieve a greater awareness of it, and in fact this is particularly useful for working with the sense of touch, as exercise can make you aware of your body in new ways. When I exercise, I wear weights, giving me more resistance and making the exercise harder to do. The more effort I exert, the more energy is produced and this occurs on both the physical level and the spiritual level.

Exercise, in relationship to inner alchemy, is quite simple in that you have to take care of the temple of your transformation in order for the transformations to be ones that are beneficial to you. Exercise is part of how you take care of yourself and will give you physical, emotional, mental, and spiritual refreshment.

Spiritual enlightenment, in part, comes through the training and exercising of the body, and using exercise to shift awareness of the self. Evola comments on yoga and mentions the following: "In other words, the use of exercise (and not just yoga) can bring about an altered state of consciousness. However these states cannot be reached if we do not actually exercise or train ourselves to work with our bodies"(1992, P.87). When you exercise, make sure you alter your routine so that your body doesn't become too used to the routine and so you don't get bored. Variety not only invigorates your body, but also your mind and spirit. I alternate between doing tai-chi and yoga, and doing taebo, which is more active. The other benefit of variety is that you can work on different sets of muscles so that you don't strain your body too much and still get in a good exercise routine.

By training our bodies, we can begin to appreciate of the various processes the body goes through, as well as what we put into our body and how it affects us. When we sweat we are purging and purifying our bodies, but do people really think of sweat in that way? Usually sweat is conceived of as an unpleasant sensation and scent, but in reality it serves to cool you down, even as it gets rid of toxins. After a really good exercise session you will sweat a lot and the smell from your body will tell you that you are actually getting rid of the toxins. And in fact, sweat can be part of an alchemical process, due in part to what you eat or drink. What you eat or drink affects the physiology of the body, in terms of how you taste, smell, and in terms of how your body cools itself down. For instance, if you enjoy giving oral sex, try going down on a non-smoker and a smoker. There seems to be a definite difference in taste. The liquid ejaculate for both men and women may look discolored if you're going down on a smoker. Now try going down on someone who eats healthy food as opposed to someone who only eats junk food. Again you'll probably find a difference in the taste of the person. This also applies to smell. What you put into your body affects the chemistry of the body and consequently the experiences other people have with you.

The substances you put in your body can also affect how it cools down. In Junius's book on plant alchemy, he mentions the custom in India of having large amounts of salt in the drinks. He eventually discovered why in the studies of a biologist:

> Repeated investigations by Dr. Kervran, which were also confirmed by other researchers, proved that the perspiration of the workers contained a very high percentage of potassium after taking the salt tablets. Table salt, however, is sodium chloride, not potassium. What had happened to the sodium? It had changed into potassium within the organism and could later be detected in the perspiration in the already mentioned high amounts. This process uses up calories ('Salt brings a certain freshness. It protects you from exhaustion in great heat.'). Hence the cooling effect, an endothermic process. (Junius 1993, p. 11)

Essentially the body transmuted the sodium into potassium and in the process produced sweat, which cooled the worker down. Truly an alchemical process is wrought by an understanding of how the body interacts with external substances. You can consciously choose what you put into your body and you owe it to yourself to carefully consider that. This does not mean however, that if you suddenly choose to become a vegetarian or a vegan you'll automatically have a healthy body. You have to carefully balance your diet. I've known many vegetarians and vegans who have been extremely unhealthy because they didn't carefully balance the diet they chose.

In alchemy there is a process where a person can actually use poison to cure poison:

> Since like repels like in physical phenomena, the homeopathic approach of curing, say, arsenic poisoning, is to use the same substance, namely, arsenic. Thus, if a physiological dose of arsenic will bring about arsenic poisoning, the homeopathic practitioner will use this same substance, arsenic, in a most minute or highly triturated form to effect a cure. Here the high trituration causes the arsenic particles to become so small that they can no longer be perceived. Because of the high trituration, the vibratory rate is greatly increased and achieves high potency in expelling the physiological dose of arsenic. (Albertus 1974, p. 54)

Trituration is the crushing or grinding of a substance into a dust. However, similar effects, in science, have been achieved in cases where a person has been poisoned by snake venom. To create an antivenom, a sample of the venom is taken from a snake, diluted, and injected into an animal. As the animal develops an immunity to the poison, the dosage is increased, leading to more antibodies which are used to fight the venom. A serum is made out of these antibodies and that creates an antivenom (http://ask.yahoo.com/ask/20000803.html, retrieved August 17, 2006). This is similar to how the like will repel like principle works. In effect, the antivenom becomes toxic to the venom. This is partially accomplished by how the body interacts with the substance put into it. For instance, the addiction of drugs is caused partially by the increased dosage of the drug, but also by how the physiology of the body adapts to the drug, which necessitates the increased dosage to continue to get an effect. Such an adaptation, however, can still have a high price, because the body is still harmed by what is taken in, as is evident by the side effects a person suffers, or by the failure of organs due to overdosing. The only adaptation that is really occurring is the body's increased tolerance toward the drug and even then it might only be the receptors that have more tolerance. The organs of the body may not be able to take increasing doses.

Sudden withdrawal of the drug will give the person a painful purging experience, though such an experience could be highly useful from a magical standpoint, as inevitably you will have to face some of your demons or personal issues as your body suffers through withdrawal. The release of physical toxins can also release mental toxins. I don't advocate doing this from a legal standpoint, however, because getting caught doing illicit drugs is not legally sound. A legal alternative is quitting cigarettes as the withdrawal from the cigarettes will also provide you a similar experience. As a person who has suffered through a withdrawal, I will say that it can lead to some intriguing experiences; mine lead me to one of my near death experiences. I vomited a lot, sweated a lot, and was in a lot of pain, as I experienced the withdrawal. There were a couple times where I lost consciousness. I kept myself hydrated, which helped. When it was over, I felt terrible, very weak, but at the same time my body felt cleaned out as well. Similarly alcohol poisoning has led me to similar states of mind, but again I don't advise it from a health standpoint. Testing your body in such extremes has the risk of death and should you purposely choose to seek such a state it is your responsibility. I've sometimes deliberately chosen that experience in my pursuit of the path of poison (i.e. enlightenment through self destruction), but it has been my choice and responsibility to do so. The important lesson to learn here is that we cannot regard the body as an object. If we do so, we are harming ourselves and perhaps even others, because of our actions. Rather we should begin to appreciate how the body can be worked with in inner alchemy and understand that what we put into our bodies does have an effect. Knowing this we can lead healthier lifestyles and raise the vibrations of our bodies.

We can also take a critical eye toward what we put into our bodies on an everyday basis. As I've mentioned above the particular food you eat affects your body. Foods with preservatives are less healthy than frozen food. Likewise organic food is healthier than food grown with hormones, pesticides, and other chemicals. Still you can only avoid the preservatives, hormones, environmental toxins, chemicals, and other poisons so much.

Likewise the habits you indulge in will have an effect on the alchemy you want to do. Cigarettes, for instance, are full of carcinogens, tar, arsenic, and other toxins. They affect your physical body and your spiritual energy. In Marcia Pickands' book, *The Psychic Self-Defense Training Manual*, she has a strength exercise where the person visualizes taking the energy from another person and then pushes on the second's arm. If the second person still has hir energy then it's not very easy to push the arm down, but if the first person has managed to take the energy then there is much less resistance to that effort. As a variation of this exercise Pickands says this:

> Tobacco is not just bad for your lungs. It will actually weaken your psychic body…have your partner hold a closed box or package of cigarettes in the left hand; then do a second strength test. The results should be dramatic. In fact, even if your partner has become accomplished at keeping his or her aura pulled in close to the physical body, just holding the cigarettes should cause significant weakness (1997, pp 40-41).

I have tried out the exercises in that book and found it to be the case that indeed holding the cigarettes causes this weakness. This is because the spiritual energy of the cigarettes is of a much lower vibration than a person's energy and consequently lowers the energy of the person. I suggest checking out Pickands' work to learn more about this particular phenomenon and then try the exercises yourself. Alternatively drinking a glass of wine a day can actually be very beneficial for your health according to some studies, but overdoing the drinking can lead to cirrhosis of the liver.

My goal in telling you all of this is for you to consider that the popular saying, "You are what you eat," may actually be true (as well as what you breathe, drink, etc.). Eating a healthy diet and choosing healthy habits affects what you can do with your inner alchemy. The choice to smoke a cigarette may predispose you to certain types of cancer, while the choice not to will lessen the chance of getting those types. But that choice also affects the internal chemistry of the body and any work you attempt to do with it. By choosing to smoke you are changing your internal chemistry (damaging it actually) and that damage must be factored in with the work you want to do with your physiology. Now extend those choices to the food you eat, and the other products you buy and you'll realize that everything you buy has an effect on your body.

Meditation is also important for the body. While meditation certainly helps with the mental and spiritual aspects of the self, it also helps the body relax. I use meditation to protect myself, to get in touch with other forces or with other aspects of my consciousness, and to balance myself. The body, emotions, and mind live on a biorhythmic cycle:

> According to the theory of biorhythms we all have a physical cycle of 23 days, an emotional cycle of 28 days, and an intellectual cycle of 33 days. The intellectual cycle affects our concentration, judgment, and ability to learn. The emotional cycle affects our moods and emotions, while the physical cycle affects body coordination, stamina, and resistance to illness. On the days at the top of the wave, energy in that sphere will be high and conversely, at the bottom of the wave, it will be low. In between there is a 'critical' period where the curve crosses the line. At these times our energy will be unstable, especially if the critical periods of two or all three cycles coincides. (Proto 1992, p. 4).

Meditation can be useful for balancing these cycles and critical moments. We can promote the health of our body by relaxing it, balance the emotions by exploring them, and let the mind travel in different directions, giving it fresh inspiration. I use meditation as a tool for balance. By doing so I am able to keep the cycle of the mind, emotions, and body working well so that the energy supporting my life is not unstable. Whenever I don't meditate I tend to be out of sorts and not as balanced. I haven't really noticed a difference in any of my cycles, beyond noting that occasionally I won't be as sexually active as I'd normally be.

For now, consider that your body is your vessel for transmutation and as such is your most potent tool for doing magic, not just inwardly, but also externally. Without a body, neither you nor I could easily affect the world around us. While inner alchemy does work mainly with what happens internally, appreciating how your body allows you to interact with the external world is also important. To some degree I've touched on that in this chapter and the previous one, but I mention it here because the majority of our focus will turn inward now. Just remember to keep yourself balanced between the inner workings of the body, emotions, mind, and spirit, and the external world around you.

Remember as well that the lifestyle you choose affects the world around you as well as your body. A smoker isn't just polluting hir own lungs, but also the lungs of other people and the air itself (though car exhaust, factory fumes, etc. put out far more pollution). Even the products you choose to buy affect the environment. If we support companies that dump pollutants in water or in the land we are only toxifying the environment and our bodies further. This certainly affects the inner alchemy we wish to work. Be conscientious in what you choose to buy, in the companies you choose to support. By doing so you support the Earth as well as yourself and as you'll come to find the relationship that you and I have with the Earth is a very intimate one, on all levels of your existence. Please see Appendix F, an Earth-friendly shopping guide for environmentally friendly products and companies you can support.

Exercises

1. If you don't exercise, start exercising. If you do exercise, change your routine every couple of weeks and note what changes as a result. Then stick with a routine for a while and note what changes occur. What kind of regime do you think is better for exercise?
2. Start noting the kind of food you put into your body. Pay attention to calories, but also to the ingredients. Try and determine how your food choices have affected your body. Does what you eat make you feel good, or does it just meet

your needs? Are you addicted to fast food? What do you think fast food companies put into their food that causes this addiction?

3. Carefully consider the habits you indulge in. How do you think those habits affect you physically, emotionally, mentally, and even spiritually? Why do you indulge in the habits you indulge in, and what benefits do these habits give you? What disadvantages do they confer on you?
4. Change your habits. Quit smoking for three months, for instance, and see if there is a difference, not only in how you feel, but in you how interact with your body. Do you think quitting smoking will affect your magical workings?

Chapter Three:
The Five Senses

The majority of cultures that exist today visually oriented cultures. This means that the sense of sight has primacy over all the other senses. Before the printing press the majority of cultures were either entirely oral or semi-literate cultures. These societies relied more on hearing than sight, when it came to communication. Presently, the majority of people tend to rely upon one sense over the other senses, to the point that they disadvantage themselves. People who have gone blind or deaf have often noted that the loss of one sense has made their other senses keener. But I believe that we can improve all five of our senses and I have found that the first step to working inner alchemy is learning to work with all of the senses as equally as possible.

One problem that is encountered with the senses though is the illusion of separation from your environment. This can partially be blamed on "civilization" and technology. When people spend most of their free time watching a television they tend to become detached from what is happening around them. And this watching of television is ironically a result of literacy, of the ability to read, so that a person uses hir eyes much more (seemingly) than the other senses. The other senses are tuned out and forgotten in the warm glow of the television screen. Literacy, traditionally considered the ability to read and write, focuses exclusively on the ability to use sight to make sense of the world. In turn this focus on what sight provides misses out on something which is very important: "The single, exclusive and intensive focus on written language has dampened the full development of all kinds of human potentials, through all the sensorial possibilities of human bodies, in all kinds of respects, cognitively and affectively, in two and three dimensional representation" (Kress 2003, p. 157). Our increased focus on vision, via written language, has detached us from being aware of our body and our environment via our other senses. All our senses allow us to differentiate and categorize various stimuli and to connect us to what we perceive in our microcosms and macrocosms.

Language does not need to completely divorce you from your reality, but can also connect you, if you acknowledge that how you make meaning occurs through more than just reading text, but also involves interaction with the world around you: "A semiotics [symbol system] which is intended to be adequate to a description of the multimodal world will need to be conscious of forms of meaning-making which are founded on the physiology of human beings as bodily beings" (Kress 2003, p. 28). We can't acknowledge our bodies if we are focused on sight to the exclusion of other senses. Sight is directed outward, but a sense such as touch can be directed both internally (to the body) and externally (to the world).

Multimodality and Body Awareness

Multimodality is the modes of existence you take on yourself, as well as the communication that occurs in such modes. A mode can be thought of as a both a paradigm of belief and thought, but also an expression, communication and experience of reality. You may not realize it, but whether you are in school, at a job, at home, or with friends, your body communicates just as much as your words do. Your body reacts to the environment around it and can tell you a lot of information from the stimuli it receives. It is a mode of existence, albeit for most people a subconscious mode. Combined with other modes of existence, such as communication through language, your body becomes part of a multimodal network, i.e. you with all of your various means and methods of experiencing life. The tone of voice, how a person stands or sits, the gestures s/he makes, causes reactions on the part of your body. For example, if your stomach feels ill walking into a situation, maybe your body is telling you to leave. Listen to what your body says, how it reacts. Try and be aware of how you sit at different places, how you talk to people and how your body reacts, and then try and change those body postures/gestures/tone of voice so that you can purposely and fully communicate knowingly with not just your words, but also your body.

The importance of body language in magic is one of relaxation and comfort. Even in situations where your body holds a yoga pose, such as the death pose, the muscles must be relaxed in order for the pose to be held for a long time. Likewise, for fans of kink, extreme bondage still requires the relaxation of the muscles to be effective. But sometimes it is also an issue of how you use gestures, specifically anchoring through those gestures the energy and meaning you send out to people. The nineteenth century magician, Pascal Beverly

Randolph, touches on the concept of body language with his approach to it, Posism. The magician would associate a specific pose with an emotional state of mind, and use the pose to send out that energy to manifest a desire into reality:

> An adept, expert in Posism, who wishes to give or receive an attacking blow, a kiss, or a caress, should place his body in a determined position and give the necessary facial expression by means of the nostrils and the mouth, as an actor in a sense. He seeks his spirit with total preoccupation and imagination, separated from his goal, and waiting for the willed realization that accomplishes that goal by virtue of the law that is realized through the higher planes-metaphysical, mental, and etheric-which, all being one, reproduces equally on the physical plane and vice versa. (Randolph 1988, p. 22).

Posism essentially argues that the magician can shape reality through using a pose. The assumption of the pose generates the corresponding emotional, mental, and spiritual energy, which is then willed toward a specific goal. This method is still very useful in this day and age, as is evident by use of poses in ritual. It disciplines the magician to call up a particular feeling or state of mind just by changing the body language, which shows again how connected the body is to the spirit, emotions, and mind. When you learn to work with your body language, you can use it to shape the moment, by adopting whatever pose is most useful, thereby expressing the reality you wish to manifest. As an example, if you are depressed, likely your body language includes a slump in your back, a frown on your face, and eyes turned to the Earth. This body language is a pose of depression, and unless it is changed will actually help to generate a reality that is more and more depressing. On the other hand, if you straighten up, look around you, and smile, your mood will brighten considerably after a few minutes. Appearance sometimes does dictate reality. Randolph's techniques, incidentally are reminiscent of eighteenth century rhetorical skills taught to orators. We only need to look at the oratory of such people as Hitler or Churchill to see how a well executed pose, along with speech, can have a magical effect on the audience.

Part of breaking down the artificial division between the body, mind, emotions, and spirit is learning to attune yourself to your senses, working with them so that you can appreciate what your body tells you and learn to work with it. Unfortunately two thousand years of indoctrination of our bodies has most of us convinced that our bodies are dirty, sinful objects. But your body isn't a dirty, sinful object. It is a gift and that gift allows you to do so much, provided you have enough sense to actually cultivate an appreciation of the body and the senses.

I do a workshop on sensory perceptions and it always amazes me how people cringe when I tell them, for instance, to smell themselves in the bathroom. The very idea of smelling yourself or your waste is considered repulsive. Yet that very same smell can tell you if you're healthy or not and is naturally a result of bodily processes that need to occur. So what if the smell is a bit ripe? That could tell you something about your health, about the food you eat and how it affects your body. You need to be in touch with your body and senses more than you are, to deprogram yourself about your concepts of the body. In *Undoing Yourself with Energized Meditation*, one of the contributors has an exercise where a person takes a shit, takes it out of the toilet and sculpts it. Willis, the contributor says: "Disgusting? Why? Simply because you have been taught from the earliest days that shit is dirty. It is not. It is that over-inflated superego that is giving you a kick in the ass and preventing you from any contact with the product of your digestive system" (2002, p. 266). Now think about this: If you have trouble even acknowledging that you smell your own shit, let alone touching it, you clearly have issues with your body. Shit is a natural product of the body. Granted, I don't go out of my way to touch it everyday, but my point is that when you censor what your senses tell you because of how you've been conditioned you've fallen into artificially distancing yourself from your body.

Animals, mammals in particular, pay close attention to their fecal matter, and to others' as well. Not only does it allow them to keep in touch with their own health, but it's also a primary form of communication among them. Many mammals mark their territories with feces and urine. We've been conditioned to believe that we are higher than animals, but this conditioning also causes us to forget that our body is mammalian. Humans depend less on smell than animals. We can detect only the most powerful of odors and only register if those odors are "nice" or "nasty." Animals, on the other hand, can determine from a pile of feces what species and sex the animal that left it was, and how long ago the animal was there. We miss all this. Scent isn't as essential to the survival of the human animal, but even though it isn't, we can still use scent to help us survive. For instance, we can access some of the information about our health from our bodily waste. If your waste smells worse than it usually does, the smell can indicate sickness or a poor change of diet.

So what can be done? The first thing is to actually start learning how to use all of your senses, including sight. We may be a sight oriented society, but that doesn't mean we even begin to fully appreciate what our sight can do for us or what we see. As an example, how many of you can see energy or auras? I've been able to see energy as dots or squiggles in my field of vision for as long as I know, but I have not met many other people who have said they have seen them. However I suspect everyone sees them, but it's always possible that as a child when you tell your parents about it you're told you don't see the dots and so you block those dots out. This happens all the time when parents tell a child: "No, you didn't see the glowing light around that person's head." Likely the child did see the glowing light or the dots, but just as likely the parents, in tune with a mainstream consensual reality that denies such phenomenon, told the child that s/he had not, in fact seen anything. They're passed off as floaters (pieces of loose blood vessel on the eye surface) or afterimages of lights, even when the child says otherwise. S/he believes the parents and consequently is divorced just a bit further from the environment around hir.

The key to getting in touch with your senses is noticing what you normally might ignore. Start, for example, with the two examples I provided above. If you can't see energy or auras try and actually look for them in dark places, where it's easier to see them. If that doesn't work for you then pick an object you're familiar with and then really look at it, noting as many details as possible. Ask yourself if you have noticed those details before, and why you may have been ignoring them. Why do you notice some aspects of the object and not others?

With smell, try smelling something that you normally consider unpleasant. Really take the time to smell this unpleasant scent. Try and figure out what makes it unpleasant to you. Is it a result of conditioning? Another exercise you could try is to smell a person you're familiar with. As an example when I see old friends I'll hug them, but I'll also smell them. It's really my way of confirming their identity, and if you watch animals you'll note that they do this all the time with each other as well. Cats will smell each other and rub their scents to mark their territory and who they consider part of their family. In my case, I like to smell the person, to confirm that this is indeed the person I know. Try it out. You may find, if nothing else, a new layer of intimacy that you've never felt before with that person (You might want to be discreet to avoid confusing your friends.).

With taste, try a new food or eat food you don't like eating. Take a breath and let your tongue feel the breath you pull in. You will actually taste the air. This is also a good way to taste just how much we have polluted our environment, as well as what we're pulling into ourselves. In a smoggy city the breath you take will not taste good, which isn't too surprising. But take the breath anyway and realize in doing so that you are putting yourself into touch with your environment. It's an environment that potentially you've helped to despoil. Taste your own skin at different times during the day, or after various activities.

Hearing is always a fascinating sense to me, despite it being my weakest sense, though I've done everything I can do to develop it. Turn off your music sometime and listen to what's around you. There are usually sounds you block out. It could be the quiet hum of a refrigerator or a subtle noise off in the distance, a slight vibration that you can barely hear and likely usually ignore. Pay attention to these noises. Learn to hear them even when you have music on or guests around. Get into your car, turn off your radio, and listen to your car. The noises you hear can tell you if something's wrong. I've often used my hearing as an intuitive soundboard with my car or the environment around me. Listen…what do you hear? Does it sound right or does it sound off?

Touch is the final sense. Every day we use this sense, but we almost never seem to realize it. Our hands have the most nerves for touching, but our entire body uses this sense. The clothes you wear every day are clothes you touch, but for the most part people don't really feel those clothes, beyond perhaps the first time you wear them. We have learned to ignore the sense of touch when it comes to the everyday sensations we feel on our bodies, but in doing so have missed out on a lot. Touch can tell you not only the texture of an object and whether that object feels good or hurts you, but it can also help you notice how you move your body. By learning to feel the body as it moves you can learn how comfortable you are with your own body and what you can do to improve that comfort. Sometime, as you are walking, try to notice how it feels to walk, how your arms move or don't move. Concentrate on the motion and on the feeling of the muscles. When you are sitting concentrate on how the feels, and how you adjust your body when it begins to feel uncomfortable. Try to get a sense of how any movement contributes to that feeling of comfort or discomfort with your body.

Touch is not just directed outward, but also inwardly, throughout the entire body, so that when you feel pain in your body somewhere (such as a back ache), you know that you need to do something to address the pain. Try running your hands, or an inanimate object such as a feather, along your body lightly; don't focus on what the hands feel, but on what the part of your body feels. Try the back of your upper arm, which I've found to be a particularly sensitive area. The hair you have on your body is part of your sense of touch. Put one of your fingers on one hair of your arm and focus on what that hair feels. You will feel something, even if it's a slight sensation. The point is to realize that by focusing on touch you'll discover much more occurring than you normally realize. Even just motioning your hands in the air will allow you to feel the air itself.

You can apply these principles to other people and likely you often do without realizing it. When you ask a person what's wrong it's usually because you've heard their voice and it doesn't sound "happy" or you've noticed their body language and instead of being comfortable, the person's posture, facial expression, or movement is different. In either case by learning to pay attention to what your senses tell you, you can anticipate how the person feels and will act toward you. Of course to some degree this is subjective, based on how well you know the person, but this also true of any experiences you have through the senses. The perceptions you have are mediated by your subjectivities. Nonetheless, it is possible to be accurate in what you sense about a person from the tone of hir voice. It just depends on how well you know the person and how much you pay attention to how other people act.

Now that you hopefully have a better appreciation of your five senses, I want to extend the sense work in the direction of the body itself. You know by now that while your senses allow you to differentiate yourself from what exists around you, they also connect to what seems to be around you. But what about within the body? Do the senses just act as stimuli receptors for the body or is there something more to what they can do?

For instance your heart beat is something you can hear and/or feel, but how many people really do? I'm not just talking about the method where you feel your heartbeat on your wrist, but being able to feel your pulse throughout your body. There is even a way to control your heart rate which Carrington & Muldoon mention in *The Projection of the Astral Body*. You first learn to sense your pulse, to feel it throughout your body: "After you have acquired the ability to lie still, and both feel and hear your heart-beat within your chest...your next step is to be able to feel and hear the pulsations in any part of your body-by concentrating upon that particular spot" (Carrington & Muldoon 1973, p. 212). Once you can do that you then focus on "telling" your heart to slow down or speed up the rate of the heart beats. This is done by consciously focusing on the heart as opposed to relying on your subconscious (Carrington & Muldoon 1973). Focus on taking over the autonomic function of the brain that usually regulates the heart and learn to consciously control the rate by consciously choosing for it to slow down or speed up. The authors mentioned above found this useful as a means of inducing astral projections. If you slow your heart beat down enough you can enter a state of near death. This takes some practice attuning your senses to hearing/feeling the heart beat, but it can be done. I see this as an example of inner alchemy, where you learn how to control a seemingly automatic function of your body consciously so that you can induce an altered state of consciousness.

All of this is accomplished through the senses, particularly touch and hearing. By learning to turn them inward you can learn more than just controlling your heart rate. Sometimes when I have a headache or some other part of my body hurts, I use touch as a way of localizing the feeling of pain. Once I've identified where the source is, I combine what I feel with the sense of color I associate with the pain. This is called synesthesia, the blending of senses. My sense of touch acts as my sight, in this case my headache translating into a bright electromagnetic green. On the other hand, when I feel really interested in a task or exercises I'm doing, some of that touch sensation translates into an image of orange. Now feeling interested in doing something is emotion, but emotion is part of feeling and translates into physical sensations. When a person feels worried about a situation and hir stomach is upset, that's because the emotion is felt on a physical level. Likewise, if a person feels happy, that sensation of happiness will be felt in the physical body, through the release of endorphins. As such emotional feeling is an extension of the sense of touch and can be part of the experience of synesthesia.

Anyone can experience synesthesia. The reason many people don't is that because they've been conditioned to treat each sense as separate from the other. It's just a question of learning how to translate one way of feeling sensation into another way of feeling sensation. You do it all the time with food, when you smell it and it incites hunger or memories of taste, even salivation. The very act of smelling is linked to that of tasting. There's no reason not to believe that you can't do the same with the rest of the senses.

One of the earliest visualization exercises I did, when I first started practicing magic, was to visualize a favorite food or piece of fruit. I would not only focus on the sight of it, but how it sounded, smell, tasted, and felt. I would treat each sense separately at first so that as an example I'd mentally touch an orange and feel the texture of the skin, feel the juice squirt on my hands as I began to peel the skin off. I'd even focus on feeling my teeth bite into the orange. Eventually I'd put all the senses together and experience the orange through all five senses at the same time. In this way I was able to provoke synesthesia both on a physical and psychic level.

In order to improve our senses, we have to understand them on a quantum level. This includes the understanding that we can sense well beyond the limits commonly accepted in our society. A good example of this is energy. While I mentioned seeing the dots and squiggles above, which I claimed was energy, I've also focused on using touch as a way to sense energy. Not everyone sees these squiggles and dots. Sometimes the ability to sense energy is found through a different medium than sight, and as I've mentioned it's important to not rely on sight as your only sense for interpreting reality.

Often magicians will claim they feel energy. If you form a ball of energy, according to traditional science, you can't see it, at least not with the eyes, and so it must not be real. Nonetheless you can "feel" the energy, which suggests that perhaps traditional science focused too much on using seeing to believe. That feeling might be a sensation of more warmth than is usually exuded by your hands, but it is a sensation that is willed by your choice to focus on creating a ball of energy. This means that sight does not necessarily determine reality. And certainly quantum physics echoes this, given that it works on the subatomic level with energy that you really can't see. You may be able to touch it though. If you work with energy, try and determine how you know the energy is there. Likely you'll realize it's through touch, the ability to feel what's around you. We even extend touch beyond the physical to the emotion when we ask each other how we feel.

Auras are another good example. When most people think of auras, they think of seeing them. However, you can sense auras with all five of your senses which extend beyond what you experience in the conventional physical reality. This occurs partially through mental visualization and focusing the mind on the task at hand, and through the willingness to experiment with the senses. For instance, returning to the sense of sight, it is possible to increase the amount of the light spectrum that your eyes can see:

> A light is allowed in by the movement of the iris, it passes through the lens and acts upon the retina. The retina is the truly light sensitive portion of the eye. It contains nerve cells called cones and rods, which serve to detect specific colors and intensities of light. When the cones and rods are stimulated, a chemical is released which helps translate that stimulation into specific colors and light intensities...The more strongly the cones and rods are stimulated, the more subtle light emanations you can detect. (Andrews 2000, pp. 41-42).

The way rods and cones are stimulated is through the eye muscles. Anyone (not just people with 20/20) vision can learn how to control these muscles and expand the range of sight in different light continuums. You've probably noticed that your eyes will dilate depending on the light density in a room. The more light there is in a room, the smaller the pupil is and likewise, the less light, the larger your pupil is.

You'll find some excellent examples of eye exercises in Ted Andrew's book, *How to See the Aura*, but here are some I use. Try letting your sight blur. Relax the muscles in the eye so that you aren't focusing on anything and your sight will blur just a bit. When you relax your muscles you are actually allowing your pupils to dilate. It's like those posters that have hidden images that can't be seen unless your eye sight blurs just a bit, allowing in different light frequencies and revealing the other image.

Another exercise that you can do involves methods similar to the Tattvas, used for elemental workings in Indian magic. Take a sheet of colored paper and put it on another sheet of paper that is its complement on a color wheel (for instance, a red piece of paper on a green background). Now focus and unfocus your eyes; you can alternate the colors you concentrate on when you do this. This dilates the pupil and creates a sensation where you feel drawn into the primary color. In similar manners the Tattvas are used by magicians to project themselves into other planes of existence, such as elemental planes. One method involves looking intently at the color combination symbol of the Tattva for a short time. Then, with the afterimage firmly imprinted in your sight, look at a blank white surface and concentrate on the afterimage, using it as a gateway for astral projection.

What's really interesting to note is how the amount of light can actually affect your brain:

> Your brain receives information about light and dark through the retinas in your eyes. The retina is evolved from the same tissues that make up the brain, so your eyes literally have a direct link to the inner recesses of your brain. When your eyes receive light, your brain thinks it's daytime and shifts your body processes-temperature, heart rate, hormone production-to match the time of day it thinks it is. And your retinas can sense light even through closed eyelids. (Perry 2003, pp. 96-97)

Clearly light has quite an effect on the ways your body functions. The amount of light you get during a particular season of the year can affect your moods, hence Seasonal Affective Disorder. SAD is caused by not getting enough light, which consequently affects the chemicals produced by the brain. Perry is quite correct in noting that even with your eyes closed, the retina can still see light. When I meditate during the day and I get really deep into it, I can still see shifting patterns of light. Often these patterns become streamers of color, which I use to explore the layers of my consciousness. Each streamer of color represents a pathway into a particular state of consciousness. By focusing I enter into a tunnel of just that color, which takes me to the altered state of mind. I've also used the streamers to get in touch with quantum/alternate reality version of myself, with each streamer representing an alternate me (Andrieh Vitimus has a space/time ritual that also operates on the same idea, by using a strobe light and string to get into the quantum matrix. See "Quantum Selves" in the *Magick on the Edge* anthology for more details on his approach). By exercising your eye muscles, you will become more sensitive to light. If you find that you have trouble sleeping as a result, try putting a dark drape over your window so you can block out the light. Wearing a sleep mask and/or shroud can also help block out the light.

You can also use technology to experiment with light density. You should be careful, however, if you're epileptic, as the technology I'm about to reference can cause epileptic fits (for more in depth information on these machines see my book *Space/Time Magic*). The dreamachine and mind machine integrate technology that uses the flickering of light to induce an altered state of mind. The light triggers chemical reactions which can lead to different states of consciousness. Both use the flicker principle:

> Flicker is the application of pulsed light to the optical region with eyes either open or closed. Research has shown that in most people flicker produces extraordinary responses in the brain. This is because the light signal causes a coded message to be distributed to its every part…The peculiar feature of flicker stimulation is that anyone looking at the light soon begins to see more than just a flicker. There is a sensation of movement, pattern, and changing color. The unexpected bonus is that the fantastic designs, movements of color and sensations of bodily involvements are in the mind of the perceiver, this also supplies a clue as to his creative potential. (TAGC-Teste Tone Liner Notes).

The mind machine, in my opinion, works better because you can adjust the frequency of strobing on the LED glasses. I've also found flicker useful for working with the body. In the chapter on meditation I'll go into this in more detail but for now I want to return to the other senses of the body and the aura.

Just as you can see the aura if you physically work with your eyes (as well as through intuition and visualization), you can also fine tune your sense of touch. For instance, when someone comes home or comes to visit and you know that person well you might feel that person's arrival before even knowing they've arrived. This is because you can feel their energy through your sense of touch, as well as any differences in the environment. This is partly why when people are robbed they feel so violated. People tend to immerse themselves, their energy, etc., into their homes, and when those environments have been touched by people who shouldn't be there, they can feel that disruption. In part this ability to feel the energies of others is based on the aura, as well as the physical sense of touch. If you've ever felt a tingling sensation or sudden warmth or a sudden chill, it's because you may be feeling some energy around you. In Barbara Ann Brennan's *Hands of Light*, note the description of unhealthy auras: "'Tentacles' are oozing, slippery, silent, and heavy" (1988, p. 106). Notice that the words chosen are sound or touch related. Clearly it's not just about seeing an aura, but also feeling (and hearing) the aura. If you're around a person and you feel drained afterwards, it's likely that the person has taken some of your energy. Your ability to touch then extends beyond just feeling with your skin. It also extends to the energetic realm. You have to be aware of not only what you feel from others, but also what you put out for others to feel—and possibly take-from you.

Even as your sense of touch extends into the spirit realm, it can also be used for tactile astral projection. When astral projection is described, it's usually regarded as a sight related activity. Even if it's not physical sight, we expect that when we astrally project, sight will be the primary (and often only) sense that we have access to. Likewise dreams are sight focused, but while it could partially be the brain's way of processing the stimuli from the day, it's also possible that the prominence of sight is a result of culture. It is possible to project by touch or sensation, and to work with energy by touch: "Tactile Imaging (T. I.) is the active use of body awareness to directly stimulate and manipulate the substance of the energy body" (Bruce 1999, p. 119). In other words, touch is also used to stimulate energy. If you've ever felt really charged up, likely you've used Tactile Imaging without realizing it, because you've felt the energy throughout your body. Also if you've done any meditation, you'll sometimes feel a surge of energy go through your body. Again, just because you don't see the energy, doesn't mean it's not there. That you can feel energy, in and of itself, is perhaps better, as it forces you to rely on another sense. You can learn to control the energy through the sensations, and then direct it toward specific areas of your body. Close your eyes and just feel your body. Focus on a single limb and then focus on feeling the energy in that limb. Then move the energy in that limb. I often feel energy as a stream or current and use that image to connect my consciousness with the energy within me.

As I mentioned above touch can also be used for astral projection: "Center your awareness hands in the middle of your chest. Reach out with both of them and grasp the rope. Climb hand over hand strongly up the rope" (Bruce 1999, pp. 254-255). As you might note, the focus is on the sensation of feeling as opposed to sight. By using your sense of touch you are able to connect with energy on a deeper level than sight alone can give you.

Besides touch and sight, there is sound. It is possible to hear the aura. This is simply a matter of being attuned to the world of subtle noises around us. Earlier in this chapter I had you try and focus on those noises you block out every day. Did you feel a tingling sensation around your ear, perhaps feel a bit of energy that seemed to come from the ear itself? If you did, it's because you were concentrating on just hearing and likely you picked up more sounds. All sound is energy. Every sound you hear is a vibration and we end up receiving those sounds and that energy because we hear them. The tingling sensation I feel around my ears, is to my mind, the reception of that energy through the sense of hearing.

Something else I've found fascinating about the ear is that if you manipulate your outer ear with your hands, you can pick up more noises. This can be as simple as cupping your hand behind your ear, so it cradles the outer ring of your ear or it can be using your fingers to push the outer lobe in different directions. You might be amazed at the range of sound you can pick up with your ears when you manipulate them. This is why other mammals have such good hearing—their larger ears capture more sound. In addition, they've learned to pay more attention to what they hear than we do.

When you use your ears to sense energy, focus on feeling an extra, energetic outer lobe. Then close your eyes and focus on hearing. Next, try and hear another person's aura, paying attention to the unique sounds you get, and then describe it to that person. The key to doing this is to let yourself hear the energy, the vibration, of the person. All of us vibrate. We don't always realize that the seeming solidity of our reality or ourselves is an illusion. On the most basic level we are composed of vibrating particles and those particles do make sound, even if we can't easily hear it. When we hear the aura, what we're really doing is tapping into those vibrations, and those vibrations are translated into sounds we know. For instance, one person's aura sounded like an alto from a violin. If you hear any dissonance in the sound you usually get, confirm this sound with hir, checking if there is an issue in hir life that affects hir energy. By checking every day you can confirm and validate the experience you're having.

Personal sounds are not limited to the aura. To some degree a person's sounds are imposed upon hir by other people, through the giving of a name. A name is more than just a word. It embodies a distinctive meaning, a reality to those people who hear it. When I hear my name, I think of myself, and when I call a friend by hir name, that sound embodies the meanings that I associate with that friend. Granted, those meanings have been formed by the relationship I have with that person and don't entirely encapsulate hir identity. They are partially created by our interaction with each other and as such s/he has chosen to accept those vibrations and their meanings. We just don't think of our relationships in terms of vibrations. A useful exercise to consider, with both friend and foe, is how much the vibrations can tell you about the harmony you have with someone. Listen to how you talk to the person, and to the meaning and emotion you put into the words. The meanings and emotions affect the vibrations of the sound and the energy the person receives. When you talk with someone you like, you may find you use a higher tone of voice, as opposed to talking with someone you dislike, where a lower tone is used. Try, as an experiment, using a higher tone with someone you dislike and note how they react to that tone.

You can also use sound to attune yourself to the energy of the land. Just as a person has a sound (through hir name), a place does as well. The name of a place conveys the meanings associated with the place. For instance, if you name your home, you give that home the power and meanings you associate with that name. Powerspots can also be named. Careful thought should be given to the name chosen. Some consultation with the genius of the power spot may also be needed to get a sense of how it feels about the name.

Naming tools, cars, etc, also is something that people do. The choice to give a name is both an utterance of sound/vibration and a personification and recognition of the object as having an essence of life to it. In fact, the vibration sets and imprints that pattern of essence into the object, because the vibration is an energy that you've put into the object by naming it. Every utterance afterwards adds to the initial vibration.

We connect to those vibrations by listening and vibrating the sound as well (if possible). Vibrating is different from regular speech.

It refers to using the lower portion of your vocal cords to vibrate the noise so that your throat itself vibrates. Everyday speech doesn't use the full range of the vocal cords, nor do people invest as much energy into it. Vibration, on the other hand, uses the vocal cords more forcibly. The sound that is made is projected more as a result. There's more investment in the sound that's made. The mantras chanted by monks or the invocations done by a magician are powerful because the vibrations of those sounds reach out and connect with other energies in the universe:

> The job, of the utterer, is to aim sonically at whatever Inner contact is sought via the hearers, whose function is to link themselves with that particular contact and not other...It means that while a skilled Invocant is emitting meaningful sonic energies directed to some category of the Universal Consciousness, those hearing them physically are acting as receptive relays sending the message backwards through themselves along their inner linkages with the Contact they are all trying to reach. (Gray 1980, pp. 176-177)

Tapping into the vibrations you hear allows you to connect with forces external to you, both in mundane reality and sacred reality. Every time you listen to a person speak, you are connecting to that person. The sounds imprint on your consciousness and register certain meanings and concepts you associate with those sounds. At the same time, speech and vibration are also projections of your aura. Good orators engage their audience because of the subject they are addressing, but also because they are projecting their aura/energy. This projection keeps the attention of the audience focused on the orator. The orator may not realize s/he is doing this with hir energy, but this can occur even on an unconscious level. The reason a person is so tired after making a speech isn't just because of the speaking, but also the effort s/he had to put out to keep people focused.

When you listen to music, you connect to the energy that music embodies. You simply need to be aware of what you hear, and learn to work with the energy in sound. Some musicians already use sound to bring about altered states of mind by stimulating different brain waves. Clearly sound has a both physiological and energetic effect upon us. An extreme example is infrasound, which is sound that can kill or harm people: "In 1960 Professor Gavreau, head of the Electro-Acoustics and Automation Laboratory in France investigated the use of infrasonics as a weapon for military purposes. He devised a siren which emitted a note of 37 cycles, the effects of which could kill instantaneously when amplified to extremely high levels" (TAGC-Psychophysicist liner notes). Infrasound is sound that occurs at an extremely low vibration. With the principle of entrainment a sound at a particular vibration can entrain other vibrations so that they resonate at the same vibration. Low vibrations for people can cause headaches and in the case of infrasound death because the vibrations in a person's body are entrained toward that low vibration.

But even as sound can kill, sound can also be used to aid people. It's a question of how we choose to use it. The sense of hearing allows us to do much more than people credit it for, even allowing us to have telepathic experiences. How does such an experience occur? There are some people you will connect with easier than others. Their vibrations are in synch with your own, making it easier to hear their vibrations. What you experience is not necessarily words; when I connect with a person very deeply it is through images. Nonetheless those images have sounds and I think of telepathy as being more sound based because sound is a primary method of communication. You have brain waves which represent frequencies of thought and mood and through those frequencies you can touch other people.

If you can listen to a person's aura, try and attune yourself to that person's thoughts. My mate Lupa and I have a deep telepathic connection, because our individual energy is synchronized to the other person. One of us often voices what the other person is thinking at the time. From my observations, this seems to be common with couples that have healthy communication between them. They learn to communicate to each other on a variety of levels. To listen to someone's mind, open your mind and energy up. Allow yourself to be receptive to the person, instead of closed off or shielded. When I'm in touch with a person telepathically I often visualize a cord between me and that person comprised of both of our energies. I can send energy to that cord, travel down it to the person, and I can hear that person, through the cord, which also acts as a sound frequency. Since this experience has been validated by people I have connected with I know it works.

Finally there are smell and taste, which are interwoven with each other. Every day we eat and drink. We smell and taste the food to ensure we like it. But there is much more to taste and smell than just that function. In the *Wraeththu* trilogy by Storm Constantine, the characters "share breath". This technique is a way of sharing and tasting each other's energy and soul. Sharing breath is also an extremely mind-blowing kiss, because you are both projecting energy to each other and then allowing that energy to mix. Even here in our reality, the very act of a kiss is a sharing of the soul, of energy. You taste each other, not just physically, but energetically. This is why people tend to feel energized when they kiss. They are sharing themselves with each other. Another level to tasting energy is through its scent.

You don't necessarily want to kiss everyone to taste a person's aura or soul. That's where smell comes in. Just as a physical scent can be pleasing or not, so too can the energetic scent of a person being pleasing or not. Generally the physical smell of a person will tell you a lot about their energy, too. Personal hygiene is indicative of how the person takes care of hirself on all levels, though a bad aroma may be caused by illness. Because of all the artificial fragrances today there's no absolute guarantee that physical smell will always reflect the energy. Even soap and shampoo leave scent residues. The way to sense the energetic aroma, since smell and taste are so interwoven, is to focus on the person and let your energy touch him/her very lightly. Open your mind and just smell/taste the energy. In other words, pay more attention to the details and sensations you get in various situations. Don't try and block the impressions. Instead write them down. Does the person smell/taste sour? Does s/he remind you of a particular food you like or dislike? Pay attention to the energy and use it as a guide as to whether you want to be around that person or not.

Exercises that develop all the senses can be found through playing games. I like to use puzzle video games. The *Prince of Persia* series (a series of games where you solve puzzles in order to progress into a castle), for example, forces you to rely on your senses, using them to solve the puzzles. Primarily you rely on sight and hearing, but even the sense of touch is affected, in terms of the eye-hand coordination that's developed and the vibrations that can occur in game controller. Playing board games with people can also be useful. By using your senses to read other players and the cues they give you can formulate your own strategies. Finally sports and other recreation activities such as paintball can also be useful for honing your senses as well as your analytical abilities. The ability to use your senses effectively to help you analyze a situation is an excellent discipline tool that will help you learn to improve your senses.

This chapter has dealt with the five senses physically and as an introduction to the energy work chapters. One question that may come to mind, particularly for the psychic level, is whether what is felt is "real" or just an illusion. My answer is that even the physical reality we sense is one which is subjective. The senses give us information, but how we choose to mediate that information is based on our own biases. So what can really be said? First, faith or belief is always useful. Faith is not deluded, as long as you think to question it and validate the initial experience with repeated practice. Second, working with other people who can validate your experiences will help you a lot, because it will give you perspectives separate from your own. Finally, an open mind is essential. It's very easy to nay-say someone else's experience, especially if you choose to close your mind to the possibility of experiencing what s/he experienced. It is much harder to approach an unfamiliar experience with an open mind, and a willingness to explore. But by doing so you can test your own limits.

Remember you are in control of your experiences. If you let them control you then you are allowing yourself to become deluded. Control involves knowing when to ground back into the ordinary mundane mainstream life, as well as knowing who you can talk with about your experiences. Rely on your senses, but also question the experiences you get with a bit of skepticism. Empower yourself, but not to the point where you believe you're the emperor of everything. Use what you have experienced to grow as a person. Inner alchemy is part of this process and by learning to work with your senses you are taking a step toward controlling who you are and what you can do. Most importantly, keep your perspective, question your experiences, and use them to grow, instead of letting them take you over.

Exercises

1. Start paying attention to how you wear your body.
   Do you feel comfortable in your body? If not, ask yourself why and write out the reasons. Observe your posture in different situations.
   Do you sit straight, or do you slump?
   How does your posture affect you?
   How does it make you feel, physically and otherwise? Pay attention to your gestures and tone of voice. Try experimenting with people by asking them how they react when you gesture with your arm or hand, or if you choose to sound sad or happy. Then purposely start controlling how you wear your body…and note how people react to you, without asking them.
2. Go out and use each of your five senses to have an experience you dislike. In this way you will learn to savor all experiences, even those that seem contrary to you. You can use the examples I provided in this chapter or find some experiences on your own.
3. Develop the five psychic senses. Again, try out the examples I mentioned above or come up with some of your own. Several of the books I've referenced in this chapter have excellent exercises as well. Keep an open mind, especially in regards to smell/taste and hearing as these senses are often not as appreciated as sight and touch.
4. Why do you think there is so much emphasis on sight, in terms of proving something?
5. Is your sight really that reliable? As an example go to a stage magician's show and try, with your sight, to figure out the tricks s/he does. If you can't, ask yourself again, is your sight that reliable?
6. Try out the *Prince of Persia* or a similar video game series or some other activity where your senses will be challenged, so that you have to rely on them to figure out the puzzle or situation. Afterwards write down your experiences.
   How if at all did the activity force you to rely on your senses?
   How is this useful as a discipline tool?

Chapter Four:
Body Fluids

I've used body fluids since the beginning of my magical practice. I've found my fluids useful for charging magical workings or as sacrificial offerings to beings I've worked with. Body fluids are also an essential part of inner alchemy; they transport nutrients and waste in the body. I consider body fluids to be a means of transmission and communication within the body, and even external to it, in the right circumstances.

Blood

When I was eighteen I used a part of my body as one of the ingredients for a ritual to the elements. I wanted to connect with them more intimately than I had before. I had worked with the hermetic model of the elemental kings, but I wanted more of a connection than just working with elemental magic in that way. Instead of doing traditional ceremonial rituals, I wanted to make a sacrificial offering. So I decided that I would offer a part of my life force, in return for part of what might be considered elemental life force.

I chose to use blood to represent my life force. I went with a friend to a park in southeastern Pennsylvania, a place that was full of what I felt was very primordial, elemental energy. We went late at night, in early spring. It was a cool night, but the shivers I had were more from anticipation than anything else. I was going to offer part of myself to the element of Earth, in return for elemental energy. I found a spot under a tree that felt perfect for the ritual itself. My friend watched as I took off my coat and shirt. I made my invocation to Ghob, the Hermetic king of the element Earth and then I took out a World War Two era knife and cut myself on the right arm. I took my blood and put it on the Earth, smearing it into the dirt as much as possible. I felt an agreement, an exchange of energy. The Earth accepted my offering and in turn I felt very connected to its energies.

Afterwards I drove both of us home. I'd actually gone into shock, as the cut was deep. I could drive, but I drove one handed and was in a shocked state of mind. We were lucky I got us home safe, but there wasn't heavy traffic that night. I recall looking at the cut later and seeing how deep it was and being surprised at the depth. To this day I still have a scar on my right arm where I cut myself. But I am still as deeply connected to the element Earth as I was that first night. I did subsequent rituals for the other traditional western elements of Water, Air, Fire, and Spirit, each time offering blood in exchange for the "blood", the life force of those elementals.

One effect I noticed from this working was that I had much higher natural affinity for elemental workings, after I had done the ritual. I was tapped into the elemental energy, a part of it now, as opposed to occasionally accessing it. I found that my interaction with the elementals was likewise more intimate and much more focused on the connection as opposed to just getting what I wanted from them. When I wanted to work weather magic or other forms of elemental magic, it became easier for me. I was identifiable to the elements as not just human, but also as an elemental.

I also always take the approach that you should work with elemental energy, as opposed to forcing it to your will. Accordingly whenever I have done elemental magic workings since then, my energy has flowed with the elements, never forcing them, but instead bonding with and imprinting my desires on them.

My example of the ritual I did when I was eighteen is one of many rituals you can do. You don't need to use a knife to do this ritual. You can use a sterilized needle for instance, or any place that carries diabetic supplies has lancets which prick your finger, though you should only use them once (I highly recommend using lancets). Or you can choose to use a knife. The knife, for me, is a much more visceral experience. The scars are reminders of the choice and offering I have made (Bear in mind though that a knife can be fatal if not done carefully, whereas a lancet will produce the same effect for a ritual). Regardless of what tool you choose to use to draw blood, make sure you clean where you've punctured or cut yourself and have a first aid kit on hand. You also want to clean the tools you use. Sterilize them with alcohol so they can be used again (except for needles and lancets). It's also a good idea to have a person on hand just in case you need medical attention, but can't help yourself.

There are other precautions you should take in regards to using blood for magic. For instance, you shouldn't scar yourself just to signify you've done magic: "Obsessive application of self-mutilation replaces the deeper meanings of blood with the frantic instability of mental illness. Carelessness with the blood of others puts the sorcerer at risk for poisoning and disease" (Seth 2003, p. 15). Keep in mind that blood is a biohazard, and can harbor a number of nasty things, such as HIV and hepatitis. Be mindful of disposal as well as use.

As with any form of magic, it's important you keep yourself disciplined and focused on what you are doing. Working with blood can be a very intoxicating feeling, as you're working with your own life force. Seth notes: "The reason blood and bones are such important parts of magic are[sic] that they are very powerful conductors and receptacles of energy" (2003, p. 19). A simple enough explanation, but consider that working with such a receptacle can lead to instability if you don't moderate what you do. A good example of this principle is that of the Roman emperor Julian who did such frequent animal sacrifices that he did overloaded on blood magic and ended up ultimately destroying himself: "The magician risks obsession if there is so much energy that he cannot focus it all. So many bulls had Julian killed; so much energy he had absorbed" (Mace 1998, p. 35). I recommend reading Mace's essay on Julian on the dangers of doing blood magic. It shows what happens when you take a potent life force such as blood and use too much of it for magical work.

Blood is an extremely effective tool to use for rituals. It transports oxygen and nutrients to all parts of the body. Without it we could not live. It is also an effective representative of DNA, in the sense that it transmits information (via the nutrients it gives to the rest of the body), much as DNA transmits information to the cell it's in. I've used blood for a lot of my genetic magic workings. The above ritual is an example of such a working, as I was seeking to exchange genetic information (with the blood as the medium of my genetic information) with the elementals. I don't think a person should ever use blood in a ritual lightly. You are offering a part of your personal energy and that's something which has to be done carefully for reasons I've mentioned above. Whether you choose to bond with an elemental or with another person or entity you should know you are offering that entity/person a key to you. However, that entity/person is also doing the same.

While blood is very effective for exchanging life force, it can also be useful for sacrifice. In choosing to sacrifice some of our own blood, we release the energy within it to accomplish the goal we seek to bring forth. In my particular case I usually use blood to charge a sigil. I'll sometimes even create the sigil with my blood. However, I usually mix the blood with some paint or whatever else I'm using to create the sigil. You can sacrifice blood to an existing entity, or use it to create a new one.

Blood magic can also be used to heal. A friend of mine who donates blood visualizes it filled with healing energy that helps the people who receive it. He actually does a vision quest and goes to where the blood is being taken from his body and then changes the frequency of the blood cells so that the energy is optimized toward healing the person. By charging the blood that is taken from him, he helps to insure that the blood can help those people less fortunate than him.

One form of blood magic that men don't have direct access to is the monthly blood that comes from a woman's period. Menstrual blood can be used for a lot of ritual work as opposed to letting it go to waste. This blood is very powerful because it is part of that monthly cycle that involves not just the uterus but the entire body of the woman. It is a sacrifice of potential life, and using that potentiality greatly enhances magic you want to do with blood. Several women I know collect their menstrual blood and then use it for rituals via tampons, pads, or a menstrual cup. The menstrual cup seems to be the best tool for women to use for magical purposes as it doesn't absorb the blood, which can then easily be used for sigils or put in paints, etc. Menstrual blood can be also used for bonding/binding rituals. Each month, Lupa and I use her menstrual blood and my cum in a binding ritual. We have a mild BDSM lifestyle where she is my dominant and I am her submissive. The binding ritual is part of how we strengthen that lifestyle choice between us. She binds me to her and then puts a very small amount of the fluids on a collar which I wear as an affirmation of the binding we've mutually agreed to.

Lupa also uses her menstrual blood for abundance magic. Because the menstrual blood is part of a monthly cycle, she feels it can be used to help work with other cycles such as a paycheck cycle, or getting to and from work safely (which is a cycle in its own way. She puts some of her blood on a small holed stone and then wears the stone in a pouch for the rest of the menstrual period, storing the energy into the stone. When she needs to do magic concerned with cycles she draws on the energy in the stone. There are other uses for menstrual blood, including purification through the body's detoxification process, and even using the cramps and directing the pain felt toward a specific goal

(Lupa 2005). The only limitation for a woman is the limit of imagination. Clearly the menstrual blood is very powerful as it embodies the life force of the woman. Men may borrow blood from an agreeable woman in order to charge items or draw toxins from them, or otherwise use the energy within it.

One aspect of blood magic that I haven't touched on is vampirism, specifically sanguinary vampirism, which unlike psychic vampirism, requires a more physical touch. People who identify themselves as sanguinary vampires drink blood to draw energy from it. This practice is a bit dangerous, especially if you don't take proper precautions. After all, such vampires are still biologically human and are still susceptible to the same diseases. If you choose to indulge in this type of practice, you should make sure the donor contains no diseases which can be transmitted by blood. You also don't want to drink too much, as that can have a debilitating effect on the body of the donor, and consuming too much blood can induce vomiting. The most important safety tip is knowing the health history of the person you're feeding off of (also known as the donor), as you don't want to get any blood transmitted diseases, such as HIV/AIDS or Hepatitis C. Make sure, you clean the donor's wound to avoid infection. The advantages of such blood magic is that it certainly creates a connection between you and the donor, albeit a less than equal connection, as the person drunk from is more or less food. Nonetheless the drinker can draw energy from the blood. What s/he is drawing on is the prana in the blood. Some (if not all) sanguinary vampires reportedly have a medical condition, which may require them to actually drink blood, but otherwise it's advisable to avoid this risky practice. There are better ways to go about getting energy within one's own body.

A final aspect of blood magic I want to touch on is the use of blood as a body paint. Whether you use the blood alone or mix it with paint (the kind you find in costume shops that's water solvent), blood can be a very effective form of body paint. Using just a little of it (a finger prick's worth of blood is all I recommend) can charge the paints you use tremendously, because you are infusing the paints with your own physical material and the energy inherent to it. I'll usually paint sigils on my body, sigils that I'll then vocalize, charging them into my aura through both the vocalization of the sigil and the painting of the sigil on the body. I'll even trace the sigil with the finger that gave blood, visualizing energy pouring from the wound into the sigil and then melding that sigil into my aura. Sigil work, in this case, can be used for healing, but also can be used as evocations/invocations of godforms or entities you work with. The blood can be understood as a sacrifice to whatever entities you choose to work with. If you choose to use someone else's blood, again, please take the necessary precautions.

Saliva

While blood is a handy fluid to use, there are other personal products of the body that can be just as useful. For instance, I like to use saliva for a lot of my workings. When I first moved to Kent, Ohio, I decided I wanted to make a power spot network that I could draw on when I needed magical energy. I walked all around, finding spots I really resonated with. At each spot, I swished some spittle and then spat on my hand. I put my finger on the ground and traced a sigil with the spit. The next day as the sun rose, its energy hit the sigils and activated the power network. I used spittle instead of blood, because it would have ultimately been unhealthy to use blood. I had plenty of spittle and it didn't represent a potential loss of health. When I would swish the saliva in my mouth I would charge it with the specific intent that I wanted to mesh my energy with the energy of the land to create a power spot network.

In ancient Greek myths spittle was also used. Apollo spat in Cassandra's mouth, so that whatever she foretold would be disbelieved. Likewise, in Christian myths, Jesus healed a person's eyes with dirt and spit.

Anytime you kiss a person you are not just swapping spit, but also energy. The next time you kiss someone, try and see what that person's energy tastes like, how it feels as it meshes with yours. Focus on not just the physical sensations, but also the mental and emotional impressions you receive. I've also used spit for healing work. I'll spit on an area that hurts and then rub the saliva in (except on open wounds). In essence, I'm treating saliva as a salve that I can use to digest the pain.

One exercise I do is called the Eight Brocades, a qigong exercise, which focuses on turning saliva into energy. Through this exercise you can raise the actual energy of the body, as the various motions of the exercise stimulate the internal energy. Perhaps what's most intriguing about this technique is the realization that we can't separate our bodies from the energy we work with. In the West, many occultists have a false division in regards to the body and energy work. They argue that the body isn't really integral to energy work, but such claims are ultimately spurious and delusional. If nothing else, the body helps to make us aware of the energy we can work with. Far eastern disciplines such as qigong, yoga, and Tai-chi emphasize a more natural approach to working with the body and energy. The Eight Brocades is an example of that. Through certain motions and postures energy is released and raised. This energy can be used to heal, protect, or for other purposes. Learning to work with our bodies and with the products of our bodies can lead to new directions in magical workings. To ignore the body, to argue that it's not essential to energy work, is to sell yourself short of the potential you could accomplish.

Below is the version of the Eight Brocades that I learned from a friend. I do this exercise every day and have found it to be very useful for raising energy. As far as I can tell the saliva is an integral part of this exercise. You are, through your movements, energizing the saliva and thus when swallowing it, you're really swallowing energy.

Sit down in a cross legged position. Click your teeth together 36 times. Next, lace the fingers from both your hands together and put your hands on the back of your neck. Make sure your elbows are parallel to your cheeks, then keeping your hands on your neck, move your arms outward. Do this nine times.

Now unlace your hands and put your index finger on top of your middle finger for both hands. Put your middle finger on the points where your skull meets your neck. Tap your index finger on your middle finger twenty four times. Next bring your hands down. Now move your head side to side, taking a breath in when you move it to the right and breathing when you move it to the left. Do this twelve times, so that you move your head to the right twelve times and to the left twelve times.

Swish the saliva in your mouth around thirty six times. Then swallow the saliva in three gulps, feeling the saliva go down to your belly. You might feel a warm sensation down there, which is good. Now rub your hands together until they are hot. Put them on the lower back and rub them on it twenty four times, with a circular motion.

Straighten your legs out now. You'll rotate the shoulders nine times clockwise and the nine times counterclockwise. Then lace your fingers together and put your hands over your head, holding them there for three seconds. Then push your hands on your head for three seconds. Repeat this two more times and then try and touch your toes.

Finally start swishing saliva in your mouth again. You want to swallow the saliva nine times. You'll likely feel more warmth in your belly and through your body. Concentrate on pushing this warmth so that it forms a sphere around you. This sphere will burn the negative energy around you, banishing it, while energizing your body.

Sexual Fluids

Another liquid I use frequently in my magical workings is my sexual fluid. The sexual fluid of a man or a woman is very powerful, particularly because it represents procreation, the possibility of life and/or creativity. Sexual fluid is often used in sigil workings. TOPY's *Thee Psychic Youth Manifesto* suggests a combination of cum, blood, and spit to christen the sigils that a person makes: "Once you have written thee fantasy on thee piece ov paper, you have to make thee paper special. To do this it must be touched by thee three liquids ov thee body. That is, spit, blood, and OV, which is thee temple name for thee fluids by masturbation" (anonymous, P. 23). The creative energies of the cum greatly empower the sigil. The energy that is in the cum is in large part raised by the act of masturbation, but also by directing your energies into the act and visualizing the sigil you want to charge while actually orgasming. It's important that you keep your focus on your goal and don't allow yourself to be distracted. Your goal isn't pleasure, but is instead focused on the totality of manifesting your desire.

Cum is also used with sex magic. Whether you are with a partner or visualizing a godform to work with, the liquid you share can be a very useful substance. The liquid is a connection, but it also is an exchange. The focus of sex magic can vary quite a bit. I've used sex magic to create a "magical child," in my case creating a Deharan godform called Kiraziel, which became a Dehar of desire (The Deharan system of magic is based off of Storm Constantine's *Wraeththu* series of novels). I've also used it as part of a death-rebirth ritual, rebirthing myself through ejaculation. I associate the act of ejaculation with procreation and manifestation so as my body ejaculated, it manifested as a rebirth moment for me on a spiritual level.

There are some disciplines such as Tantra and Taoism that frown on ejaculation, arguing that ejaculation causes you to lose life force. It can be useful to restrain yourself from ejaculating, in that it can lead to more pleasure and orgasms, which can be used to power up a magical working you are doing. The building up of energy by not ejaculating becomes a cumulative effect. Ejaculation is not orgasm and if you're desire is not to ejaculate, then actually ejaculating will short circuit the magic you are trying to do. When I've chosen to use sex magic, and not ejaculate, I've used it for trance purposes, building the energy to the point where I've altered my state of mind and then either done a vision quest, astral projection or some trance work. It is important to note that Tantra and Taoism differ from each in terms of the overall goal of such work: "For the Tantrics the goal of the work on the subtle body is Liberation from the round of birth, death and rebirth. For the Taoists the goal is Transformation-the strengthening of that body so that it may better manage life in this world and, perhaps, maintain its identity through the whorl of death and so carry its power over to the new body to come" (Mace 1996, p. 60). The difference is important to understand as the exercises with the muscles are different, in terms of the visualization and where you wish to direct the energy. If you want to learn how to restrain yourself from ejaculation pick up a book or two on Tantra or Taoism that focuses on muscle exercises you can do with your perineum and genitals. I recommend Mantak Chia's books as they are fairly comprehensive guides for this kind of work. These exercises are also useful in terms of just learning how to build energy up by working with your muscles.

Anytime you ejaculate, do not waste the liquid. The liquid isn't a waste product, but is full of protein. If I don't have a sigil I'm charging or I'm not doing a sex magic working, I will swallow the liquid, taking that energy back into me. If you waste the sexual fluid, you have wasted some of your own energy. You can perceive the swallowing as a form of taking a eucharist, so that you are partaking of the sacredness of yourself and honoring that sacredness by doing so (Mace 1996).

Body Hair

Body hair, whether it's pubic hair or hair from your head, is also very useful to use. I take hair clippings from my razor and offer them to the land, so that I can bond with its energy by giving something of myself that will be absorbed by it. I visualize the energy in those hairs melting into the land's energy, connecting me closer to the elements. I've also used strands of my hair to do bindings on people; long hair is useful for that kind of working. Wind it around the object that represents the person and visualize the hair act as ropes that bind. Of course your own hair can be taken and used against you, if you're not careful. Even if the hair is dead, nonetheless it still contains something of you, though you can remove your energy from the hair. I usually just imagine any leftover energy in it coming back to me. This can be applied to anything that comes from your body. However, I don't absorb energy from my waste materials, but put it to a different use, as I explain below.

Hair can also be used for sacrifice. In one ritual I did, I took some of my side burns, shaved them, and gave them to the elements, in return for helping me to access my subconscious in a dream. A person can also chop off all their hair and make an offering of it. The act of chopping it off can be especially useful for personality aspecting, because people often associate physical features with their personality. A haircut can facilitate taking on a new persona. In a kink magic (BDSM sex magic) context the choice to cut or shave your hair can also be an act of submission to someone else. Offer the hair to a person as a sign that they have power over you. Finally you can combine your hair with another person's hair for a magical working, such as a handfasting. Something Lupa and I've done is exchanged pouches with each other's hair as love tokens that enhance the connection to each other in our relationship.

Hair dye is also something you can use for magical purposes. Lupa and I dye our hair red with henna every so often as an evocation of Fox, who we consider our family totem. Temporary dyes such as *Manic Panic* are useful for short term workings, but long term dye jobs can be used as well. I personally advocate using material such as henna to avoid chemicals, but some of the dye colors such as green or purple need the chemicals so your hair color can be changed. You can use dye jobs for evocation, invocation (though this depends on how long you want the invocation to last) or for charm purposes. With charms, you are accentuating your aural energy by using the hair dye to draw attention to you (Of course, the color determines what sort of attention you get; blonde will probably attract different attention than bright pink.).

Skin

Skin is another product of the body that can be useful for magical workings. I've taken my skin and hair, put it on a doll, and then used the doll as a familiar. I'll glue the skin and hair onto the doll and in effect put a piece of myself into the doll. Application of personal fluids can also be used if so desired. The doll can be used to attract any negativity that people feel toward you. It essentially acts as a scapegoat and a shield all at once. I always take such dolls and move them away from my own home. Alternatively the doll can also be used as a sacrifice. Create the doll, add your skin or whatever else and then sacrifice the doll. The purpose in this case might be to work a death-rebirth ritual with yourself, with the doll being a sacrifice, a death of yourself, or the purpose could be for behavior modification, with the doll containing a specific behavior which you feel is damaging you. Regardless of what you use the doll for, it becomes an effective fetish. The most important aspect of working with the doll is to make sure you distance yourself from it. While the doll can serve as an effective foil in terms of drawing negativity away from you, you probably don't want someone to get a doll you've created and use it against you. Make sure that whatever you use the dolls for, that you keep the dolls in a safe and hidden place.

The skin on your body can also be used for a variety of purposes. For instance your skin is a shield, protecting your internal organs from the environment. You can take that further and use the skin as a psychic protective shield. Because skin conducts the innate energy in your body, it's easy to direct that energy into a shield, while also using it as a filtering device.

When I shower, I see the cleaning of my skin as a purification act. If you use your skin as a shield the shower can be especially useful for cleaning off any psychic muck leftover. Cleaning also opens your pores up, freeing up any other toxins. So when you clean just visualize the water and soap pulling away any psychic gunk from your skin. Body paints are also useful in this context. Lupa and I once painted on each what we felt represented the emotional issues that we were dealing with. The paint was used to evoke the pain of those issues. When we showered, we cleaned off the paint and washed away the pain, helping us to begin healing the issues.

A lot of body modification occurs with skin as well. I've never pierced my body, as I feel the piercings disrupt the energy flow, but some people could use the piercings as attractors of energy or for ceremonial purposes. Often, in magic, body modification is used to indicate a rite of passage or to represent a magical act, or connect with an entity. For instance, the phoenix tattoo on my right arm represents rite of passage for me, the ending of one cycle and the beginning of another, but is also my connection to the power spirit of phoenix. The green wolf paw tattoo over my heart also represents another rite of passage, into marriage with Lupa; for the same rite, she has a dragon's claw holding a pearl with my personal sigil on it. She also has two wolves, one on each arm. They represent her connection to the totemic Wolf, but also represent her masculine and feminine aspects. Another way tattoos can be used is for specific magical workings. In the *Deathgate Cycle* by Margaret Weis and Tracy Hickman, one of characters had sigils tattooed all over his body. He could do magical workings with those tattoos. There's no reason a person couldn't do so in real life as well. Design the tattoo to evoke a certain energy and use it as a form of storage, for lack of a better term.

One final aspect about skin is its sensitivity. Run a feather on it, or use a flogger to hit it and you will different sensation of pleasure and pain. These sensations can be used to charge magical workings or stimulate altered states of mind. Lupa and I go into much more detail on this in *Kink Magic: Sex Magic Beyond Vanilla*.

Waste Products

The last type of product you can work with from your body is your waste, either your shit or piss or snot. There are three approaches you can take for using these products. The first approach is through purification. Every time you shit or piss, or blow your nose, visualize the negative energy in your life going into your waste and being flushed out of your life. Not only are you getting rid of physical waste that is harmful to your body, but with this approach you can get rid of emotional and mental waste. You'll certainly feel better in more ways than one.

A second method is to use your piss and shit as a tool for cursing someone. Because these products are waste they already embody a lot of negativity. Shitting or pissing on a picture of a person you hate is an extremely effective way of sending negative energy to that person.

You are saying that person is waste. Of course you need to consider the moral ramifications of doing this act. You are shitting on that person's life, focusing on making that person's life go to shit. The question is: Is it worth it? To some people, if they are vindictive, it could be worth it, but at the same time that's a lot of energy being put toward making another person miserable as opposed to bettering your own circumstances. Remember that it's your call and you do have to deal with the consequences of your actions.

The third approach is to use your waste to mark your territory, much like a dog or cat would. By marking your territory, not only are you saying that this territory is yours, but you're also depositing if you will, some wards and/or protection. It's a matter of focusing the energy, and pushing it toward protection. Something which is not welcome in that territory will catch your spiritual (and perhaps physical) scent and will know that to enter into the territory is to possibly encounter you. I recommend using urine, because fecal waste can contaminate ground water, whereas urine is sterile. While some people may consider this disgusting, animals have marked their territory to good effect and often other animals will respect those territories. The fights that occur are resolved and one either loses hir territory or keeps it. Regardless you can use your waste to create a shield around your homes. Just don't get caught with your pants down.

If you want to work with waste products that aren't as toxic, you can use snot. Snot still has germs on it, but it's not overly toxic, unless you're sick. I will occasionally put a bit of snot on a doorframe or somewhere else to mark territory, but also to create a magical ward. A magical ward is a protection that filters out certain types of energy. By using my snot as a ward I basically charge what energy is in it toward protecting a specific place from something I don't want entering that place.

Conclusion

One final question might be whether what I've described in this chapter is inner alchemy. While we aren't working internally with the body, I think that using your body fluids and products is a form of inner alchemy. You are taking your waste, fluids, etc. and charging them with intent and desire. There is no reason you can't use your body to work magic and no reason you can't take what comes from your body and incorporate it into the magic you do.

Certainly by working with the products of your body you may end up overcoming societal taboos that have been ingrained in you. If you winced when I discussed cum or shit in a magical context, consider that your reaction may possibly be a result of societal expectations. Overcoming such expectations and norms is part of inner alchemy. If you can become more comfortable with your body as a result of working with its products, then your change in attitude will certainly affect the inner alchemy you work. And if nothing else, being more comfortable with your body is a wonderful feeling, because all too often society views the body as sinful or dirty, or as something which is removed from spirituality. The body is part of spirituality and the products that come from the body are also part of such spirituality. Reclaim your body and your comfort with it, instead of giving into quaint, provincial views of the body.

Exercises

1. Try out the Eight Brocade exercise I included in this chapter. It may take a while to notice overt effects (it took me approximately a month of everyday practice and even longer before I noticed a regular effect). The effects can include sweating and a rising or lowering of the body temperature, which indicates that your energy is being raised. How does working with the body tie into working with your energy? Or does it?
2. Did you wince or get embarrassed working with your shit or cum? If you did try and figure out why you did. What do you think causes this attitude and do you think you'll actually try to work with these things?
3. If you've never worked with your blood, sexual fluids, spit, etc., do a magical ritual of your devising with one of those fluids or products. In your opinion, is there any difference working with part of your body as opposed to not? Do the same ritual without the body product and then compare and contrast the rituals. Which was more intense, and useful and why?

Chapter Five:
Neurotransmitter and Metabolism Magic

Knowing about the processes of the body, how something happens, is just as important as making it happen. Maybe you think it's just a movement of muscle and tendon against bone, the proper tension creating the necessary movement so that you can gesture with your hand. That's certainly part of what is happening, but there's also the central nervous system which uses neurons, and specifically axons, to send electrical impulses that generate the necessary energy for the body to move: "The axons are usually bundled together in thick multi-stranded cables called nerves. These lead from one part of the body to another carrying messages" (Dawkins 1989, p. 49). We are walking electrical signals and these signals allow us to do everything we do. These signals control our muscles, often involuntarily (in that we don't think about the choice to move the muscles), but of course they can be controlled. It's just a question of understanding how the muscles are triggered by the impulses and tracing those impulses back to our brain.

One analogy that is often used with the brain is that it's like a computer. However, this analogy is faulty as Dawkins points out: "The basic units of biological computers, the nerve cell or neurone, is really nothing like a transistor in its internal workings. Certainly the code in which neurons communicate with each other seems a little bit like the pulse codes of digital computers, but the individual neurone is a much more sophisticated data processing unit than the transistor" (1989, p. 48). The question then is why do we use computers to understand the brain? In part, it's convenient. The computer seems to think--or so we believe. Of course what's really happening is that we're humanizing the process that's occurring. This notion of the brain as a computer also comes from John Lilly's choice of naming the brain the human biocomputer, which inevitably colors the perceptions of what the brain is, let alone what it does. Contemporary science shows that any divisions of the brain's functions are artificial (See Talbot 1991, Restak 1995, McTaggart 2002, & Lipton 2005).

But regardless of whether your brain is a biocomputer or not, you need to understand it as much as possible as it is the key to the temple of your body. Through your brain you can consciously control what your body does as well as the electro-chemistry of your body. So let's define the brain as a biocomputer, because it is through Lilly's work that I got my start in inner alchemy: "We are general purpose computers that can program any conceivable model of the universe inside our own structure. Our general purpose computer can reduce the single self metaprogrammer to a micro size and program it to travel through its own model as if that reality were real" (Lilly 1968, p. 17). Now if we approach the brain as a biocomputer, various programs (the models of the universe) can be engaged in the biocomputer. These can be explored by the metaprogammer: "In a well-organized biocomputer, there is a critical metaprogram labeled 'I' for acting on other metaprograms and labeled 'me' when acted upon by other metaprograms" (Lilly 1968, p. 16). In other words, the metaprograms are versions of ourselves, and are part of the models of the universe and so can be changed. As one model of the universe informs another model, so too will the version of the self in the first act on the second version of the self. Does this sound confusing? Consider it this way: In all of us is the potential to be more than just one person. In society, there is this focus on the person as a singular entity. However, likely when you go to work you are at least a slightly different person than when you go out to drink. You will likely find that you change clothes, habits, even the way you speak based on the environment you are in at the time. To some degree this is because you are reacting to environmental and societal expectations, but it is also in part because you have an established model of reality for each environment you go into. In other words, you have an identity, a personality you associate with that environment. This personality may not differ very much from your other personalities in your other models or environments of reality, but even the slight differences are created in part by you to help you fit into each environment.

But what does this have to do with the body? Your body is also an environment toward which you have certain attitudes, created by your reaction to environmental (cultural) influences and by your interaction with your body. The dieting magazines that you see, as an example, have an effect on you, even if that effect is to simply choose not to have anything to do with them. What's most important, though, is that your body is a model of a reality. It's a very complex model even if it doesn't seem like it on the surface. Of course, to some degree the model is based off your perceptions, but as you delve further into what the body is and can do, you quickly realize there's a lot more going on that you don't notice—which is true of any model of reality. Neither you nor I are the sole creators of the models we exist in. We help to create our models, but we don't necessarily know all the dynamics occurring in the background. But as your body is a model of reality, you can explore it, miniaturize the self and discover what the reality of your body has to reveal to you.

When I was twenty and I first read Lilly's books and realized this, I decided that I would do a combination of a shamanic vision quest and his idea of miniaturizing the self, which also happened to be mentioned in Barbara Brennan's *Hands of Light*. I lay down and counted a hundred breaths, while visualizing myself walking down stairs and getting smaller as I did so, until I saw myself enter my body and become a blood cell. I used Brennan's visualization as a guide for doing this: "Now imagine yourself very tiny, like a point of light, and enter your body wherever you choose" (1988, p. 165). The reason I used this visualization is because I felt that as a light I could mesh with the energies of the aura and also merge with the cell. At the time I knew nothing about biophotonic energy, the concept that cells emit light to communicate with each other, but becoming a small being of light had always intuitively made sense to me.

As a blood cell, I traveled through my entire body, visiting all of the organs, until I came to the brain. At that point I moved into the brain itself and began to explore it. I noticed there were areas of the brain that had too many chemicals and others that didn't have enough. I needed to modify my Serotonin, neuropeptide, and Dopamine levels. By doing so I could readjust the electrochemical flow. I also interacted with my neurons, exploring how they worked and shot electrical impulses. I then changed where some of those neurons shot the synapses so that instead of maintaining the electro-chemical composition that had existed, I created a new one, which no longer had me suffering at the whims of my manic-depression.

What I was doing was changing the receptors that got activated in the brain: "A neuron sends a message to another neuron by releasing a neurotransmitter across the synapse to a receptor site on the membrane of the target neuron. That receptor is specialized to receive that neurotransmitter. This is how the nerve cells of the brain communicate, both within the brain itself, and outside of it, within the entire body" (Restak 1994, pp. 4-5).

We don't need drugs to control this communication, though they can be helpful in controlling the more extreme aspects of mental illness. What I do is visualize my brain with a network of energy. I explore that network which involves exploring the receptors, and then I get a feel for where the energy isn't quite connecting in a way that feels right. I change that connection, routing the energy to different receptors until it feels like the brain is connected the way it needs to be connected. The entire time I'm listening (for lack of better word) to what my brain is communicating to me. By keeping a journal of my own behavior I can determine the differences between how I acted before and after the workings.

The key to controlling this communication is to understand that receptor sites can be changed. We can focus on a specific type of receptor and neurotransmitter and favor that neurotransmitter/ receptor combination over other types: "Neurotransmitters, like all chemicals, can be described by their structures-the ways in which their component atoms come together to form molecules. Each neurotransmitter molecule has a unique three-dimensional structure that differentiates it from all others. The receptor molecule on the target neuron also has a specific structure, and it is into its 'lock' that the specific neurotransmitter 'key' will fit" (Restak 1994, p. 22). The more a specific type of neurotransmitter is produced and the more the receptor for that transmitter is stimulated, the more receptors arise for that neurotransmitter. At the same time we can slow down the reuptake (the process of reabsorbtion) of other neurotransmitters back into the brain, essentially lengthening the effect of the neurotransmitter. In other words, the specific need generates the specific receptor. However, you have to be careful. You don't want to imbalance yourself. The goal for this kind of working should be to stabilize the neurochemistry of the brain. As a personal example, when I was suffering from depression, I focused on causing a faster reuptake rate of Dopamine and Norepinephrine and slowing down the reuptake (reabsorption) rate of Serotonin and Neuropeptides transmitters. However I only did this to correct the chemical imbalance. I didn't want to reduce the amount of Norepinephrine (which induces depression, but also anxiety, and ecstacy) to the point that my brain wasn't producing any. This would only cause further imbalance.

But how does one go about changing the levels of receptors and neurotransmitters? As I mentioned earlier, I used Lilly's model of the human biocomputer, Barbara Brennan's visualization and the shamanic vision quest. As I traveled through my brain, I experienced how it worked and, for lack of better word, communicated with the brain cells. Through that communication I came to understand how the cells interacted with each other. And through that communication with the cells, I could also transmit my own needs, in this case reducing the level of neurotransmitters that induced depression. I programmed the cells in the brain to change the directives so that more neurotransmitters were produced that would regulate the depression-inducing neurotransmitter and consequently balance the rest of the neurotransmitters. This happened through meditation, specifically the ability to miniaturize my consciousness so that I could communicate with my cells. Lilly recorded an experience of communicating with his cells that is somewhat similar to my own: "There was microcircuitry within the membrane at a molecular and atomic level. There were energies moving in prescribed paths in multiple directions within the membrane" (1967, p. 93). Lilly's model of understanding the cell involves seeing it as circuitry. My model of the brain was one where I communicated with the cells and became part of the sparking energy that erupted from synapse to synapse. I became a neurotransmitter and sailed into a receptor, programming the specific emotion needed into the receptor so it could be evoked in the body. This concept of communicating with the cells in your body is not as far-fetched as it may seem.

In Tantra, this communication with the cells is something that is noted, and understood: "Tantra holds that each cell is a living being, that it is totally conscious, endowed with a mind, with emotions, and memory" (Lysebeth 1995, p. 7). A text about Tantra that draws from traditional sources, instead of modernizing the concept mentioned above, still manages to convey a similar idea:

> The various samskaras correspond to an inner, transcendental prefiguration toward which the discriminating and individuating activity of manas is oriented...Samskaras are eventually picked up at a later stage, as a result of the election, coalescence , and appropriation following the merging with the samsaric current. This current includes predetermined forms and various legacies (whether biological or pranic), which refer to previous elements, whether

> connected or not. In this sense, samskaras actually exist in the subtle body in which the causal body is manifested. They are also responsible for imparting direction both to manas's selective action, through its organs, and to the life that supports, nourishes, and shapes the physical form. (Evola 1992, pp. 50-52).

I understand and define the samskaras to be the consciousness that directs the manas or energy within the body to the various patterns that best support the life of that body. My understanding is, of course, based on my own biases, but reading the above passage and applying it to my own work with my cells resonates with what I've been doing.

Intriguingly enough recent findings in biology suggest that the actual brain of a cell is the membrane. Such findings have also found that a cell has similar organs to what a human body has and that cells can be considered intelligent and able to adapt to their environments: "Single cells are also capable of learning through these environmental experiences and are able to create cellular memories, which they pass onto their offspring" (Lipton 2005, p. 38). What is even more fascinating is that the electromagnetic charge that is put into a protein can shape the function of the protein (Lipton 2005). This seems to fit with biophotonic theory, which also argues that the function of a cell can be changed by the shift in frequency of biophotonic energy. In other words, if an electromagnetic charge is given to a cell, the frequency of the biophotonic energy will be shifted, which affects what the function of the cell is.

The cell's communication isn't entirely based on DNA, and is geared toward getting information from the environment as opposed to the genes. This occurs through receptors and effectors, with the receptors acting as antennas that pick up information (Lipton 2005). This information includes physical signals from the various neurotransmitters and hormones, but also includes getting information from energy fields. "Receptor 'antennas' can also read vibrational energy fields such as light, sound, and radio frequencies. The antennas of these 'energy' receptors vibrate like tuning forks. If an energy vibration in the environment resonates with a receptor's antenna, it will alter the protein's charge, causing the receptor to change shape" (Lipton 2005, p. 83). The energetic resonance isn't limited to light or sound, but also to various other forms of energy, which includes energy that characterizes the identity of a person. I'll discuss my own theory and approach to resonance in the advanced energy work chapter, but suffice to say that a cell's ability to resonate with energy does allow it to be genetically altered and in turn can alter what you consider yourself to be, depending on how in tune you consciously are to the energy you emanate. The effector proteins take in the energy from the receptors and channel that energy effectively into the cell, as well as emanating the energy to other cells, "Instead it is the membrane's effector proteins, operating in response to environmental signals picked up by the membrane's receptors, which *control* the 'reading' of genes so that worn out proteins can be replaced, or new proteins can be created [italics are his]" (Lipton 2005, p. 86). In other words, the genes respond to the signals picked up and accordingly are sequenced toward what is best for the survival of the cell and of the body.

If you approach the cells as units of consciousness in and of themselves, you can begin to appreciate how the model of your body is much more intricate than you thought. The key then is to interact with the cells on the level of consciousness they exist in and also be aware that you can shape the programming of these cells by being aware of the environmental influences that are introduced to them. In the next chapter when we focus on DNA and biophotons we'll learn more about how this communication works. This is entirely possible for you, through the medium of meditation, and eventually the medium of your everyday life. Below is a meditation exercise you can use to move your consciousness into a cell in your body.

First you should be in a comfortable position; I usually lay down on my back. You'll want to take deep breaths, in through the nose, and out through the mouth. When you inhale your belly should puff outward from your body and when you exhale the stomach should move toward your body. You should feel a sensation or tingle that spreads through your body when you breathe like this. This is the energy stirring in your body. With each breath focus your awareness on the act of the breath, the movement of the lungs, and the stirring of the energy.

You will explain to yourself the purpose of your meditation and then you will say the following (You can also use a pre-recording if that's helpful): "As I count from one to ten, you will feel a tingling, healing, relaxing energy start at the tip of your toes and spread to your ankles, healing and relaxing your feet and ankles." After every breath, count until you've gotten to ten breaths.

Next say: "As I count from eleven to twenty, the healing, relaxing, tingling energy will move up from your ankles to your knees, relaxing your calves. At the same time your feet and ankles will feel more relaxed." Again after each breath, count.

"As I count from twenty-one to thirty, the healing, relaxing, tingling energy will move up from your knees to your hips, relaxing the thighs with healing, relaxing, tingling energy. Your calves and feet will relax as you feel more tingling energy."

At this point you shift your awareness to your hands, while still being aware of your feet and legs. By now you should feel this tingling, relaxing energy in your legs. "As I count from thirty-one to forty, the healing, relaxing, tingling energy will start at the tip of your fingers and move through your palms to your wrists, relaxing your hands with tingling, healing, relaxing energy. At the same time, your legs and feet will feel more and more relaxed as I count from thirty-one to forty." Remember to count after each breath.

"As I count from forty-one to fifty, the healing, relaxing, tingling energy will move up from your wrists to your elbows, relaxing your forearm, even as your hands, feet, and legs more and more relaxed as I count from forty-one to fifty."

"As I count from fifty-one to sixty, the healing, relaxing, tingling energy will move up from your elbows to your shoulders, relaxing your upper arms, even as the tingling, healing relaxing energy intensifies in your forearms, hands, feet, and legs."

"As I count from sixty-one to seventy, the healing, tingling, relaxing energy will spread from your shoulders into your chest, down into your stomach and groin, relaxing all of your torso with healing, relaxing, tingling energy, as the legs, feet, hands, and arms feel more relaxed."

Now you may find as you are saying this and focusing on your breath, and feeling the relaxing, tingling energy that you have trouble remembering what your count is. Focus on the matter at hand, which is to keep yourself cognizant of your body, but also aware of the count.

"As I count from seventy-one to eighty, the healing, tingling, relaxing energy will spread up from your shoulders into your neck, relaxing all the muscles in your neck even as the rest of your body becomes more and more relaxed."

"As I count from eighty-one to ninety, the healing, tingling, relaxing energy will spread from your neck to your head, relaxing your face and scalp, with tingling, healing relaxing energy, even as the rest of your body feels more and relaxed, as I count from eighty-one to ninety."

"As I count from ninety-one to one hundred your entire body will become more and more relaxed."

Once you've reached the final count of one hundred, your body will feel incredibly relaxed and full of tingling energy. At this point, visualize a doorway before you. When you open the door you will go to the destination you had chosen for the focus of the meditation. In this case, the destination would be a blood cell within your body that you've chosen to embody your consciousness. You become a small being of light and enter into your body.

Whenever I have entered one of my blood cells I feel a sensation that I can only describe as flow. It's not even that I'm in one cell, so much as my consciousness is transmitted from one cell to another. The advantage of going with a blood cell is that it does travel through the body, coming into contact with the various organs. In this case you want to move your consciousness to the brain so you'll ride the blood cell until you get to the brain.

Once you're in your brain you can closely observe the specific chemical compositions that currently affect it. For example, when I was depressed, it was the result of a chemical imbalance. My brain felt like a cocktail or soup. When my consciousness traveled through the brain it would go through the synapses, neurons, and receptors. I was able to identify the kind of chemicals predominantly affecting the brain and detect any imbalance in the chemicals. I went to where this imbalance was and visualized switches in the brain for the neurotransmitters. I switched on the endorphins and Serotonin, and turn the flow of Norepinephrine and Dopamine down. I felt a pleasurable tingling sensation in the center of my brain. I found that anytime I wanted to stimulate the endorphins I could focus on the switches I'd installed.

If you choose to do this, use caution. I usually switch the endorphins on (beyond the normal level) for instance, when I'm focused on writing or being creative, as this seems to stimulate my creativity, but I don't put the switch on all the time. Nor do I shut off the Norepinephrine or Dopamine switches. I lower it, so as to lower reaction to stress, focusing on a more calm approach. Although Norepinephrine is a hormone released from adrenal glands, it should be noted that feelings of anger and rage while using adrenalin can lead to depression, particularly if such feelings are not able to be expressed. Certainly my depression was in large part due to genetics and repression of anger and rage. But we should never stop any of the chemicals in our brain. What we are really doing is making the Norepinephrine and Dopamine stay in the synapse shorter and making the Serotonin stay longer. But stopping could lead to permanent harm. Remember, those chemicals are there for a reason!

You can also, when you're in your brain, travel through the synapses, exploring how the brain works. When I initially sent my consciousness into my brain I traveled through it, learning how the energy that the synapses shoot worked its way through the brain. By learning how the signals in the brain were transmitted and where they went I could control what neurotransmitters were stimulated. I sometimes will focus on that central area of the brain and will a bit of energy into it, visualizing a specific change, stimulating the neurotransmitters so that they hit the receptors and induce a high and/or trip. The most interesting aspect about the brain is that once it's achieved a state of altered consciousness, whether naturally or through entheogens, that state can be experienced again by knowing how to stimulate the brain so as to produce the transmitters that will create that altered state of experience. As an example, I have had some experiences with entheogens, which I detail in Appendix A. I have been able to replicate the highs and/or trips from those experiences because my brain has the memory of that experience in it. If I stimulate the memory by remembering what the sensation felt like, I can replicate that sensation in the brain, stimulating the neurotransmitters that will produce a similar affect to what the drug did. In other words, I deliberately put energy via the synapses into certain neurotransmitters which then hit the receptors and create the experience of being high or tripping.

Entheogens, natural ones anyway, are not radically different from the chemicals our brains produce. If we can use external drugs to stimulate an experience of being high or tripping, we can also use the chemicals our brains naturally produce to have similar experiences, and fortunately Johnny Law can't regulate how we choose to internally stimulate our brains. It's also much easier to self-regulate neurotransmitters than entheogens, as you have much more control over the effect. Even if the effect becomes overwhelming you don't have to sit through it like you would with entheogens. The key to doing this is to travel through your brain, to experience it on a level of consciousness that is not your everyday consciousness, but on the level of the brain itself. The meditation I've provided above is a good starting point, but don't think that one time will do it. Take time to explore your brain and the rest of your body. Even nine years after I started exploring the consciousness of the body through meditation, I'm still continually going back and experiencing new sensations.

You can experience vision quests with each specific transmitter, working with its spirit, and learning more of how it works. If you visit http://en.wikipedia.org/wiki/Neurotransmitters, you'll be able to get detailed information on the different neurotransmitters and what they do. You can then invoke yourself into the neurotransmitter and get a closer feel for what it does by embodying your consciousness in it and journeying with it as it goes through your body. The neurotransmitter acts as a spirit guide, showing you how it affects your body. Remember that the transmitter has it own consciousness that you are interacting with. That interaction will likely not occur in a manner that we think as conventional communication. For me, the sensations have been tactile and are the effects the transmitter has on the body. In other words, I am feeling how the neurotransmitter interacts with the body to produce effects. We must always remember that our conception of consciousness is biased by our own consciousness. Anything else, including a cell, will likely have a different concept of consciousness from our own. Keep yourself open to this idea and working with the neurotransmitters as spirit guides will be easier.

Using the meditation technique I mentioned above or a different form, the goal should be to contact the neurotransmitter of your choice. I will usually say: "I invoke myself into [name of neurotransmitter]", or simply allow my consciousness to merge into the neurotransmitter, much the same as with the blood cell example above. When I dive into my brain, in a blood cell, I perceive it as a vision quest, a journey I'm taking into the brain to find the spirit guide which represents the neurotransmitter. When I meet that spirit guide, it usually picks a symbolic form that is appropriate to it and to my perception of it. The spirit guide for Dopamine, for instance, was an old man, while the spirit guide for Serotonin was a six eyed snake with three eyes on each side. The archetypal appearance of these spirit guides enables you to work with the neurotransmitters on a level of consciousness that you can approach. We think in symbols and our conception of the world is mediated by them. I focus on traveling in the cave of brain flesh (which is how I perceive the environment I'm questing in). While questing in this meditative state, I focus on the specific neurotransmitter and its unique energy. I'll vibrate its name, calling for it to appear in my meditation. When it does appear, it assumes a form I can relate to. I've noted that the first connection with a given neurotransmitter can take up to a week to occur or happen the very first time you focus on finding it.

Once I've made contact with the neurotransmitter of choice, I'll ask for a symbol from it. This symbol represents a contact point, making it easier to connect with the neurotransmitter. I draw on the alphabet of desire as the technique to use for the symbolism. The Alphabet of desire is a personalized symbol system created by the magician. Each symbol represents a subconscious power of the psyche or an entity that the magician wishes to work with (Mace 1984). In this case we are contacting the consciousness of each neurotransmitter and getting a symbol from it that acts not only as its representation, but also as a key to working with it. And we can work with the neurotransmitters to change our consciousness.

Once I've obtained the appropriate symbol, I usually go from the meditation technique I described above to one which is more extreme. For instance, I like to use a bathtub of very hot water (but not scalding water), with salt thrown in, for meditations at this point. The bathtub serves as a sensory deprivation tank of sorts. While it's true my senses are still working, the hot water serves to negate the sense of touch. I'll usually keep most of my face under water, save for my nose and mouth. I'll vibrate the name of the neurotransmitter and this works well with my ears being underwater, because the vibration is much more powerful in terms of what I hear. While I'm vibrating the name, my eyes are closed and I'm focused on visualizing the symbol, projecting it along with the words I'm vibrating to the neurotransmitter I seek to contact. Below I've detailed what happened when I contacted Dopamine. All journal entries are in italics.

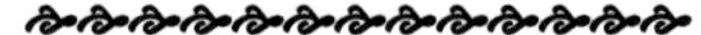

My first working with Dopamine was me lying in my bed, meditating, using the one hundred pranic breaths for meditation. When I focused on meditating, I focused on Dopamine and came across this old man, sitting in a cavern of brain, looking at me. He smiled and said he was glad to meet me, he was Dopamine. He than hands me this symbol...says write it down, this is how you get ahold of me. Then he told me to go on my way and use the symbol to get a hold of him. I left the cave and came out of my meditation.

I took a bath this time. Very hot water, but no oils in the water. In my desire to commune with Dopamine, I wanted to avoid attracting any substances that might be similar, but from an outside source. When I got in the water, I focused first on the symbol, channeling my pain from the heat to the symbol, charging it with energy. I then submerged most of myself, including most of my head, just leaving my mouth and nostrils clear of the water. I vibrated the word Dopamine, five times. In the water, the vibrations were much stronger and the word sounded more like a buzz. Oddly enough Maryam (my roommate at the time) thought she heard me hissing the word. I could hear my heart beat, and suddenly I was dancing around my heart. It was a giant fire. And Dopamine showed up, appearing like an old trickster man. Smiled at me in an odd kind of way, fish smile, if fishes have smiles. He watches me dance and occasionally I vibrate Dopamine again. Then he takes me to my brain. The drum of the heart is less loud, slower, but I'm still dancing. In the brain, we are again in a cave of wrinkled brain. Synapses fire and I can hear noises, tinkling noises mixing with my heart drum. I feel a massive pressure around my head building up, a wave of heat. He tells me I can trigger him, trigger Dopamine...but he also warns me to be aware of balance. Everything has it's balance...push carefully. So he's there and he's asking me how long I'll keep my head in the water. Once in a while I feel tempted to pull it out, I do at one point, but then stick my head back in. I'm going for sensory deprivation as much as possible to focus on the internals. Feel the pressure build up...balance it, but not too much. I need an edge to start the synapse. Feel my head against the bottom of the tub, but I keep my nostrils above the water. My breaths are slow and deep, my heart drum steady. Then I feel the synapse fire and Dopamine is gone, surging through the network to find the receptors, sirens for his chemical soul. He tells me to work with the others as he leaves, but to come back to him as well.

I raise my head out of the water and sit in the tub, not really moving. I'm just starting to feel the Dopamine hit. I see what I would guess are hallucinations, some swirls in the air, nothing too fantastic. Call Maryam and she helps me get up...I'm feeling rather high at this point. I dry myself off, my skin tingling, my eyes noticing shifts in reality, slight shifts, but ruptures or ripples maybe in reality. As I write this now, I feel high, my brain is suffused with a pleasant white glow. At the beginning my crown chakra was wide open (still is now), but it had green, a spiral of green rising out of it with a bit of gold coming in. Now it's white, but the spiral is still there. The orgone in the air is thicker than usual, or maybe I'm just aware of more. The pleasure is not painful, just a warm glow, suffusing everything, a kind of numbness, but nonetheless a sensorial awareness of that numbness, paradox perhaps? Whatever it is, feels damn good...but I'm well aware of what Dopamine said...balance. I'll come back to him, but I want to work with the other neurotransmitters, and keep his advice in mind.

I recommend for the bath tub deprivation working to have someone on hand, just in case. Have the person watch when you do the ritual, so your head doesn't go underwater and you drown...it's easy to lose yourself in the meditation. Also having a minder on hand, in case of anything else is good common sense. The goal here is to use the deprivation to focus on the internal workings and specifically with the neurotransmitter, so that you can then induce the neurotransmitter to spark, happen, fire, whatever else you want to describe it. Why is the bath tub sensory deprivation? Okay technically it's not, but it's as close as you get to a sensory deprivation tank, when you don't have one. The water, even really hot, provides a kind of haze for the senses, a numbing of them, so that you focus more inward and less outward. I kept my eyes closed the entire time, and hearing went toward the inner world, tactile sense focused on the heart/lungs/and brain. I also had the bath curtain pulled, so no light coming in. So, for me, it worked as a sensory deprivation device, as best it could and certainly seemed to get me going on the path I wanted

A couple of other effects I noticed from the Dopamine working. After I finished writing up the report, I went to play a chess video game. I found that the patterns for playing the game worked out really well, more so than usual, so that even when I hadn't knowingly planned for something to happen, for a specific to make a move, when the sequence started up this would sometimes occur. I can only guess that in my state on some level I was more aware of the patterns and was able to influence this through pushing the buttons, which doesn't really require conscious control. Yesterday for most of the day I still felt the glow, the high from the Dopamine. Occasionally I would see patterns form and shape in the background. After I took a long nap, this glow dissipated.

As you can see from this entry above, the working I did was very dynamic. The high lasted much longer than any entheogen could and was much more intense. When you work with your body, you will find that the processes in your body are the best to work with in comparison to relying on foreign substances. Still it's important to be disciplined in your approach to working with neurotransmitters. Doing these workings for a high or a trip ultimately demeans the inner alchemy you might seek to work. Remember Lilly's principle of discipline: "The easily evoked pleasure of the entheogenic state may be a major goal for some persons. The external reality struggle to obtain pleasure from the environment has rules of its own which must be met realistically and with intelligence and balance. Discipline in the self-metaprogrammer is absolutely essential when exploring the further reaches of consciousness and alternative realities" (1967, p. 133). I might add that Lilly was not successful in being disciplined when it came to using K (ketamine). Although by working with the neurotransmitters you are not working with entheogens, you are nonetheless producing similar effects. You must be wary of these effects, in the sense that you shouldn't come to depend on them just to get high. Focus instead on using these workings when you really need them, as a way of deepening your understanding of your consciousness and also activating states of creativity. Remember to balance yourself. As you may note in the above entry, I mention the cautioning that the spirit guide of Dopamine told me, the need to be balanced. Keep your workings with the neurotransmitters balanced.

Below I'm going to also include the experiences of someone who read a rough draft of this work. Caroline Reece graciously agreed to try out these ideas and I'm very thankful to her for allowing me to include the notes of her experiences.

I found the website you suggested, Wikipedia, to be extremely useful. Once I began to read about the various neurotransmitters and their purposes, I immediately realised there was a correlation with the nature of two characters I had previously come across in meditation. Neither of the two figures in question had told me anything about themselves so I knew very little about them. All I did know was that even without interaction with them, they had a strong effect on my mood and energy levels.

The first is a character I named Euphorn. He is a well-built yet agile coloured man with a tribal look to him. He has tattoos and wears a sarong but no top, just some kind of bone symbol on a necklace. He has cats eyes, which seem to change colour from yellow to green to red and draw me in. Sometimes I think he may have a forked tongue though I have never seen it. He is in a constant dance, moving so smoothly, his energy never fading. He has two large drums that he plays as he dances. Whenever I have seen him I have always felt a rush of serene energy, which I was soon able to liken to the effects of Dopamine. I was also pleased to read that Dopamine has a dark pigment – it seemed to fit so well!

Then there is Euphorna. I named her this as I found her after Euphorn and upon first meeting she appeared to be the female equivalent of him. When I examined her more closely I realised that she was in fact quite different. She dances too, on a podium. She has quite an extreme appearance – numerous unusual piercings adorning her face (including some metal spikes made to look like whiskers), heavy make-up, false eyelashes and long false nails. Euphorna's head is bald, though she has appeared to me on separate occasions with a small pink Mohawk and small cone-shaped horns. She enjoys the buzz of heavy industrial dance music – it courses through her veins and mine as a result making her come to life. I discovered that she also got this quickening from knife-throwing and riding a fast bike. I have decided that she must be my Epinephrine.

I meditated focusing on Epinephrine after reading your chapter, Cell Magic, and she appeared for a short time only. She was dancing on her podium, smiling. She was holding two fire sticks, one in either hand, and for the first time she seemed to notice me. She gestured and traced the shape of a symbol unknown to me in the air with fire. I made a note of this symbol as soon as I came back to ordinary consciousness.

Later, I decided to do some work with Euphorn (or Dopamine). I tried your bathtub meditation. It sounded like a fantastic method to me as I love my baths! It was every bit as good as I had hoped. I found it really easy for my mind to reach the desired meditative state; partly due to the fascination of hearing my heart beat so loudly, and partly due to the sensory deprivation. As I began to see Euphorn drumming away I was aware of the blood pumping around my body; most intensely my brain. Euphorn was in a remote place where the ground was neither soft nor hard. I felt as though there were spectators but I could see nobody. There were tents positioned around a fire, and Euphorn drifted over and led me into one. We sat down and he held my hands. I could feel his energy rushing through me. He offered me a large rectangular sweet as though he were offering me drugs. It became clear that he was offering me the choice of a deep hit (the sweet) or a gradual increase (the tap outside of the tent). I chose the latter for safety. We left the tent. Euphorn seemed to laugh at me and continue dancing.

As I slowly turned the tap, I felt my blood circulating again and became aware of myself once more in the bathtub. I surfaced and opened my eyes slowly. My first thought was that perhaps the tap had actually been an exit rather than a Dopamine switch. Then I hallucinated a white spiders' web on the bath taps with a huge silver spider on it. Then I saw some words that make no sense. Charlie-Dog-44. I felt a little sick when I got out of the tub and my ears hurt. I slept. It felt as though the meditation had been very short – perhaps only ten minutes. Gary later informed me that it had actually lasted around forty-five minutes. Such are the effects of Dopamine I guess!
(Caroline Reece-Personal Communication September 29, 2005)

Besides using the bathtub as a sensory deprivation tank, you can also use sex. With sex, you aren't focused on suppressing your senses, but rather on exciting them to the point where through visualization of the symbol and vibration of the name, and through the act of sex you excite yourself to the point where you contact the neurotransmitter and have a mental orgasm. The goal in this working should be to avoid having a physical orgasm right away. Hold back for as long as possible, focusing on building up the energy for yourself and your partner (if you have a partner involved). As you stimulate yourself or are stimulated by someone else, keep your focus on the symbol of the neurotransmitter and vibrate the name as well. You may also wish to paint the symbol on your body. When you've made contact with the neurotransmitter and you get to the point where you've reached the edge, where you know the neurotransmitter could spark and you need that extra push, let yourself physically orgasm and push the energy into triggering the neurotransmitter activation. I've found this technique works as well as the bathtub technique for connecting with and activating the neurotransmitters.

Further workings with the neurotransmitters have occurred with Zachary Walters and several other experimenters. Zac has even created a mythos, which while different from my own shamanistic mythos, still has some intriguing synchronicities. For instance, both of us had similar descriptions for Melatonin as an ebony woman. Some of this work has been done independently and some of it has been done together. For instance, we did an experiment where we worked with the neurotransmitter Serotonin, with an emphasis being on examining its role in stimulating the pineal gland and consequently aiding astral projection. We ate food with lots of Tryptophan to stimulate the production of Serotonin and we also used natural and artificial light sources, varying the amount of light received to determine if light had an affect. Some days food with little Tryptophan would be eaten, also to determine if there was a difference or not. We ended up finding the days with more light exposure or Tryptophan did have a better affect on the magic we were doing.

As an extension of that work I ended up connecting with Melatonin and did a spirit guide working where I had Serotonin and Melatonin perform an alchemical marriage, which resulted in an encounter with DMT. Below are the details of two of those encounters.

Today I did a working with both Serotonin and melantin (Melatonin). I had only low amounts of Tryptophan, some milk this morning, and last night cheese. I used the mind machine (with strobe lights which provide a lot of light) and Coil's Constant Shallowness Leads to Evil. I once again focused on astral projecting through the pineal gland, but this time projected my AOD symbols for Serotonin and Melantin. I encountered them both...The ebony skinned Melantin and the crimson six-eyed serpent Serotonin. They eyed each other askance and asked me the purpose of summoning them together. I told them I wanted to see what happened when they combined. Serotonin promptly proceeded to have sex with Melantin, making her pregnant with his seed. After the act, she was only pregnant for a moment before she birthed DMT-Dimethyltryptamine. As I watched he grew quickly and he told me he was the time shifter. His body changed ages rapidly from young to old and back again. Around this time my body began to vibrate and the patterns of light that the mind machine was showing me gave away to fog which was around DMT. He took up a black spear, with the tip having very precise geometrical shapes. Then he threw the spear at me and it hit my third eye. At that point, my third eye ignited and opened and I began to experience hallucinogenic visions of probably futures and pasts. This entire trip lasted for approximately forty or so minutes, a little over half the Coil album. the entire time I was aware of DMT in the background, but the visions I saw and experienced held my attention, showing me what was to come in my life. I saw a long black haired woman kneeling before me and pulling me from my chair, to her. Even after I finished the session up, my head still feels tingly and for lack of better word on fire, albeit in a very pleasureable calm way. My next step is to replicate this experiment without the mind machine and the music to see what happens without the aid of external props.

❧❧❧❧❧❧❧❧❧❧❧❧❧

Today I redid the experiment with Melatonin (melantin) and Serotonin, but without the mind machine and music. I projected through my pineal gland their symbols and almost right away the symbol of DMT was transposed on topic of them and DMT was there. I felt his many pointed spear touch my third eye and I once again began to have experiences, but not as focused on the visual hallucinations...this time I felt more tactile hallucinations, such as a feeling of vertigo, but also lots of tingling warmth that gathered through out my body. When I came out of the meditation, this warmth stayed with me and even now is still around me. An intriguing circumstance, to say the least. I suspect the mind machine focused the hallucinations on a more visual end before because of the light.

❧❧❧❧❧❧❧❧❧❧❧❧❧

The work in this case produced more than just another spirit guide, but also an understanding of how the different neurotransmitters interact with each other to produce more neurotransmitters. Tryptophan is essential for the production of Serotonin and Melatonin, which in turn creates DMT. Another thing we learned through these experiments was how external sources of stimulation such as food and technology could be used to purposely evoke neurotransmitters. It's a fair point to note that you can never entirely cut out of the equation the reliance on other sources of stimulation. The very food we eat has an effect on the chemistry of our body. But a purposeful choice in diet can lead to some intriguing experiments with the neurotransmitters, much like the experiment above.

My goal is to eventually create personae for all the neurotransmitters that I can then evoke or invoke with the alphabet of desire that I'll use for them. I'm also currently taking the chemical formulae/molecule formations and turning them into evocation sigils for calling the neurotransmitters, much like using the sigils for the Goetic demons, albeit without forcing the neurotransmitters to come, but instead respectfully working with them. This evocation is useful for helping heal other people and even healing yourself. I have, for instance, used Tyrosine to get rid of headaches. Tyrosine is the controller of the rate of the signals in the brain, and also controls your eye color, hair color, etc. Besides working with him to turn my hair red (an ongoing process), I've also worked with him to get rid of my headaches, to shift the rate of the signal, or vibrate the energy into a different frequency. Evoking him for this is easier than invoking him, what with the pain in the head. I've even taken his technique of changing the signals and used it as a healing technique, where I will vibrate the patient's energy away from the energy level of the pain, excising the pain.

I've accomplished the work with Tyrosine in a couple of different ways. I've dyed my hair with henna to make it red, but henna usually only last for six weeks or so. As a way of testing the work with Tyrosine, I chose to invoke him and go to the roots of my hair. I had Tyrosine manipulate the genetic information to draw out the red in the hair. Consequently it takes much longer for the red color of the henna to fade. It does help that I already had natural red highlights in my hair as Tyrosine draws on this genetic information to make the color stay in longer. With a headache, I've evoked Tyrosine, having him work more independently. He vibrates the energy, essentially changing the frequency that's causing the headache. This technique has also been used by me to vibrate pain out of the body. By changing the frequency of energy the pain is no longer sustained.

My latest work with the neurotransmitters has focused on working with multiple NTs at the same time while using different breathing techniques. Pranayamic breathing is good upper body and head work, while Taoist water meditation breathing techniques (these techniques will be discussed in chapter seven in further depth) are useful for lower body health. As an example I've used the Taoist breathing in concert with Arginine and testosterone. Arginine's symbol is a V with pulsating strands between the branches of the V. This is appropriate because Arginine regulates blood circulation. Testosterone is a sexual pheromone that stimulates adrenaline and can determine the overall masculinity of a person; its symbol is that of a sword. The Taoist breathing involves breathing with your diaphragm in a way that involves getting your back to move as you breathe, pushing your torso forward, sideways and backwards. This stimulates the blood vessels and internal organs, increasing the flow of energy to them (Frantzis 2001a). Using these breathing techniques, I also visualized the symbols of Arginine and Testosterone and called the neurotransmitter entities to me. They then further increased the stimulation of the blood cells. The result was a warmth that spread through my entire body. As a result I was able to increase my libido substantially.

One final aspect of neurotransmitter workings that I want to note is that after I've gotten the symbol from the neurotransmitter and worked with it I've always had physical sensations occur that one would associate with the neurotransmitter. For instance when I worked with Norepinephrine, my body felt numb. I was sitting at the computer and I felt my limbs go to sleep, even though I had only been sitting for a couple of minutes. Norepinephrine is similar to morphine in that it's the body's natural painkiller and can numb the pain if activated. These physical sensations tell me that I must be triggering some process associated with the neurotransmitter, and by working with our neurotransmitters as spirit guides we can activate these processes in our body. We are interfacing with not just a physical body, but also with our own consciousness and the other forms of consciousness present within us. Doing that allows you to do far more for your body than any drug can do. What is learned as well, through this, is how to direct your consciousness toward working with the other consciousnesses that reside in you, "Thoughts, the mind's energy, directly influences how the physical brain controls the body's physiology. Though 'energy' can activate or inhibit the cell's function-producing proteins...The fact is that harnessing the power of your mind can be *more* effective than the drugs you've been programmed to believe you need [italics are his] (Lipton 2005, p. 125). Indeed by working with your neurotransmitters in a conscious manner you can use them to lessen your dependence on drugs by learning to work with what is naturally part of your body and has always been meant to be worked with consciously. You essentially reinstate the natural balance of the brain. A receptor that is addicted to a drug must be weaned off of the drug. By using a neurotransmitter, you can work to get the receptor to accept it again and decrease the need for the drug.

Truly, the work you can do with neurotransmitters is multiple and probably will not even be fully mapped by me. Still, it's fun experimentation and allows you to know your body much more intimately, on a level that most people take for granted as being autonomic.

You can also extend your workings past neurotransmitters; for example, you can affect your metabolism. Metabolism controls your digestive and waste processes, turning food into energy and getting rid of whatever is left and is also involved in the processes of the cell. It modifies and regulates the cell's biochemical processes, basically digesting the nutrients and neurotransmitters. My workings with metabolism have been concerned with making my digestive and waste processes more efficient, particularly geared toward getting more of the toxins out of my body, though I have also done a lot of work specifically with the metabolism of cells. As with the neurotransmitters I've used my consciousness to investigate my metabolism and learn how it works so that I can turn it up or turn it down. A good time to do this particular pathworking is right after you eat a meal. You will feel very grounded so you may find it harder to get into a meditative state; nonetheless, by doing so you can actually experience the process of metabolism at work, which is helpful if you wish to modify it. I usually think of metabolism as a dial. You can speed it up or slow it down with a flick of the dial, once you understand how the process works. Again, do the deep breathing and counting exercise included above. Your body settles into relaxation because of the grounding that is occurring. Once you're very relaxed, send your mind toward your belly and focus on the process of digestion that is occurring. Become that process to the exclusion of anything else around you. Your goal is to understand exactly what's happening in as much detail as you can so that you can then visualize the changes you want to make. Make sure you've read up on the processes you want to change, so that way you can use that information to help you fine tune your body and the visualizations you use.

Mitochondria are organelles of a cell that act as power plants and have their own DNA. They are integral to the maintenance of the cells and indeed of the metabolism and processing of information of the body. To learn more about mitochondria I recommend checking out Wikipedia and other sources (I've included several books on biology in my bibliography), but also doing some meditation focused on them. Mitochondria tend to refer to themselves in plural form. They said that to summon them I should think of the color blue-green and explained that they were the light dancing in the cells. They also said that they helped metabolism, processed neurotransmitters, and routed environmental information that came to the cells and modified the genetics, physically and energetically, within DNA. Mitochondria are basically batteries and processors of raw energy and can be worked with in that capacity. In the processing of neurotransmitters, the mitochondria can be used as filters, selecting certain neurotransmitters over others. This should be done carefully and moreso with an aim toward healing a person than for altered states of mind.

In my further workings with mitochondria I've come to think of them as the cell's subconscious, in a sense, because they contain so much more information than the consciousness of the cells could handle. Mitochondria decide what becomes conscious and needed for the cells, and then processes and sends it out to the cellular consciousness.

Workings with Taoist breathing techniques have yielded some intriguing results with the mitochondrial subconscious. Taoist energy work focuses on connecting the energetic pathways to each other. I have contacted the consciousness of the mitochondria while doing the energy work and each time have been lead to the pineal gland, which the mitochondria uses to attune the energy of the body to different frequencies of energy. Given that the pineal gland does process Melatonin and likely Serotonin this makes sense as each of these neurotransmitters responds to the frequency of light, i.e. energy.

In my meditations, I also worked with the bacteria of the body, which appeared as a young woman and told me to summon her by thinking of sunlight shining on golden hair. She mainly discussed the importance of interconnection in the body, showing me how every organism in the body works together for the mutual benefit of all. Her discussion can be applied microcosmically to the body, but also macrocosmically to our own placement in relationship to the Earth and indeed the universe. She explained how important it is that mutual cooperation occurs, because without it, life wouldn't be maintained in the body. Everything connects together by the functions that are performed as a process that enables life to continue, but when that process is disrupted life cannot be maintained. Applied to our own interactions with the Earth, it's worth considering that our disruption of life on Earth can only do us harm despite any short term gains we think we've acquired. This working is particularly intriguing given that bacteria are mostly recognized as separate beings that live in symbiosis, or occasionally parasitically, in our bodies.

Another process I'm currently working on with my brain is the reduction of stress to my eyes. I occasionally get headaches when my eyes ache from looking at a screen too long. The back of my brain, the occipital section, will start to also ache. I'll stop looking at the screen, but I also do energy work for this problem. What I have found is there is too much uncontrolled energy connecting the pathways of the eyes to the brain. Remember that our eyes are always taking in light and so the light from the screen is being gathered. Your eyes aren't just a means for you to see, but also act as energy receptors. When I close my eyes, I'll "look" inward and usually see bright sun yellow jagged energy trails or a grass green color. The jagged yellow energy trails are excess energy. I take the excess energy and remove it from the energy pathways of my brain. What has happened is that too much energy was collected and there was a need to get rid of it. I'll usually put the excess energy into an entity or sigil I'm working on.

In the case of the grass green color, it's a disruption of my electro-magnetic energy. We all have a personal EM field. But when I work with computers all day that field can be disrupted by them, creating an imbalance, which results in a headache. I'll step away from the computer and turn it off. I'll then usually meditate on the headache, with an effort being to change the color I perceive into a different color, or change the electromagnetic balance, so that the pain is healed. I also travel through the brain, checking all the energetic connections and getting rid of any excess energy or unblocking any energy which is stagnant. In both types of headaches, I also work on slowing down the blood that's going to the brain. You may note that when you have a headache your heart beat is easier to feel if you touch your temples or other parts of your head. By slowing down the heart beat, you can induce a state of relaxation, which will ease the pain in your head. Sleep also helps with this, allowing your brain to go into repair mode.

Another situation I have dealt with involved a person who had unfortunately been poisoned with crystal meth by someone staying with her. Ground up crystal meth was put her in food, without her awareness. This systematic poisoning disrupted the functions of her brain and eventually she began to have epileptic seizures. (It should be noted that anyone can get seizures, if the right circumstances are created to cause them). With such seizures, there is again an excess of energy which causes the connections in the brain to misfire leading to the seizure itself. When this person came to see me (after having seen a medical professional), I ended up doing some healing work on her. I went into her brain and began to fix the energetic connections. I could not fix them all right away, but what I could do was set up a program of healing; as different connections became healed, the energy would target another connection and begin healing it. The reason I could not heal all the connections at once was because too much healing could cause a system shock. The body gets used to the states of health that it is put in. Consequently changes must be gradually done. A quick cure-all could be much more dangerous if the body chooses to reject what you've energetically done to it.

The aforementioned person did end up getting better. After several sessions of healing she could actually stop herself from having a seizure. I had helped her to create a system of venting her energy, so that her excess energy did not go back into the brain, but instead was distributed to either her body, or projected outward, by her own choice. When I last spoke with this person (approximately two years after I did my healing treatments on her) she had regained complete coherency with her mind, and the damage done by the drugs had for all intents and purposes been cleaned up. She still has occasional seizures, but not nearly as severe as they used to be.

I have also heard of cases where people suffered nerve damage to a part of their body and were able to heal the damaged nerve, despite what doctors told them. A daily regime of energy work with the affected nerve enabled the people to gradually reconnect the nerve to the central nervous system. However, such work, from what I have heard took years (Leyborn 2006). It is important to remember these workings take time. You can possibly aid the effort if you choose to do retroactive magic, with the goal being to work with your past self to retroactively heal the nerve repair right from the beginning of the accident. I direct readers to my book *Space/Time Magic* to learn more about retroactive magic. A person who chooses to work on a nerve every day of the year may only see limited results in the first year, but it is important to persist. Any of us can choose to accept what modern science says, that we can't heal certain ailments or injuries, or we can choose to defy modern science and attempt to will ourselves to heal. You have resources in your body and with energy work that can be applied to different injuries. The real question is do you or I choose to empower ourselves, to take our healing in to our hands, albeit still consulting with your physician, or do we choose to allow the injury to decide our reality? The choice is always in your hands.

Exercises

1. Try out the meditation techniques I described above. What are your results? Have you connected with the neurotransmitter of your choice and how has it affected you? What physical effects have you noted?
2. The next time you have a headache try to see if you can work with the connections on your brain and stabilize the energy. Also map your brain out through meditation. Travel in and visit and then record how it works. What could you change? What do you feel needs to be changed?
3. Do you think that cells have their own form of consciousness? Why or why not? What evidence and experience do you have to back up your answer?

Chapter Six:
DNA Magic

The next layer of working with inner alchemy is through the cell. While to some degree in the last chapter you've begun to do some work with your cells, this chapter is going to focus more intensely on the processes that occur in the cell, and with DNA.

In science, recent focus on cells has been on genetics and also on biophotonic energy, which is emitted by cells. Perhaps the most fascinating aspect of this research is how cells communicate with each other:

> Benveniste's experiments decisively demonstrated that cells don't rely on the happenstance of collision but on electromagnetic signaling at low frequency. (less than 20 hkz) electromagnetic waves...According to Benveniste's theory, two molecules are then tuned into each other, even at a long distance, and resonate to the same frequency. These two resonating molecules would then create another frequency, which would then resonate with the next molecule or group of molecules. (McTaggart 2002, p. 67)

This resonance in the cells is something that probably seems automatic, but there's no reason we can't harness its energy. This energy is also referred to as biophotons: "Photons switch on the body's process like a conductor launching each individual instrument into the collective sound. At different frequencies they perform different functions" (McTaggart 2002, p. 43). I think it's possible to work with biophotonic emissions and even learn to control the frequencies that are emitted.

A basic definition of biophotonic energy is as follows: "Biophotonic energy is defined as extremely weak light that is radiated from any living system due to its metabolic activities, without excitation or enhancement" (Takeda et al 2004, p. 656). Since biophotonic energy is light, it's likely that we not only process it through the metabolic functions of the cell, but that it may even be responsible for the metabolism that occurs. Regardless the biophotonic light does serve as the means of cellular communication, and relies on a specific structure: "Deep within the cells that make up our bodies are structures called microtubules, minute, hollow cylinders constructed out of spiraling stands of protein" (Keith 2005, p.123). These microtubules support the cells and have a diameter that is just large enough to support the passage of water molecules and, more importantly, light wavelengths. These light wavelengths are essential to cell repair, "A certain wavelength of light was known to actually aid in cell repair, a phenomenon known as *photo-repair*; and, second, that carcinogens absorbed the photo-repair wavelengths and reemitted them at a different wavelength [italics are his]" (Keith 2005, p. 123). This different wavelength diffuses the photo-repair capabilities of the cells and essentially causes cancer. The healthy light that is emitted occurs in synchronicity with the biological rhythms of the body, but the light that has been altered by the carcinogens no longer allows communication of the cells with the body, creating ripe conditions for cancer (Keith 2005). Yet the communication that occurs between the cells and the body, through the light emissions, happens on an even deeper level.

To understand that communication we need to understand the relationship biophotonic energy has with DNA by exploring what DNA is and how it interacts with RNA. DNA is our genetic code. It contains and transmits that information within the nucleus of a cell:

> The DNA molecules are built up of two chains of nucleotides entwined in opposite directions to form a helix. Each nucleotide in a chain has a complementary nucleotide in the other. They bind together in a pattern in which Adenine always couples with Thymine, and Guanine always seeks out Cytosine. The sequence of these base pairs and their three-dimensional conformation along the double helix determines the hereditary information. (Restak 1994, p. 96)

The DNA interacts with the RNA in order to develop the structure of the cell: In essence, the RNA transmit the appropriate information to other parts of the cell, which start generating what is necessary genetically as a result of the information. (Restak 1994) The DNA and RNA work together to create the cells and from there the building blocks of what is considered the human body. Dawkins speculates that DNA/RNA, or replicators, do this to build survival machines (1989). The human body is a survival machine that can survive in a variety of environments, while serving as a host for the genes and keeping them viable.

We want to work with our bodies and our genetics, to fine tune what is happening with intent. Yet Dawkin's concept of the body is ultimately mechanistic, that of a machine: "A body, then is not a replicator, it is a vehicle...vehicles don't replicate themselves; they work to propagate their replicators" (1989, p. 254). The replicators are genes that survive long enough to imprint their existence, to pass on a trait that keeps them viable (Dawkins 1989).

But is this paradigm of survival really what happens? Is this the sole reason of communication/transmission from cell to cell, to create a human machine that allows for the carrying of genetics? If this is the case, the DNA/RNA have accepted a bad deal overall. There's not much autonomy for them in the body. I find such an approach to be lacking, if only because it represents a commodification of genetics, a consumer mentality at work. The focus is on how one organism takes advantage of another, while offering little in regards to symbiosis or cooperative living. We aren't looking to commodify ourselves, commodify our paradigms until they hit the commode, a waste tissue no longer needed.

If we settle for such an answer, the alchemy we seek to work is futile, because we are focused on survival and not on evolution. We aren't agents of change for our bodies, so much as pawns for our genetics. The inner alchemy we seek to work with our bodies, with our genes, is one of intent, desire, and will. Still we shouldn't overly mystify DNA as occurs in the following passage: "It may be DNA that communicates to the magician in the language of synchronicities, confluence of life events, awakenings, satori, peak experience, and other occult events. DNA is implicit in the use of blood and sexual fluids in reifiying wishes, by the combination of the esctasis of orgasm or bloodshed with intent, along with our strongest magical link to our own beings, the little microscopic bits that contain the code for everything we are" (Louv 2006, p. 263). The problem with such mystification is that it draws too heavily on the modality of traditional biology that argues that genetics determines everything, even how we adapt to the environment we live in. It suggests that magic is not an environmental force, but instead a genetic code, when in fact it may actually be both. It also leaves out of the equation free will, suggesting that even our occult experiences are coded into the genetic structure without any variability, which is rather dull, if that's the case.

Accordingly, for me, a different paradigm is in order. This paradigm relies on more than just the communication between DNA and RNA to construct a cell, or for the replication of genes. Rather, it concerns body modification and evolution, a willful change of what we have, into something better. It is also an acknowledgement of the role that the environment plays in genetics, something which has been ignored far too much within traditional biology.

Biophotonic energy and DNA are interconnected, and it is through this connection that I have done a lot of my magical workings with DNA. I've always noticed a sensation of light around the DNA in my visualizations. The light changes frequencies as the DNA is worked with. Interestingly enough, if DNA is unwound it emits more biophotonic light:

> It is known that when you apply a chemical called ethidium bromide to samples of DNA, the chemical squeezes itself into the middle of the base pairs of the double helix and causes it to unwind...Popp discovered that the more he increased the concentration of the chemical, the more the DNA unwound, but also the stronger the intensity of light...He also found that DNA was capable of sending out a large range of frequencies and that some frequencies seemed linked to certain functions. (Mctaggart 2002, p. 44)

DNA, in essence, acts as both a storehouse and emitter of biophotonic energy. That energy likely contributes to the genetic functioning of DNA, but beyond even that enables the magician to work directly with the DNA, and specifically the frequencies that the biophotonic energy emits.

DNA is understood as mainly conveying genetic information, but with my approaches to magic, I've never really approached DNA in that way. It's always been my thought that DNA can be modified and worked with and that the environment plays a role in this (Note: When I refer to genetics and DNA and the idea that genetics can be changed I'm not referring to the idea of changing the number of chromosomes in your genetics, but rather to modifying and working with the genes that are available. The only way to tell a difference is through observing the body as a whole). Part of this mentality comes from my refusal to accept that I would always have to deal with the genetic aspect of my depression, but it also comes from my desire to experiment. In traditional biology the argument that has occurred is that the environment is shaped by genetics, "The doctrine of the extended phenotype is that the phenotypic effect of a gene (genetic replicator) is best seen as an effect upon the world at large, and only incidentally upon the individual organism-or any other vehicle-in which it happens to sit" (Dawkins 1999, p. 117). This doctrine unfortunately is quite unsound. It essentially argues that the environment is shaped by genetics, and yet fails to factor in how changing environmental conditions demand adaptation on a physiological level. Lipton aptly points out that genes aren't destiny and that environmental influences including diet, exercise, etc., will have an impact on the genetics that influences yourself and future descendents (2005). In other words, genes do not determine the reality of our body.

Nor, however, should we think that the environment has complete control over the development of our body or the genetics. Rather, what happens is that the cells process the environmental information via their organelles and then determine what genetic characteristics are most useful for adapting to the environment. What is even more intriguing is that genetics can be shared, "Living organisms, it turns out, actually integrate their cellular communities by sharing their genes...Now scientists realize that genes are shared not only among individual members of a species, but also among members of different species" (Lipton 2005, p. 44). Thus genetics responds more to the environment, adapting life forms through the information obtained from the environment, as opposed to dictating what the environment should be.

My first experiment with DNA was a bonding of the five western traditional elements to the DNA bases. The bonding of the elements correlates to the order of the bondings of the DNA except in the case of the RNA strand Uracil, which represents spirit and can interface randomly with the DNA. Guanine bonds to Cytosine and Adenine bonds to Thymine. When I bonded the elemental energies to my DNA, I bonded Earth to Guanine, Fire to Cytosine, Adenine to Air and Water to Thymine. To some degree this is a subjective and arbitrary bonding. I'm certain that if someone wanted to bond fire to Guanine for instance that it would be just as workable. Alternatively bonding all of the elements to each DNA segment, for instance Earth, Water, Air, and Fire to Thymine, is quite possible. My initial bonding of the elements to the DNA was done as a further experiment of the blood letting ritual I'd done (see chapter four for details). I figured that if I had already exchanged life essence with the elements, there was no reason I couldn't take that essence and bond it to my genetic structure, making my access to elemental energy more genetic and natural than before.

The reason you can bond elemental energy to your DNA is because of biophotonic energy, which has different functions depending on the frequency that is in place for it. One example is the bonding of elemental and other varieties of energy to the person. Because magic is an environmental force, it can affect your genetics and indeed has shaped them so as to be able to interact or interface with the different frequencies of energy (such as elemental energy) that is available to you to work with. Another example of this is Reiki energy. When you get an attunement, the frequency of your energy is being widened to make you aware of the energy frequency of Reiki. Once this awareness is achieved, the practitioner can channel Reiki energy. What I find interesting about Reiki is the symbols that can be used by people to enhance the Reiki workings. There are, of course, the standard Reiki symbols that people learn when they get the second and third Reiki attunements. But there are also Reiki symbols that different people have received for specific functions, such as curing cancer. In Christopher Penczak's book on magic and Reiki, the author mentions that he has received from his students symbols that they used for specific situations. These symbols modify the Reiki current, focusing on a particular frequency and applying it to a specific problem. The symbols serve as a focus for the alteration of the frequency, attuning the person to the specific change that occurs in the Reiki when it's focused on a specific kind of ailment (Penczak 2004).

Just as Reiki can be adjusted (or if you will, just as a person can be attuned to Reiki) so can a person use the biophotonic energy to attune him/herself to different frequencies of energy. We already do this to some degree naturally, but this function of biophotonic energy can be used purposely, so that you bond different frequencies or types of energy to your DNA and can access those energies by changing the frequency of the biophotonic energy. Or there's what I like to do, which is widening the frequency (bandwidth) of the energy so that you work with multiple forms of energy at once. So for instance you can meld elemental energy work into Reiki healing that you are doing for someone. Likewise you can narrow the frequency of biophotonic energy. I suspect that at least in some cases of psychic vampirism the frequency of biophotonic energy is too narrow or deficient, causing the need to leach off of other people. This can be corrected through increasing the types of energy the psychic vampire resonates with. Much as the body can slowly adapt itself to different forms of poison, so that the poison is eventually neutralized, so too can s/he take in different frequencies of energy, gradually getting used to those energies, so that s/he no longer needs to feed off of other people.

The real question is how you meld your own energy to elemental or other forms of energy. I initially determined a correspondence that wasn't based on a systematic thinking, but on intuition. It was as if I could see the DNA strands in my mind and I could see where each element should mesh with each strand of DNA. Since I had already offered my blood to the elements, I figured I could take what they'd given me and mesh it to my DNA. I spent approximately a week on each element and each DNA strand. The first week, for instance, was dedicated to exploring the relationship between Earth and Guanine. Everyday I did a meditation where I would visit all the Guanine strands on my DNA and bond the frequency of Earth to the strand. In the meditation, I visited a cell and then descended into the cell itself to where the DNA was in the nucleus. My goal was to find Guanine, so while I was doing this meditation, I was vibrating the word Guanine at different pitches. The goal is to find the pitch that Guanine vibrates at for you. Once you have found this pitch, in your meditation you'll see the DNA segments that are Guanine vibrating. Visit those segments and apply a hermetic symbol of Elemental Earth[1] to the strand. Evoke Earth, while meditating and attach that elemental energy to the symbol you have put into your DNA strand. Now comes the hard part. You need to visualize the hermetic symbol for Spirit Earth (Spirit Earth is the gateway to the raw elemental plane, while the Elemental Earth symbol is the connection to our physical reality) and connect the vibrating strand of Guanine to that energy. This creates a tunnel from the first symbol of Elemental Earth to the Spirit Earth symbol. This tunnel acts as a gateway, sending Earth energy into the Guanine. The biophotonic energy takes the frequency and adds it to the usual frequency of energy that you already possess: your energy signature.

I also did a ritual at the end of the first week where I played music that reminded me of the Earth. The music was mostly industrial and the sounds ranged from the clashing of tectonic plates (*Coil – How to Destroy Angels 2*) to Tibetan monks chanting to bells and then silence. The ritual involved summoning the spirit of Guanine and the spirit of

---

[1] You can find these symbols in any book on hermetic or elemental magic; I used *Enchantments of the Faerie Realm* by Ted Andrews.

Earth and through sex magic consummating their joining in my own body. I used the hermetic symbols for Elemental Earth and Spirit Earth as a gateway to evoke the Earth spirit. For Guanine, I focused on a double helix and vocalized the word Guanine at a pitch that would cause the Guanine strands to vibrate. Through that vibration I called forth the spirit of Guanine. I ejaculated and asked both spirits to meld their energy into the semen. I then proceeded to take the cum as a eucharist. This would make the elemental energy of Earth a natural, genetic part of me, allowing me deeper access to that energy frequency. I used semen instead of blood for its reproductive energy and rich blend of hormones, protein, and other building blocks of life. I associated these building blocks with the fertile aspects of Earth, and wanted to encourage that in the genetic assimilation of the elemental energy.

I did variations of the meditation and ritual with each strand and element and likewise used music that evoked the element being worked with. (I particularly like the band *Rapoon*, which has some excellent elemental themed music.) In each case I found the period of a week was useful because it allowed my own energy to adapt to what was for the most part an alien energy. However, you should take as much time as you need to do this working, as your ability to adapt your energy to another frequency may vary. It never hurts, either, to be overly cautious in your approach to this work, as changes to your genetics and energetic signature can take some to be undone.

Most recently, I've decided to take the working I've described above to the next level. Instead of just applying one element to one DNA segment, I've focused on applying all elements to all DNA segments. This is done partially to balance the elemental energy within the DNA, but also to incorporate that energy further into the biophotonic energy. In the case of these workings, I've made a sacrifice of hair trimmings shaved to each element, placing the hair in the hermetic symbol for each element and then making the sacrifice in a manner that accords to each element. Earth's sacrifice was buried, Water's sacrifice was given to a lake, Fire burned, and Air blown into the air. Spirit's sacrifice was made to a composite symbol of the other hermetic symbols and then left where it was, for Spirit to take away on its own. The sacrifice of the hair is a sacrifice of DNA, a giving of energy for another kind of energy and, if you will, a template by which the elemental energy can be mapped onto the actual energetic structures of the person. The hair is a sample of your genetic code, and when it's given to an elemental energy form it acts as a template for the elemental energy to use when it's mapped to your genetic code.

After the sacrifice has been made, I've used inhibitory meditation to cut off my senses as much as possible and focused sending myself to the DNA. I have imposed each set of hermetic symbols on each DNA strand, strengthening the connection between the elemental energy and the DNA, as well as balancing this energy further with the biophotonic energy.

While I've been doing this work, the meditations have also focused on personal issues that might be considered elemental. As an example, when I was working on this process with the Earth element, I got into a conversation that was focused on what my plans are for the future and what do I want to do for a career. My work with Water yielded up dealing with issues in a relationship I was involved in. My work with Air has focused on creating flexible mental habits, and Fire has focused on using creativity effectively, while reining in destructive urges. So the balance was not merely physical and energetic, but also emotional and mental. The end goal of the working was to not only attune my DNA to the elemental energy, but use the DNA as a gateway for that energy on multiple levels of my being.

You can also use other forms or frequency of energy besides the elements. For instance, you can work with the seven main chakras extensively and apply their symbols/sounds to the DNA, causing them to resonate with each other. Likewise Otherkin[2] who use magic may introduce dragon, faerie or other energies into their DNA, particularly by applying the theory of resonance (see chapter nine) as it applies to meshing their genetic structure with their Other energy Finally, DNA manipulation is also useful in invoking godforms, if you desire to bond their energy to your own.

The meshing of the DNA with different forms of energy is one way to use DNA magic, but another application is the enhancement of our cells as power generators. By meshing the different frequencies of

---

[2] Otherkin are people who feel that they aren't quite human in a spiritual manner and identify themselves as something different such as an elf, dragon or animal. For more information please refer to Lupa's book *A Field Guide to Otherkin* (Immanion Press, 2007)

energy to DNA, you are already processing more energy through your cells then you might otherwise do, but through manipulation of the frequency of biophotonic energy you can also increase the energetic output, the metabolism, of the cell. This turns each cell in your body into a mini-chakra. It functions the same way a normal chakra does, and utilizes the DNA strands and double helix, and the mitochondria, for its energy routes. The way the DNA is constructed actually allows for the possibility of shaping the cell into a mini-chakra, because as you will see in conventional models of chakra work, the nadis form a double helix spiral, which surrounds the main chakras. By working with your cells as mini-chakras you are taking the next step, and learning that the chakras are not limited to seven major chakras or even tertiary chakras in your hands and feet. The chakras or energy centers of the body can literally be every cell in your body.

A further advantage of creating these mini-chakras is that you can use them for concentrated healing work. As an example, by attuning one of your cells to Reiki and then attuning that cell to elemental energy, you can mix the healing work you do with both elemental and Reiki energy, without having to do a convoluted ritual to call up the elemental energy. Since the elemental energy is already a part of you, when you do a healing with Reiki, you can also channel that elemental energy through all of your chakras. This type of healing can also be applied on the cellular level, through the mini-chakras. The mini-chakras energize the cells and increase their consciousness so that it's easier to work with. Consequently, when doing healing on a cellular basis, it is easier to direct the focus of the consciousness of the cells, which at this point are used to working with you as energy centers.

The principle of replication can be extended toward the very creation of the mini-chakras. As one mini-chakra cell produces other cells, it also produces other mini-chakras, with all the attunements replicated as well. Naturally you will need to factor in environmental effects on these chakras, but since this is occurring already by adapting the genetic structure to process these energies the replication will likely continue. The difference here is that you are consciously directing this development, consciously shaping the health and adaptation of your body through this process.

Healing on this level can take a variety of forms. If dealing with cancer, for instance, instead of allowing the healthy cells to feed the cancerous cells, you can redirect the energy toward maintaining the defense and deny the cancerous cells oxygen and nutrients that would normally be passed on to them. The energetic cells can drain the energy from the cancerous turning them into waste, which will eventually be expelled by the body. The goal is to avoid allowing the cancer to seed other cells, to replicate itself so that it continues to live. At the same time the cells learn to protect themselves and your body as a whole (Davis 2003). However, once the cancerous cells are starved you will need new cells to replace the old. The healthy cells will replicate with the mini-chakras in place, so the new cells protect themselves and go on to produce more healthy copies. Additionally, the mini chakras balance the cells and their DNA, so that junk DNA does not turn the cells into cancer again. The addition of other types of energy enables the cell to fortify its defenses with more than just your own energy. It can then fight off the junk DNA and various viruses with an increased energy spectrum. This provides more angles to combat the potential problem, because there's more variety to the energy and it's harder for the junk DNA to adapt to.

Replication can be useful for dealing with other forms of disease, such as infections. One magician I know attuned a bone marrow cell, which produces blood cells, with Reiki. The consequent blood cells produced were attuned to Reiki and spread the healing energy of the Reiki to the rest of the body, particularly the infection he was fighting, which enabled him to successfully counter what would have otherwise been a life threatening illness (Vitimus 2005). Additionally, ridding yourself of carcinogenic and toxic substances will start to change the type of wavelengths emitted in your cells. You'll want use a detox regime to help begin that purging process, such as fasting or a diet. Do some research and keep in mind your own bodily needs and what you can handle. You can speed the healing of these wavelengths by using your mini-chakra cells to emit and amplify the healthy wavelength energy throughout your body. This aids in healing a wide variety of ailments.

Another technique you can use with your DNA is to create a DNA sigil. Take the drawn formulas (i.e. the diagrams) for each strand of DNA/RNA and create a sigil out of it. This can also be done with the formulas of neurotransmitters. One result is to spread the genetic work you've been doing to other cells in your body, and even to other people, using the genetic magic to help heal those people or strengthen them. You can also evoke the spirits of the neurotransmitters, amino acids, mitochondria, etc., outside of yourself, so you aren't just working with them internally. The evocation can be useful for healing work, as a way of getting to know these entities, or for other inner alchemical work. Evocation of these entities may be helpful in terms of learning more about your physiology and how it works, and can direct you toward useful information in books and other sources, when you look up that information to verify what the entities have told you. Remember that the various consciousnesses that reside in your body are resources that can be utilized to help you with your health, physically, emotionally, and mentally.

There are key aspects to remember in these workings. The first is the principle of equivalent exchange (And this is not gotten from the show *Full Metal Alchemist*, but instead learned through hard earned experience). What you are exchanging is equal to what is being offered to you. If either side fails to live up to its obligation what was given can be withdrawn and should be. Even though, for instance, I have offered hair clippings to the element of fire and those clippings are now burned, what I really offered was energy. If the element of fire fails to do an offering in return that energy you offered can be taken back. It is your energy. The hair clippings are only a physical form that encapsulates your energy. You can, of course, take that energy back, but personally it's an offering and exchange, I've made and prefer to honor that.

The second principle to remember is that by doing this process you are undergoing transformation on all levels of your body. You are inviting the influence of other entities into you. Make sure you trust those entities.

The final principle is the goal itself. What is your purpose in doing this work? Why do you want to do it? For example, my goal is to change my cells into chakras that will allow me to process even more energy and store it as well, which will increase the ability of my mitochondria. I want to maximize the role of my cells as power generators, even as I use that energy to keep my cells healthy and balanced. But I make sure to ask permission. Remember that cells have their own consciousness as well and it should be respected. What you change within you will change you overall.

These examples show it is possible for you to work with your DNA and cells. And the implications of this work extend beyond the cellular level into a new approach to energy work, and how you interact with the world and universe. In your own way, you are a cell for the planet, a DNA spiral for the universe. The question is, are you a healthy cell with a strong DNA spiral, or a cancerous cell filled with junk DNA, ready to destroy your own habitat?

Exercises

1. Do some research on biophotonic energy and learn how it is used to treat cancer and other illnesses (You might wish to begin looking in medical journals, such as *Cancer Science*). Focus as well on how the cells use biophotonic energy to communicate with each other. Now, doing a meditation, try and communicate with the biophotonic energy in your cells. If you are ill, try using the biophotonic energy to speed up your healing (in conjunction with your present medical treatment).
2. What other types of energy might you be able to meld with that I haven't mentioned here? How do you think my approach to DNA magic applies to energy work, if at all? If you use energy work, how might DNA magic help you?
3. Besides bonding with elemental energy or shaping your cells to become mini-chakras, how else can you apply DNA magic?

Chapter Seven
Basic Energy Work

In contemporary magic, there is a movement to dispel the notion that energy work occurs. One post modern magician argues that: "Of course, energy is a useful symbol, but it is absurd to say there's some hitherto undiscovered energy that shares none of the other characteristics of other energy we know. Saying this energy is somehow responsible for magic is absurd" (Dunn 2005, p. 29). While Dunn is correct that energy is not entirely responsible for magic, as we do rely on symbols and a variety of other means of expression in practicing magic, he's incorrect in presuming that energy itself is just a symbol. Although I mediate a lot of reality through symbols and language, I can't mediate the feeling of tingling or heat that emanates from my hands. I can say it tingles, but I can't entirely define the feeling as a symbol, and it would be foolish to do so, because you limit your reality if you only approach it as symbolism. It's the same as seeing deities and spirits as only symbols; through experience I have found they have independent existences outside of my perception. Also advances in science with the finding of biophotonic energy suggest new forms of energy that cannot be detected by conventional means. Whether or not they share characteristics with other types of energy is something that can only be discovered through experimentation. Dunn also argues, "Scientific literacy and pseudo-scientific explanations aside, mages should work with the concept of energy in an intuitive sense, understanding it not as a literal truth, but as a handy symbol for power. 'Explanations' in terms of biological electricity, brain waves, vibrations, and so forth, often do more to obscure than to illuminate" (2005, p. 30). While I agree that working with energy in an intuitive sense is a good idea, the problem that occurs with Dunn's argument is that he is essentially asking magicians to cut out vital areas of research and experimentation and limit ourselves only to symbolic magic.

This inevitably takes away from the efficacy of the magic done, because symbols are only one aspect of reality when it comes to magic, "It is all right to understand it metaphorically but the [totem] animal needs also to be related to in the immediacy of its existence, not merely as if it were a message 'about'. To treat it as if it were <u>only</u>

a metaphor about other aspects of one's life is to miss the fact that it is also the nucleus of the connection to those other aspects [Underline is his emphasis]" (Gallegos 1989, p. 148). The various theories that are drawn on and put into practice by magicians are highly useful for advancing magic beyond where it is. The explanations do not obscure but, as with science, serve to illuminate until such a time as further experimental work unveils a new direction to go in. To limit our directions of magical research and work is to narrow all the possible avenues of exploration and does more to obscure magical practice than to illuminate it.

Even so, some magicians feel the energy model is outdated and yet struggle, at the same time, to find some term that explains how magic works, particularly energy work. Others want some kind of sensational term that will make energy work seem more mysterious or dare I say, less New Agey. Perhaps the real problem is that the term energy has become generic, even as, in a sense, the term magic has also become generic. As with anything, we should not focus on terms to the point where we exclude practice. Otherwise, we engage in an academic circle jerk that goes nowhere fast.

The biggest obstacle I've encountered with energy work is explaining what energy is to someone who's never experienced it on a conscious level. Many people are trapped in a nineteenth century scientific empiricist mentality and need to "see it to believe it." But what if you can't see it? What happens then? As it happens, I can see the static, multi-colored bits of energy that some might call auras, and others orgone, Wilhem Reich's term for energy. But not every magician sees this energy. For those who don't there has to be a way to sense it. As I discussed in chapter 2, our senses connect us to our environment and not all of us need to use sight to notice energy or other phenomena we know exist. For instance, you can't see the air around you, but you can feel it. Likewise you can't see the heat of the sun, but if you close your eyes and slowly spin in a circle, you'll eventually feel the warmth and the direction it's coming from, on your face. That warmth is energy, but you can't see it. You can only feel it.

My answer to this problem of learning to sense energy involves more than throwing an energy ball at you like a water balloon. After all, if you can't even feel energy, you're not going to notice an energy ball. You aren't attuned to that reality. An energy ball might work if the person realized s/he was feeling energy, but unless the person knows what kind of sensations to expect, s/he might write it off. Any lingering aftereffects would be passed off as emotions, environmental stimuli, or impending illness. And the key to really explaining energy to someone is to give hir an experience or two that pushes hir out of whatever mindset it is that doesn't allow hir to acknowledge energy within and without. The following exercise is a useful starting point.

First have the energy worker place hir hands about twelve inches apart and parallel to each other. The person who hasn't felt energy should place a finger between the hands, but should not touch either hand. S/he should also close hir eyes. The energy worker now concentrates on sending energy from one hand to the other. The goal of the person who hasn't felt energy is to basically concentrate on feeling the finger and specifically any sensations that occur. This could be tingling, heat, or even cold. The energy worker should switch sending energy from hand to hand and even send energy from both hands. Each time the goal is to get the person to feel what direction the energy is coming from. I've never had this exercise not work with a person.

Once a person has successfully felt energy, the next step is to actually get the person to not only feel energy, but also project it. There is a fallacy in the magical community that the right hand is the projecting hand and the left hand is the receiving hand. It doesn't matter which hand you use to receive or send energy--you can send or receive with both hands, though some people have preferences. I mention this because the next exercise has you create a circuit with a partner.

Sit comfortably across from each other and hold hands with each other. The more experienced energy worker starts up the circuit by sending energy into the other person through one arm and then receiving the energy from the other arm. The person who is having energy pass through hir should focus on feeling that energy, and specifically feeling the sensation that denotes the passage of energy. This sensation will give hir an idea of what it feels like to work with energy in the body. Usually the feeling I get when I have energy sent into my body is of a tingling surge, and this seems to be similar for other people. After a little while the more experienced energy worker should stop sending energy and allow the less experienced person to send energy, so that s/he can get a feeling for both sides of the equation. An additional note for the person who is sending energy--don't focus on pushing the energy. Instead, focus on flowing with the energy. Let your awareness of the energy guide you to it. Move your consciousness within the flow you feel as opposed to pushing it. If you push your consciousness you'll be forcing it as opposed to directing it gently. It takes a lot more effort to push against energy than to flow with it toward a result. Another way to think of this principle is to apply it to water. You can close your hand in a fist to try and contain the water, but it'll just flow around your hand, leaving drops in your hands. On the other hand, if you keep your hands open and cupped you can hold some water in your hands. A lot of it will still flow past you, but you'll have some water that you can drink.

Both of these exercises are useful for beginners, because they not only give you an idea of how to sense energy, but actually teach you to send and receive energy. The cycle technique can also be used for other purposes, which I'll explain in the advanced energy work chapter. For now, if you've never felt energy, concentrate on getting used to feeling and working with it. The very fact that you can now sense energy should show you that it's not just a New Age fad. The key thing to remember about energy work is that energy is real and can be worked with. It's not just a symbol, but has its own reality. Granted, symbols can be useful for energy work, particularly in working with and personifying archetypal energies (Judith 1996). But energy work can't be ground down to just symbols. Even in the interactions you have with other people, energy can play a much more subtle role than what symbols themselves provide. You may note that sometimes you feel stronger connections toward some of your friends and loved ones than others. Partially this is due to the kind of relationship you have and the intimacy involved in creating and sustaining a friendship and/or romantic relationship. But partially this is also a result of how well your energy meshes with the other person's energy. When I get into a conversation with someone else, it's always intriguing to note how much the person and I engage each other on not just a verbal or physical level, but energetically, too. You can usually tell if it's a good conversation if you're both energized by the exchange. And this energy is conveyed in part by the words and actions, but also by how your spiritual essences interact. Basically, in a good conversation a cycle is created, like in the exercise above, which keeps that energy flowing between you. Conversely, when you hang out with someone who is an unconscious psychic vampire, all depressed and attention-seeking, you'll feel drained afterwards for no apparent reason.

Another reason there are such issues with energy work comes down to the mind/body split, which to some degree still pervades much of Western occultism. The idea that the mind is separate from the body creates an issue when doing energy work. After all, you have to wonder which you are affecting, the mind, the body, or both? Suffice it to say this paradox often leads to the kind of conclusions that I've quoted from Dunn. Also, Western occultism relies far too much on a psychological model when it comes to magic; it's no surprise, then, that many occultists have issues with energy work. It's not something which fits conveniently into a psychological model, because it has applications that go beyond any psychological work.

I don't limit myself to a psychological model of magic or to the mind-body duality that pervades Western culture. I prefer an integrated approach that perceives the body, mind, energy, spirit, etc. as one and the same. No one part is greater than the others and is not even divisible beyond the artificial labeling that is used to differentiate the ideas. The problem with such divisions is summed up as follows: "Some religions describe the body as the root of all evil while others tell us that it is merely an illusion or at best, simply insignificant. Medical practices treat the body mechanically, as a set of disconnected parts divorced from the spirit that dwells within. Standard training for psychotherapists completely ignores the role of the body in mental health" (Judith 1996, p. 55). It should be no surprise that ignorance of the body also leads to ignorance of energy. And while many people may feel the body isn't important, I have to wonder how they can expect to work magic if their physical health is not exactly up to par. It should be no surprise that generally there are also psychological and/or spiritual issues that create problems for the magician reflected in hir physical health.

Despite this problem energy work can be integrated into inner alchemy provided you realize that much as the body and mind are not separate from each other, neither is energy an isolated phenomenon. If you've done the exercises above you now know what energy feels like. But what is even more important is to get a sense of the different systems of energy work that are used. I don't particularly feel that any one system is right. At best such systems are descriptive as opposed to prescriptive and as such can be altered with experimentation. For now I'll present the energy work systems I'm familiar with in a basic context, but with an eye toward moving past that context.

Chakras

This system of energy work is probably the most well known. I will admit I've never learned the traditional East Indian words for the chakras, so I use the English terms. My main focus has been on working with the information I have and using it to understand my energetic body. I personally don't feel that not knowing these words affects my ability to work with this energy system; the chakras themselves exist outside of a particular culture. In fact it is possible to find similar parallels of energy systems through disparate cultures (such as the Tan Tien and Meridians of Taoism, or the Sephiroth of Kabbalah).

One way to define chakra is, "The word chakra literally means disk. How fitting that in modern times, disks are the common storage unit of programmed information. We can use this analogy and think of chakras as floppy disks that contain vital programs" (Judith 1996, p. 9). This definition is overly simplistic and doesn't really begin to encapsulate what chakras are or what they do. They do process specific types of information. The root chakra, for instance, processes and channels Elemental Earth energy. In other words, chakras aren't really floppy disk; they do much more than just contain information. Judith does provide a better definition, "Swirling intersections of vital life forces, each chakra reflects an aspect of consciousness essential to our lives...Chakras are organizing centers for the reception, assimilation, and transmission of life energies. Our chakras, as core centers, form the coordinating network of our complicated mind/body system" (Judith 1999, p. 4). In other words, chakras are confluences of energy that also direct that energy and monitor and maintain it. In fact, chakras are the energetic equivalent of a cell in the body. This is why it is so easy to make cells into mini-chakras.

But chakras have other functions as well. As I mentioned above, they process specific types of energy. This energy is expressed in our emotions, behaviors, and even in our physical health, but the chakras are not just a psychological gateway as Judith portrays them (1999). They are quite literally gateways to other dimensions of reality. The Earth Chakra is an actual gateway to the elemental plane of Earth.

What's truly fascinating is that you can actually use your chakras to access these other planes of reality via astral travel and also through the use of tattvas. A person stares into the tattva until s/he sends hir consciousness into the symbol, and through it finds access to the plane of existence the symbol represents. However, you can use the chakras to do this, meditating on the location of the chakra and the corresponding symbol and opening that chakra up, so as to travel into the plane of existence that the chakra is a gateway to. I've used the gateway technique effectively to meet the animal spirit of a given chakra via Gallegos' personal totem pole paradigm, as well as the elemental/DNA pathworkings in the previous chapter. I will go over the gateway chakra technique in more detail in the next chapter.

Another intriguing aspect about chakras is the system of energy that keeps them balanced and functioning in relation to each other. The nadis are energy currents that balance the chakras by working together to keep the chakras spinning, "The ancient tantric texts that depict the chakras show their major *nadis* as figure eight patterns that wrap around the chakras. The two nadis, *Ida* and *Pingala*...begin at the first chakra and meet again at the sixth, polarizing each of the chakras in between and contributing to their spin [Italics are hers]" (Judith 1996, p. 372). What's so fascinating is that these nadis form a double helix around the chakras, representing a DNA spiral that effectively contains and channels the elemental energy that each chakra processes. These nadis not only keep the chakras functioning, but also distribute the different types of elemental energy throughout the body.

I've devised an energy raising technique that utilizes the nadis and the chakras that I perform while standing up. I first take deep breaths in through my nostrils, drawing energy up each chakra with each breath, until I feel the connection between all the chakras. Next I draw energy up through one of my legs, left or right, and then circulate it through one of the nadis. If I draw energy up the left leg, the energy will reach the Earth chakra and then go up the nadi that starts on the right side of the body. Likewise if I draw energy from the right leg, that energy will go up the left nadi. The energy is circulated through the nadis, but I also raise my hands above my head, and circulate the energy through my hands so that it's connected not just at the sixth chakra but also above, in my crown chakra, where the energy is directed and then brought down to the sixth chakra so as to re-enter the nadi system.

I've found this technique to be useful for not only raising energy, but also maintaining the balance between the chakras. It's important to maintain this balance, because without it the energies of the chakras will become distorted. As a personal example my third chakra was blown out (i.e. too large), while my second chakra had almost been entirely bypassed so that it hardly moved, the energy going instead to my Earth chakra. This resulted, for my physical health, in having no libido and also having stomach issues in terms of what I could eat. My fourth chakra seemed normal, but my fifth chakra had a large blockage in it and my sixth and seventh chakras were healthy.

As it would turn out a lot of my problems originated in the fourth, or heart chakra. I felt a need to protect my heart and accordingly the energy of the fourth chakra tied up the energy of the second chakra while blowing out the third chakra, in order to protect me from interacting with people on a sexual or power level. Likewise my seventh chakra was affecting my fifth chakra, causing the blockage in it. Although the seventh chakra seemed normal, my intellect felt stifled and this consequently stifled my ability to speak. The above technique I used helped me to become aware of these blockages and begin balancing the energy, though I also relied on another system of energy work (discussed below) to dissolve the blockages. The important thing to note is that although some of the chakras appeared normal they not only were affected by the blockages, but in several cases were actually the cause. It's important in working with chakras, or any other system of energy work, to not only consider the obvious symptoms, but also find the underlying causes of those symptoms (Judith 1999). Only in doing that can real healing occur.

Barbara Ann Brennan School of Healing

Brennan's paradigm is primarily focused on healing. I've used this system in my own energy work since 1995. It primarily deals with how to manifest events in your life and how to fine tune that manifestation so as to avoid repetition of patterns that aren't beneficial to you. Through conscious awareness of how your energy interacts with these patterns you can utilize the energy effectively to grow past them,

> Incarnation is organic soul movement in which, higher, finer vibrations or soul aspects are continually radiated downward through the finer auric bodies into the more dense ones and then finally into the physical body...As growth takes place, the individual opens her

> ability to sustain higher levels of vibrations/energy/consciousness coming into and through her vehicles, her auric bodies and chakras. (Brennan 1988, p. 61)

Such a focus in energy work is highly useful for healing and inner alchemical work, in terms of working through unhealthy habits and repressed emotions.

Brennan notes that unhealthy beliefs and habits can be perceived energetically as well as manifested in the actual behavior itself. These habits and beliefs are perceived energetically as thought forms, which essentially are built up thoughts that have come to possess their own energy (Brennan 1998). Thought forms will try to sustain themselves by continuing to feed into the person's belief about how a particular situation will turn out or how an interaction with another person will end. This can be worked through by learning to recognize the subconscious reactions and choose a conscious action instead. Energetically thought forms can be dealt with by working through the energy blockage that continues to divert energy to them.

Another aspect of Brennan's system is that she identifies types of energy--known as energetic defense systems--that manifest in a person's aura and they will shape how a person energetically interacts with other people: "We all create blocks because we see the world as unsafe. We block in patterns that involve our whole energy system. Our energetic defense systems are designed to repel, to defend aggressively or passively against an incoming force. They are designed to show power and thus scare off an aggressor, or they are designed to get us attention indirectly, without admitting that is what we want" (Brennan 1988, p. 104). In short, energetic defense systems are subconscious defenses we build and use to deal with different situations in our lives. They are built into our auras and when we are in situations where we feel threatened, our auras activate those defense system to deal with the situations.

Some of Brennan's descriptions of energetic defense systems are similar to psychic vampirism. One example is the oral sucking defense system, where a person sucks in energy from around them in order to fill s/he own energy field. Brennan notes that, "There is something amiss in the person's ability to metabolize the orgone supply from the surrounding atmosphere, causing him to need predigested energy from others" (1988, p. 104). This description of the need for predigested energy is similar to that of a psychic vampire. Both

Belanger and Kaldera notes that a psychic vampire also can't process just any energy, but needs the vital life energy of another person, which is already processed (2004, 2005). Similarly Brennan's descriptions of tentacles echoes that of Belanger's and Kaldera's description of tendrils and the purpose for each is also similar, namely to draw in energy from other people.

Of interest to me is the notion that such people, whether they are conscious psychic vampires or not, can't take in or metabolize energy that isn't already processed. As I mentioned in chapter 6 it's possible that the biophotonic energy of such a person is on too limited a frequency of energy. Maybe the metabolic processes of the cells and specifically the mitochondria have been damaged when it comes to processing different frequencies of energy. Or perhaps the light wavelength of the cells has been altered to a point that it can only communicate limited amounts of information, as compared to a person who has healthy cells. This in turn would suggest that there is even potential genetic damage, that the inability to process energy would also limit the ability to environmentally adapt. This is only speculation, at this point, but research and experimentation should be considered to see if there are any parallels between the inability to process energy and the biophotonic energy of psychic vampires.

While I've never described myself as a psychic vampire, when I was much younger I did suffer from an energy imbalance and would try and draw energy from other people by touching them. Even in the last year and a half I've been dealing with energetic blockages and found that after I dissolved those blockages and the emotional issues that accompanied them I had much more energy to access. What is most important is dealing with the root cause of the issue. Symptoms, Brennan points out, are messages indicating something is wrong (1993). A scan of your body's energy can actually tell you if there is energetic blockage, which could be causing the energy to stagnate. This stagnancy can lead to disease, because as we've seen energy is linked to cells and the genetics of the body and such blockages do affect the flow of nutrients and vital information to the affected area.

Brennan's focus on health and energy is an argument that unhealthy imbalances first manifest energetically and then continue to shift downward until they appear physically. They occur in large part, according to her, by the beliefs we choose to have and accordingly how those beliefs then affect our health (Brennan 1988). I partially agree with Brennan's assessment. Beliefs, attitudes, and emotions do have an effect on the overall health of the body and indeed the reality a person manifests. However I don't think of this manifestation as coming down from a higher source of energy (which sounds overly New Agey), so much as coming from within the subconscious and/or psyche of the person, which is where beliefs, attitudes, and emotions tend to be expressed the most. These beliefs can manifest in our energy, but even our energy is integrated into our bodies. In other words, separating the body from the energy and using a hierarchy to explain the health issues will only continue to focus on the overt symptoms as well as promote the mind-body duality. It is better to approach energy and the body as part and parcel of each other and integrated into each other as a whole. Thus the focus is not on symptoms, but rather on the root cause of the disease, and specifically on healing that disorder on all levels as opposed to approaching it on an only an energetic or only a physical level. Then too, we must be cautious of overly assigning responsibility for health issues to our attitudes and beliefs. These do play a role in health, but external situations that are out of your control will also manifest in your life. Getting hit by a car, for instance, and breaking your leg, may not be something you manifested, particularly if you looked both ways, but the driver who happened to be speeding and came around the curve wasn't able to stop in time. All you can control in those situations is how you consciously choose to approach the situation. This is important to remember, because the notion that belief is entirely responsible for your health can be a trap in the sense that you may begin to feel overly responsible for events that happen to you that you simply don't have control over. Learn to assess and wisely consider your options in a situation and know where to accept responsibility, but also be kind to yourself.

Another way to consider this problem as well is that although the energy of a person exists before and after a body dies, the body acts as a field of limitation and manifestation. The body gives energy shape and provides it a vehicle through which to manifest, but at the same time, in giving energy shape, the body also encapsulates and embodies that energy. As such healing, via energy work, needs to occur on all levels of the person, not just with the energy. When healing is approached in this manner, with a focus on all of the body, a person can move past not only the physical or energetic harm, but also the emotional trauma or mental psychosis.

Brennan's paradigm gives us a sense of how energy work is approached in healing work. Her paradigm is useful, but it still focuses on dividing the body from energy, emotion, etc. This division, in inner alchemy, isn't useful, because this split needlessly divides a person's effort in healing hirself. Energetic healing is useful, but alone will not fully complete the kind of work a person needs to do. An approach that unifies energy with the body will also factor in what a person eats and other habits that have a material and energetic effect.

Astral Paradigm

Traditionally astral projection is concerned with the projection of the spirit of the person outside of hir body. My interest is not in the actual act of projection, but rather on some new approaches to energy work that have been developed that lead a person to successfully astrally project. I've already discussed in chapter three a technique used in astral projection for the control of the heart beat rate. Just as the physical body can be controlled for the purpose of projection, the energy within a person's body can also be used to help. And though the approaches in many astral projection books are focused solely on projection, this doesn't mean that those techniques can't be used for other purposes. Controlling the heart rate can be useful for learning how to control the automatic functions of your body. Likewise, learning the energetic techniques can give you new perspectives on how to work with your energy.

I must admit as well that, to my mind, astral projection is not so much a projection outward, as it is a projection inward to the different layers of consciousness that a person has. Some of these layers of consciousness can connect with the overall collective consciousness that embodies the phenotype of humanity, which thus explains the encounters people have on the astral planes with each other. But whether the astral planes are entirely external to us, or internal to us, or a mixture of the two, what's important is that if they can be used for inner alchemical work, there is a definite advantage in doing so.

The astral body is usually considered to be the etheric double of the physical body and is made up of energy (Carrington & Muldoon 1973). Astral projection seems to incorporate the physical body into the act of projection. Muldoon mentions the pineal gland, found in the brain, in relationship to projection, "My incorporeal self rushed to a point in the pineal gland and hurled itself against the imaginary trap-door, while the golden light increased in brilliance, so that it seemed the whole room burst into flame" (Carrington & Muldoon 1973, p. 35). I experimented with Zac Walters and several other people with the pineal gland in this capacity, using it as a gateway for energy work and for banishings. I also found it useful for projections as it focuses energy for that purpose. Whenever I directed my astral projections through the gland I noted that they were more vivid, as if the gland was directly located to the sense of space/time anchoring me to the astral plane. Muldoon argues that the gland serves as the connector between the spiritual world and the physical world (1973). Basically the pineal gland controls the vibration of energy that the body is set at, so that by working with the gland it's possible to alter the vibration of energy in the body. It also has connections with biophotonic energy, acting as a resonator of the energy.

Robert Bruce's approach to astral projection echoes my conception of the astral as being partially connected to different states of consciousness, "It is the downloading of the projected double's shadow memories into more *accessible* levels of the physical brain that normally occurs during the reintegration of the projected double with its physical counterpart [italics are his]" (1999, p. 23). For this process to work, it is essential to understand and be able to remember the altered state of consciousness you are in when you project. If you can integrate that awareness and experience into your everyday consciousness, on some level, you will be able to remember the experience of projection, instead of forgetting it.

Bruce's energy work takes a somewhat mechanistic approach. He describes the energetic connections in terms of five types of energetic circuits that perform different types of tasks, such as the processing of raw energy that is collected by tertiary circuits that he identifies as ports (Bruce 1999). This description can't be overly faulted as it is the main paradigm by how Westerners approach the body and the various aspects of it. Energy is not computer circuitry though. It's better to consider it from a more natural perspective, so that the "circuitry" is actually the veins of energy that run through your body and the "structures" are organs. This natural perspective allows you to reintegrate your awareness into your body as opposed to making it a distinctly separate machine that you just happen to reside in.

One point which Bruce makes that I agree with is the over-reliance on visualization in energy work. Visualization is not actually directly working with energy, so much as it is imagining what's occurring with energy. While visualization is useful for psychotherapeutic work, it doesn't begin to touch the reality of energy work, because it is the use of imagination, as opposed to increasing an actual awareness of the energy in your body (Bruce 1999). Bruce gets past this handicap, by having users of his system focus on body awareness, "*Mobile body awareness* (MBA)-the ability to focus body awareness on any specific part of the body...enables the dynamic manipulation of the energy body and its energy centers, or chakras, allowing specific parts of the energy body to be directly stimulated, and the flow of energy into and through it to be increased in a controlled way" (Bruce 1999, p. 114). What is involved with MBA is learning the ability to focus on a specific part of your body, say a finger, and be able to sense and/or direct the energy in the finger.

Bruce's idea is similar to Franz Bardon's approach to the accumulation of energy in a specific organ or part of the body (covered in the next chapter). But the difference is that Bardon's approach involves the accumulation of external energy, whereas Bruce focuses on the manipulation of internal energy. Bruce relies on the ability of touch and also being able to direct that ability inward. To some degree you already have this awareness. Every time your body feels pain or pleasure you are aware of it. Every time you breathe, the feeling of the air going into your lungs is noticeable. The problem, however, is that you come to take these sensations for granted because you feel them all the time. Consequently your awareness is limited, unless you consciously choose to focus on the sensations.

Bruce argues this is essential in order to successfully project. I agree with him, but as the focus of this book is on inner alchemy, my concern is on using that awareness not only to help with your energy work, but to also be aware of your body in general. Taking some of the exercises discussed at the beginning of the chapter, it's possible to use them to come to an awareness of the energy in your body. The cycling exercise can be done with yourself, and you can cycle the energy through your body, feeling how it travels through the pathways and discovering any blockages in them. When you do this exercise, focus on the feeling of the energy. Don't visualize it, because that will distract you from actually achieving an awareness of the energy. Feel the energy. It may feel like a tingle or a sensation of movement. Follow that sensation wherever it goes. Notice, as well, if there is any temperature change, if that part of your body feels warmer or cooler than usual. Localized temperature changes indicate the presence of energy. Then when you're ready try and direct that sensation to a specific part of your body. Finally, see if you can spread it throughout your body and maintain an overall awareness.

Learning this awareness of energy will not only help you learn to manipulate it, but will also increase your overall awareness of your body. This will help you use that energy to heal problems with your body. You can also use this awareness to learn how to wear your body more comfortably in terms of posture, muscle tension, and even facial expressions. Try, for instance, changing facial expressions and note how your face feels. Lengthen and shorten the gait of your walk or the overall pace. Move the muscles in your belly and note how it makes you feel, in terms of your emotions and their connection to your body image. That kind of awareness can be useful for disguising (i.e. hiding your reaction from other people) or discovering how you feel about a situation or it can be useful for learning to be more comfortable with your body, enjoying what it can let you experience when you don't tense up. It's not surprising to me that the people who aren't in touch with the sensations in their bodies have the most trouble learning energy work.

One aspect of astral projection I want to mention is my own theory on it. From my experiences and reading up on various sources (some of which I've cited above), it seems to me that astral projection is an individual experience, which varies due to the subjective experience a person has with it. But I also think that the astral plane isn't so much an external plane as it is a quantum sea of possibility, which a person can access and experience through projection. We might think of the astral planes as a nexus of all potential realities, a place of thought, imagination, and consciousness. Our consciousness is anchored to our body, and the body keeps the sanity of the person intact, by providing limitations. Otherwise it might be easily possible to get caught up in all the possibilities that the quantum astral plane offers.

The levels of the astral plane aren't limited to seven or structured in a specific way. As a function of consciousness, the astral plane allows us to surf the wave of probabilities and explore what potential outcomes could be. It is a nexus of reality that allows interaction with other people and entities and might even be conceived of as a virtual space/telepathy as experienced through an altered state of mind. I cover this in much more detail in an article I published in the very first issue of *Konton Magazine*.

Taoist breathing practices – B.K. Frantzis

My first exposure to Taoist breathing practices was through the Eight Brocades, which I described in the body fluids chapter. The manipulation of breath, saliva, and body positions was all designed to stimulate the meridians (power points) of the body, releasing energy held in them. This energy was used to not only vitalize the body while purging toxins, but also used as a banishing/protection ritual. The exercises banished the toxins and negative energy from my life, while also vitalizing the natural energy and putting out protective energy, in the form of heat, which would form a shield against negative energy. I've continued to do this exercise for the last eleven years and have found it to be highly useful for protection, and also for teaching me that the body and energy are not separate from each other. Taoist approaches to energy work integrate energy and the physical body together, arguing that the two are not separate, but rather interconnected.

Much more recently I've been using Taoist breathing meditation techniques daily. These techniques are useful for dissolving energetic blockages and the resultant body tension. I've also used them to deal with emotional issues, because the energy that is dissolved isn't just rooted in the body or itself, but also in the emotions. In fact, emotions are a form of energy and can be thought of as energy in motion, which is why they're effective catalysts for magic. The purpose of the breathing exercises is to learn to control that energy in motion instead of letting it control you and your reactions. In other words, you learn to become conscious and responsible for your emotions as opposed to letting them dictate your actions. It's fair to say that until recently I often let my emotions control me, and tended to react to a lot of situations. It was only through the dissolving practices of the Taoist breathing meditations that I've really begun to engage in an inner alchemy of the emotional issues and traumas in my life. This process has been circular, a gradual dissolving of the energy and release of emotions, but then a discovery of another blockage and beginning the dissolving process again. It's been powerful in bring out that which has been repressed, sometimes for years. Still, I have found that these practices never push you past what you're comfortable with, provided you're willing to be responsible for what you experience. I cannot stress enough that taking personal responsibility for what you feel is integral to this process.

In the Taoist practices, energy is referred to as chi. This energy is life energy; it keeps your physical body functioning. But chi goes beyond that as well, having other layers which affect the emotional, psychic, and even space/time-related energy of a person, making it instrumental in all aspects of being. Chi is what animates the flesh, but also allows for manifestation of spiritual reality into physical reality. Taoist practice is focused on cultivating internal awareness of chi and using that awareness to live life in a manner that connects a person to the Tao (Frantzis 2001a).

According to Frantzis there are two types of Taoist energetic practices involved with breathing, water and fire, though more people are familiar with fire. Water, which I've been using, is explained as follows, "The water method is a practical way to release blockages in the whole mind/body so one can fully transform and ultimately experience conscious harmony with the Tao...The water practice are based on a philosophical perspective that is relevant to everyday life: *Whatever you do must feel comfortable* [italics are his]" (Frantzis 2001a, p. 64). It is that last point which is particularly relevant to water practices of meditation. Nothing is forced. The energy instead is encouraged to flow, without strain. This is done so that the gradual dissolution of an energetic block is not harmful, but instead incorporates the energy back into the person, without the attachments that created the blockage. The flow of the energy also allows a person to go deeper into hir psyche, while also being able to experience a deeper appreciation of external reality (Frantzis 2001a). It is important to remember that what is within you does manifest externally as well internally, and learning to resolve inner issues allows you to deal with external realities without reactive triggers.

The fire method of Taoist meditation takes a much more forceful approach, arguing that the way past energetic blockages is to force the blockage to break apart (Frantzis 2001a). The fire method tends to lead toward more extreme practices with energy work,

> Fire approaches include the extremely physical and emotive Hindu tantric and kundalini yoga traditions, with 'kriyas' where people spontaneously shout, speak in tongues, do spontaneous yoga postures, curl into fetal positions, weep, yell, and growl like animals. Fire approaches include the Western psychological cathartic methods, such as encounter therapy, psychodrama with encouraged and guided screaming…and releasing the full range of human emotions in dramatic ways. (Frantzis 2001a, p. 73)

These extreme practices can be useful; indeed for most of my practice in energy work I've used more of a fire approach. These practices involve externalizing your energy, pushing it outward toward manifestation. But pushing your body and energy time and time again can also have negative consequences. I have had seven near death experiences. Six of those experiences have occurred in the last decade, and all have had an effect on my body's health, because each experience has been a system shock. The sixth near death experience, where I was given a hallucinogen (without my knowledge) and then performed sex magic, which caused the drug to trigger, was particularly traumatic for my body and my sense of self. I literally felt as if my body had dissolved, during the experience, and I had to rebuild it. The violation of trust via the drug, but also what I've come to view as a rape of my energy and body, also damaged me. The effect on my body was that I was physically ill for quite a while after the experience and even now under the right circumstances I can become physically debilitated as the experience damaged my energetic body and consequently its connection to my physical body. I have, over time, through a variety of energetic practices been able to undo much of the harm caused by that experience, and may manage to do so fully some day, but I will say again that pushing your body's limits is unwise as that particular experience taught me in full.

When learning of these two different approaches it occurred to me that the majority of energetic practices that occur in the west are fire oriented, with an emphasis on forcing energy, pushing past obstacles, instead of gradually dissolving them. As such the majority of Western energy work has no counter balance. Of course, because so much of Western culture is consumed with materialism this is not so surprising. Even the metaphysical practices of much of modern Western occultism are more obsessed with the result than with the actual process. This perspective forgets that results are merely road signs, confirming that the process is working or not working. Even when a positive result doesn't occur, nonetheless a result has manifested, and what the magician must do is go back to the drawing board and change the process so that it achieves the desired goal. However, with the focus only being on the result process is forgotten. Instead you have practitioners that advice people to just do magic, and not worry about how to do it. But how can you do something if you don't understand the dynamics, i.e. the process? This is a question chaotes, in particular, ignore all too often. Manifestation of a result is not the do all and end all of magic. Understanding the process of magic and knowing the role of that process in your life is far more important because it allows you to focus on what you truly want and need, as opposed to just reacting to a result.

As is, the energetic practices tend to suffer because the focus is more on results than on learning how energy works and the variety of purposes it can be used for beyond the obvious. It doesn't surprise me that some Western occultists express dissatisfaction with energy work, but this may be due to the lack of understanding the full potential of what it can be used for. Instead of focusing on an obvious result, consider how energy work can be used to raise awareness of yourself (for example conscious manipulation of your internal organs) and the environment around you (how you are connected to the environment), or consider how it can be used to connect intimately with someone, as well as for the more obvious application of healing. Or consider how much energy plays a role in the actual acts of magic you do. You invest energy in every magical act you do, even if you're not aware that you're investing it.

Another difference between the Taoist water meditation techniques and other approaches to energy work detailed above is that the means of working with the energy is through inhibitory meditation, "Meditation is not the mere contemplation of an idea or belief. Often in meditation insights or creative capacities are unleashed spontaneously, springing from somewhere other than logic or analytical thought" (Frantzis 2001b, p. 25). Meditation, when done with energy work, forces you to face your innermost demons. The energy work dissolves the blockages that keep the emotions repressed, and as the energy is freed, the emotions are experienced through the meditation and processed. Through this you learn to come to peace with them, as well as accepting yourself more. And the energy work you do ends up having benefits in terms of what you can do with it. I found when I began doing the water meditation techniques that how I worked with energy changed a lot. I used to force my energy, pushing it outward, but I found with the dissolving methods that it became much harder to push. I had to learn instead to flow with it. Once I got used to that movement I was able to direct it, but always in a manner that was more of a gentle flow than a forceful push. In other words, my thinking and indeed my ability to feel the energy changed as I changed techniques. As an example, when I used the cycling technique with another person I'd always push my energy, forcing it to flow into the other person, but once I learned the water techniques I would instead feel the energy flow gently into the person. I found that when I forced energy, it was much more tiring for me, and sometimes the effects for the person weren't beneficial, causing a vague feeling of sickness or unease. Gradually I learned I could direct the flow by concentrating on merging with that feeling and using that merged consciousness to "suggest" where the energy could go. What's fascinating, with the water method, is that the energy work occurs on a cellular level, dissolving the energy right down to the cell and perhaps even beyond (Frantzis 2001a). This process is done to free yourself of the memories, which may infect the health of your cell (possibly a cause of cancer, see below for more details). Painful memories are poisonous to our health on all levels of our being, because they catch us in a cycle of reaction and pain and are not necessarily resolved by external confrontation. Only by confronting your own role in the situation and taking responsibility for it can you move past the pain and toward new patterns of behavior, where you are more conscious of your words and actions and they affect you and others.

Frantzis also discusses the connection that emotions have to the body, "Our glands release substances that make us angry and depressed. By energizing or enlivening your body, Taoist meditation practices can enable you to experientially understand and control the connections between your physical body, glands, and emotions" (2001b, p. 36). I have found that the water meditation techniques have not only been helpful for revitalizing my energy, but made my body healthier. For instance, the Taoist breathing involves learning to breathe in a manner where you not only push your stomach muscles out, but also your sides and back, expanding your entire torso with your breath. This stimulates and massages the internal organs and deeper blood veins, causing more circulation of blood and energy. The meditation also helps to clean out those emotions that are poisonous for the body (Frantzis 2001b). Thus these practices greatly benefit your overall health.

The water method also helps detach meaning from events. By learning to disassociate meaning from situations a person becomes much less attached to those events and can evaluate just how relevant the actual situation is to him/her. This is important in dissolving energy blockages, because meaning is often associated with the blockage and by unraveling the meaning you can deal with directly with the trauma of the situation (Frantzis 2001b). It does not, however, promote complete detachment from the world around you.

The energetic anatomy in Taoism differs from the chakra system. The main paths of energy flow not only the through the torso of the body, but also through the arms and legs and the energetic power points are spread throughout the body. Nor is the push of the energy focused upward, as it is with the chakras. Instead the energetic pathways are directed toward the maintenance and health of the body, with the energy circulating throughout the body. There are also three major points, called Tan Tien, that are used for balancing and processing the energy of the left and right channels, but are also used to keep the energy flowing to the internal organs of the body. One is located slightly below the third chakra and is usually what would be a person's center of balance. The second is located at the heart chakra and the third is located in the head.

Taoist Breathing Practices - Mantak Chia

What I've presented so far is one version of Taoist energetic work. But there are other Taoist systems of energy work. Chia and Winn, for example, argue that Taoist energy work is similar to tantric work with the focus of directing the energy upward. The only difference they note is that Taoism does not employ all of the visualization, imagery, chanting, and other rituals that are involved in Tantra (1984). I've found so far that this statement is correct. The primary focus is on the body and the energetic interactions that occur within it, as opposed to visualization that focus on external sources of energy.

Chia's system of energy work is different from Frantzis's system. Instead of dissolving blockages and having the energy descend and then cycle upward, Chia focuses on sexual energy and cycling the energy up from the perineum (kundalini) and down to the belly, where it is safe to hold that energy (Chia 1983, Chia & Winn 1984, Chia & Abrams 1996). His approach would probably fit under the fire version of Taoism because it's more forceful and focused on retention of sexual energy as opposed to letting it flow. He notes symptoms that could be the result of a fire approach to energy work, "Human energy tends to flow upwards during meditation and may cause immense heat to accumulate in the brain coupled with bodily sensation, visual and auditory hallucinations, emotional outbursts, and various delusions (Chia 1983, p. 7). His solution for these problems is to have the practitioner circulate the energy to hir belly, where it can be safely stored. I would note that some hallucinations are a result of achieving altered stated of mind and that feelings of extreme temperature variants usually indicate that you are working with energy. With that said I've only worked with some of Chia's ideas on energy work and am continuing to explore his system.

So far my focus has been on his breathing techniques and to a lesser degree the sexual energetic work. Like Frantzis, Chia relies on the tongue to complete the energetic circuit. The tongue is placed on the roof of the mouth and allows the energy to be circulated. The Microcosmic circuit focuses strictly on the energy that is moved from the perineum up through the spine and down the front to the belly. The belly, where the lowest Tan Tien is located (also your center of balance) is the safe place to store energy (cite needed). The macrocosmic circuit includes the energy found in the arms and legs. With each inhalation the energy is pushed to the arms and legs, while each exhalation brings the energy back in. I recommend reading Chia's work to get a fully fleshed out explanation of the processes involved in the breathing. You'll learn a lot about how the muscles in the perineum contribute to the dynamic of breathing and energy work.

Both Frantzis and Chia advocate a dissolving of sexual energy, but their methods are different. For Frantzis it's a dissolving of tension and psychological hang-ups (2001b), while for Chia the focus is on retaining youth and vigor by not allowing sexual energy to leave the body. Chia explains this as follows: "The Taoist method of cultivating sexual energy recirculates to the body the hormones, proteins, vitamins, enzymes, minerals, and electrical energies of the semen. When they are transformed, one enjoys a marvelous sexual life, improved health, deep inner balance, and rising spiritual consciousness" (Chia & Winn 1984, p. 5). In other words, retaining energy involves also retaining body resources present in the sperm. Ejaculating the sperm causes the body to lose the physical resources, which must be reproduced by the body to make up for what has been lost. It's important to note that Chia associates energy with the physical resources, so that a loss of one is a loss of the other. He does have a good point here, in the sense that the body does use up some resources when ejaculation occurs. However those resources are also replenished by eating and drinking a healthy diet. Humans are not contained self sufficient biological systems, but must instead interact with the environment to get sustenance.

However, the real benefit of sex is how long it lasts. On both an energetic and physical level sex that lasts for longer than a few minutes gives a person better health by strengthening the immune system and providing needed chemical changes, "A moderate amount of sex tends to repair hormonal disturbances, to reduce cholesterol and blood pressure levels. Sexual activity alters the body chemically. The reason this happens is because each gland in the body affects all the others" (Chia & Winn 1984, p. 26). Sex that occurs in only a few minutes doesn't give the people involved the maximum benefits. The changes that occur are minimal. Sex that lasts longer gives the body a healthy saturation of the hormones and chemicals that can keep it healthy. Longer sex is also good for the emotional and psychological health of a person. This in turn rejuvenates a person's energy, causing it to circulate throughout the body.

Chia offers some excellent exercises for the genital muscles and the prost Tyrptophan ate. For men, it's important to exercise these muscles for the health of the prostate, but an added effect is learning how to control those muscles when it comes to sex. The ultimate effect is that through learning control of the perineum a person can circulate the energy through the body, "this system stresses the circulation of energy called 'chi' along certain pathways inside the body. These pathways help direct the 'chi' – also known as prana, sperm, or ovarian power, the warm current, of kundalini power – to successfully higher power centers (chakras) of the body" (Chia 1983, p. 1). The energy is directed up the spine and then to the rest of the body. Another technique I personally like is the inner smile technique where a person converts negative energy in the body into positive energy, by directing an inward smile via the circulation of the energy. The inward smile is simply smiling inward to yourself, directing the positive energy of a smile into your body.

Chia's system is useful to explore because he covers a wide variety of topics within it. There are more systems of energy work in Taoism and its important to not stick with just one perspective, but instead a multitude of perspectives out on such systems. In my sequel to this book I hope to cover more extensively some of the other thoughts and approaches as well as revisiting the two systems I've discussed here.

Conclusion

There is no real right or wrong way to doing energy work. I will admit I currently favor the Taoist breathing practices for my personal work, because they have been very useful for helping me deal with many internal issues of physical, emotional, and spiritual natures. But I will also say that each system I described above has been useful and prominent in my magical life at one time or another and each system continues to inform my energy work practices. Undoubtedly, as well, other practitioners will find other approaches to energy work more useful than what I've mentioned. It is up to each person to find the tools that work best for hir at a given time. There are many approaches and systems out there. You just need to research, practice, and experiment with what you find. What I have included here is what I am most familiar with as well as what I feel is most relevant to alchemical practices of energy work.

However I have also developed and modified several approaches to energy work through experimentation. One approach, inspired by Zac Walters, is modification of the residual self-image. The residual self-image is Zac's term and he details his own work on body dynamics in the anthology, *Magick on the Edge* (Megalithica Books, 2007). A basic rundown of his work involves using your awareness of your body to physically shape and change it and to also externalize that awareness through symbolism. Zac has used a wrestling video game, for instance, to give him an idea of how he wants his body to look, creating a character that fits the image he wants to manifest for himself and using that character as inspiration for his body image. The character served as both a diagram and inspiration for his physical workouts. As he exercised he visualized the character being mapped to his body, while contributing all the energy put into it into his exercising. The result was a much more fit physical body. His method has worked well for him.

My own variation of his method relies on the Taoist dissolving methods, which emphasize body awareness. Instead of externalizing the residual body image, I use my meditation and breathing to internalize the residual body image, with the goal being to imprint on my cells the ideal body image I seek to cultivate. I breathe in the residual image I want, and breathe out any negative body images or issues I have. This approach is useful for health purposes, in that you can breathe in the healthy energy and body image you want to cultivate and breathe out the body toxins you don't need. The awareness that is cultivated by the process of breathing and meditation allows you to connect with the consciousness of each cell, as well the energy in it, and program/explain the changes you seek.

When doing this meditative work, I've sometimes focused on purging the body and found that afterwards it has felt temporarily worse as it works to get rid of the toxins. This is because the toxins are being released instead of stored away. However, afterwards I feel much better and my body is much healthier. Additionally because the Taoist breathing is focused on massaging the internal organs of your body, it allows you to imprint on them the desired changes to the self-image of your body. The internal organs communicate that change to the rest of the body. In this way you aren't focused solely on your muscles, but on the entire health of the body. So when I work with the self-image of the body, I will meditate on how I want my body to appear, and on the overall health of the body. I'll breathe in and send that energy to the body, with a focus on the awareness I have of the body extending to the cellular level, so that my cells are bathed in the self-image. At the same time, the consciousness of the cells can communicate with me, to let me know if what I have in mind is healthy for the body. Occasionally the self-image has been modified by the cells and always for the better. When I exhale, I breathe out what is unnecessary for the body, and either put that energy into my shields or release it to be recycled in the environment.

Exercises

1. Do all the basic energy work exercises in this chapter. Try pushing the energy and letting the energy flow, both alone and with another person, and note the differences. Which works better for you?
2. Explore some other energy work systems, not covered in this book, in detail. As an example, examine Norse belief systems (the *Rune Gild* book through Runa-Raven Press would be a good place to start) and how they approach energy versus how psychic vampires approach energy work (Belanger's *Psychic Vampire Codex* or Kaldera's *Ethical Psychic Vampirism* would be good guides for this). By exploring a variety of systems you will learn not only what works for you, but how to integrate those systems into your practice.
3. Ask yourself whether energy is a symbol or whether it is a valid reality, in its own right. Defend your answer and then opposing viewpoints.
4. Take the body-image exercise and work with it. You can use Zac's methods as detailed in *Magick on the Edge*, or my own, or try a combination of the two. Or if you're really feeling ambitious, come up with your own method of body modification via self-image.

Chapter Eight:
Intermediate Energy Work

One of the most important aspects of energy work involves learning to balance both the internal and external energies. In this chapter I deal with the external energy, the energy we process from a variety of sources, through elemental systems. The key is learning to balance these energies in our lives, knowing when to call on them and use them to help us as opposed to being subject to them.

The elemental energies aren't composed of just Earth, Air, Fire, and Water. Instead elemental energies are basic building blocks of your own energetic system. In fact, it's fair to say that all external energies have some degree of influence in the energetic makeup of a person. We are connected to the universe, talk to it, and inhabit it. We exist in a web of life, each delicate strand relying on the participation of all to continue that existence. In this chapter, while I'm talking about forms of energy that may seem to be to external to a person, I'm showing how those energies can be used to balance the internal energy and create a better state of conscious awareness in a person. Let me provide a personal example.

In the fall of 2004, I got a cold and although it eventually went away, my throat continued to remain sore. This happened with every cold, and the sore throat would not go away for weeks or even months at a time. I was fed up with this and decided to do a ritual where I would balance the energies in my throat and get rid of the soreness. I based this ritual on hermetic principles of elemental energy, but I also didn't want to work with the Judeo-Christian angels and elemental spirits. Instead I chose to work with pop culture versions of elemental beings. To fully understand how I put this working together, I'm going into a tangent into hermetic theory and practice to explain the dynamics behind the working.

My inspiration when it came to the hermetic practices arose from two sources. In *Enchantments of the Faerie Realm* by Ted Andrews, the last appendix on astral gateways provided hermetic symbols through which you could access elemental realms or planes of existence. But more importantly Andrews advocated an idea, which still appeals to me to this day.

> Each kind of elemental reflects a basic energy pattern of the faerie realm as it builds and manifests in nature. They interweave to create and sustain all matters on Earth. All four kinds of elementals exist in every aspect of nature and in every person. We cannot exist if any of them are missing from our life. These are not mere labels, symbols, or even concepts. They are vital actual forces bound within ourselves and within nature. (1993, p. 3)

The concept that these elemental forces exist both externally and within us, but also independently of us, was something I always felt was inherently correct. When I initially got Andrew's book many years ago, it was my first introduction to hermeticism. It specifically dealt with elemental hermeticism, which is often ignored in favor of what is consider "high magic", the focus on planetary influences, godforms, etc. The book gave to me the understanding that the elemental spirits interacted with me far more intimately than I realized. I initially imagined tiny elemental faeries (gnomes, naiads, salamanders, and sylphs) working on my body and keeping it in balance with elemental energy.

The second source, one I'd only recently been introduced to, confirmed a lot of my ideas about elemental energy. Ironically I did not read Franz Bardon's *Initiation into Hermetics* until after doing the elemental workings I'm going to describe, but the principles in his book hold true to the concepts and forces I worked with. Bardon's approach focuses on elemental accumulation in the body, drawing in elemental energy to a specific part of the body. Essentially the magician focuses on the type of elemental energy s/he wishes to use and then draws that energy into hirself, uses it for a time and then releases it. The energy is accumulated through a process called pore breathing,

> Now concentrate and think that not only do your lungs breathe or inhale air with every breath you take, but the entire body as well. Be completely convinced that your lungs, simultaneously with every single pore of your body, absorbs vital energy and supply it to the body. Imagine that you are a dry sponge which is immersed in water and which greedily absorbs the water. You must have the same feeling when you inhale. (Bardon 2001, p. 91)

Through pore breathing a person is able to accumulate not only vital life energy, but also the elemental energy. Intriguingly enough a chaote named Black Rabbit has a similar idea, "Create a sigil for some attribute you desire – strength, wisdom, power, or whatever. Now go into gnosis and strongly visualize your sigil on the appropriate part of your body. Do this as often as it takes for the association to feel strong and natural" (2005, p. 5). In this case, the difference is that you use the sigil to accumulate a particular energy and then you keep that energy, integrating it into yourself. This technique can be refined into my own technique with the DNA so that instead of just focusing on the body, you actually imprint the sigil into your genetics, incorporating the attribute into your genes. This makes the magic much more natural, while also focusing your genetic development into specific areas. Care should be taken with using this technique, whether you use Black Rabbit's approach or my own. You need to have a very good idea of not only what you're changing, but the degree of change as well, so you can measure its success, but also to avoid any potential genetic mishaps. Tinkering with your genetic code, if unbalanced, can lead to health problems via retroviruses found in junk DNA.

According to Bardon, for the accumulation to occur, the person focuses on how the elemental energy should feel. The fire element for instance is heat, while air is perceived as cold and breezy. The focus is on sensation and using that sensation to identify the elemental energy you feel (2001). This can be a good basis for determining whether elemental energy is accumulated. The Tibetan exercise of *Tumo*, which is the igniting of psychic heat (internal energy), is a useful example, as through a series of breathing exercises the person accumulates and then ignites the psychic heat throughout hir body. This focuses the breath, but also attunes the mind toward a specific kind of energy with the help of visualizations. Likewise, with Bardon's method the focus on sensation, breathing, and some visualization is useful for the accumulation of elemental energy. This balances your own energy, but also gets you used to working with elemental energy. The accumulation of a particular type of energy allows you to balance it with other energies that are present within you, but are from external sources. One difference between my own work and Bardon's is that I do not subscribe to the notion that you should get rid of elemental energy when you're done with it. Instead I incorporate it into my own energy.

Returning to the case of the cold in fall of 2004, instead of using the traditional angels and elemental kings, I chose to use pop culture archetypes that embodied, for me, the elemental energies I wanted to work with. The crew of the anime series *Cowboy Bebop* particularly appealed to me because of the color schemes and the actions and personalities of the characters, because all five characters neatly fit into an elemental category.

I associated Jet with Earth. Not only does he have a metal arm, but he's a skilled mechanic, cook, gardener, and is always focused and worried about the practicalities of a situation. He is always trying to come up with a strategy and is focused on making the resources that the crew has last as long as possible. The colors for his character are also mostly earth tones.

The character of Spike Spiegal fits water. He is a very intense character, but not in a fiery passionate way. His intensity is like that of water, flowing into the places of least resistance. His eyes, which seem so dead to people, are like stagnant bodies of water, deep and murky, with unknown depths. Spike even describes his fighting style as that of water, where he flows with the enemy to find an opening. Likewise his spontaneity in different situations can also be likened to water, because you can't necessarily predict its movement. His color scheme is blue.

Faye Valentine fits the fiery passion of fire. Her colors are red and yellow, and she constantly smokes. She is impulsive, with a quick temper, and is very creative and quick to seize an opportunity, but doesn't always examine the factors that surround that opportunity.

Edward is a classic air elemental. She's all over the place, flighty, and never very focused. At the same time she is intelligent and is able to make intuitive leaps of understanding that allow her to make tangential connections to the problem that she's trying to solve. However, she is not incredibly grounded. Her color schemes are white and blue, which match a sky with clouds, and her actions are spontaneous and unpredictable.

Finally there is Ein, the data dog, who represents the element of spirit. Spirit moves in mysterious ways and likewise Ein also moves in mysterious ways. He does the right thing at just the right time to solve a problem, but otherwise stays in the background, and acts only when it's absolutely necessary.

For my purposes, I decided that these characters would represent the elemental energies I wanted to use to balance my energy. I envisioned tiny versions of them working on me, scanning my body, and finding the cause of the continued sore throat. Then they decided on what needed to be done to balance the elemental energy and create a healthy stability for my throat. I evoked rather than invoked them, though I could have used invocation by studying the actions and persona of the characters and coming up with a chant or other method that tapped into their energies.

Instead, for the evocation, I took a bath and in the course of the bath meditated on the characters and on the elemental energy in my body. They scanned my body, finding energetic blockages that needed to be dissolved so the energy could be balanced. In my throat they found I had too much fire and air. The air stimulated the fire to the point where my throat was sore from. I decided to use Jet to ground both fire and air, with Spike serving as secondary support. I envisioned Jet putting his metal arm to the Earth and pulling on earth energy, while grabbing the elements of fire and air (Faye and Ed) with his other hand and grounding them into the earth. Spike made sure the elements of fire and air didn't fight back too much. Finally I used Ein, the spirit element, to create a solid link among the other elements so that they were balanced out. Almost immediately my throat stopped being sore. In fact, since I've done that working, I've rarely suffered from a sore throat and the soreness only lasts for a little while when it does occur.

Naturally this type of energy work can be extended beyond dealing with sore throats. Scan your body using elemental energy to find any blockages that draw on the elements and then use archetypes of your choices to balance that energy. The reason I chose to use the archetypes of *Cowboy Bebop* is because those characters are culturally approachable and relevant to me, in a way that the elemental kings and angels are not. I want to work with what I identify with, because it creates a strong resonance of identification that aids in the efficacy of the working. I find that it's not the symbols that make the magic, but the magic that makes the symbols. In other words, use the symbols that you identify with, as opposed to what someone else tells you to use.

A second type of working that utilizes the principles mentioned above involved a pathworking ritual I created for a college pagan group that was used to get a person in touch with the elemental energy s/he felt s/he was weakest in. It might be assumed that whatever the strongest element was for a person, the weakest was its opposite. As an example, I had a very strong fire element, but felt very weak in water; likewise a person strong in air might have a weak earth element. However, this is not always the case. Generally how I determine what my weakest element is, is based on the attributes assigned to a given element. Fluid adaptability and emotional strength were attributes I lacked and so I used that as a guide for determining that I should work with water.

For the ritual, I had the quarter callers, me included, come together several weeks in advance and begin a pathworking journey. Each person was to focus on the specific element they were going to call. I gave everyone a series of tattvas based off the hermetic symbols of the elements that I'd gotten from Andrews's book. One symbol represents the elemental gateway into the element, while the other symbol represents the spiritual gateway; the use of both symbols connects the user to the elemental plane of choice. Once the elemental plane was reached, the person traveled there until finding a spiritual guide that served as not just a guide, but a teacher who explained the elemental energies and helped the person become a conduit for those energies. The spirit guide, in whatever form it took not only explained the elemental energies but gave the seeker a symbol to work with. Also I found that instead of using standard invocation chants, it was better to have each person come up with their own invocation that would best summarize the relationship that s/he was had with the spirit guide.

The goal was to have the quarter callers act as conduits of elemental energy, channeling it to the other people so that those people were connected to that energy and could find their own spirit guides. By acting as conduits, the quarter callers essentially removed the step with the tattvas, while also supplying a source of elemental energy that the other people in the ritual could focus on. This was useful because each person who was not a quarter caller was placed in the elemental quarter where s/he felt weakest. By having a source of elemental energy there, that person could attune to it and use it to strengthen hir connection to it. The quarter callers worked for several weeks with their spirit guides, taking journeys and merging some of their consciousness with that of the elementals so as to become a conduit.

When the ritual occurred, each of the quarter callers had been given symbols by the entities they worked with (These symbols took the place of the tattvas, personalizing the working for the people involved), which were painted on their foreheads and served as a gateway to the elements. I called Spike Spiegel for water, while another quarter caller called Jean Gray for fire and yet another one called the spirit of a dead cat for Earth; I forget what the air element was. Spirit wasn't called, though it could have been. We focused on the four traditional elements for this working. Once the calls were done, each caller went to the center of the circle and faced outward toward the people in the circle. The rest of the participants faced inward toward the callers and after I led them into the pathworking, they began meditating on finding an elemental spirit that could help them work with and grow stronger in the elemental energies they felt deficient in.

At the beginning of the ritual I warned people that by participating they were agreeing to a year long commitment to that element's influence in their lives and that likely they would be changed by it. A full year later, people continue to evolve through the elemental energy they worked with.

As an example, my friend Maryam, who called on the dead cat for Earth, became much more grounded and also came to the realization that her path of magic would need to be alchemy based on grounded scientific principles she'd learned. I, by calling on water, ended up breaking up with Maryam, because the flow of our relationship didn't work in the direction it was going. I also started to dissolve a lot of the inner demons within me, as well as learned to become more adaptable to situations and more emotionally aware of myself and how I choose to act in situations. Other people reported similar experiences with the elements they chose to work with.

After the ritual I devoted my year's time to Water because, in my experience, you can't fully feel appreciate the effects of working with an elemental influence unless you're willing to devote a decent amount of time to actually working with it. It's very important that if you choose to do this kind of working that you realize you are committing yourself to changes in your life and to working with a specific elemental energy that will have an impact on you. I cannot emphasize this enough, nor the need to keep yourself balanced while undergoing this year of work. It's easy to get caught up in a particular element and take on the negative aspects that it represents.

My work with Spike as a water elemental, for example, resulted in him occasionally popping up in my intuition and telling me to go to a specific place and do a specific thing and then work with the situation as it developed. Perhaps the best example I can give was being at a festival where I was presenting workshops and being told by Spike to get out and walk around and visit the campfires the first night I was there. Shortly after I did this, I met a woman who was able to read my energy and described accurately (without me saying a word) everything going on in my life and told me what I needed to do to get rid of the stagnation I was experiencing. Within a couple of months I had broken up with my partner of two and a half years and shortly thereafter met my magical mate. It was a case where I was introduced to a situation and then had to flow with it and see what resulted.

You can use just about any elemental paradigm for balancing your energy. Although I used the four (or five) classic Western elements, I have adapted this idea to the seven elements of the chakras. For my own workings, I've modified the ritual to incorporate the chakras for several reasons. While most are familiar with the four (or five) Western elemental energies, Sound (the fifth chakra), Light (the sixth chakra), and Spirit (the seventh chakra) are essential elements for us as well. The amount of light a person gets has a physiological effect on the body, and likewise sound can also have a physiological effect. Spirit contains all other element, but is not defined by them. It is infinite possibility, but needs a choice to become manifest reality.

This ritual is still for all intents and purposes similar to the group elemental working. All that's been added are a few more correspondences to new elements. As with the four elemental working the goal is to balance elemental energies, by picking a particular element to work with for a year. As an example I worked with the Water/chakra from October 2004 to October 2005, with the fifth chakra/Sound from October 2005 to October 2006. I plan to work the first chakra/Earth after Sound, from October 2006 to October 2007. The Sound chakra had the most blockage in it, which I discovered when I did my chakra-totem workings.

The Personal Totem Pole by Eligio Stephen Gallegos inspired the idea that the chakras could be used to balance external energy. Since the chakras process energy coming into us all the time, it's important to keep that energy balanced and working with energy that is already within us. It's important to note that though Gallegos employed the concept of the personal totem pole as a primarily psychotherapeutic technique, it does have energetic extensions. The animal spirits you work with are not just psychological constructs or aspects of yourself, but also connections to the actual animal totem spirit. The animal for a given chakra may, over time, change to one which works better with that chakra. The mutability of the totem spirits is an aspect of this system I particularly agree with,

> The fundamental function of the mind is to vitalize the world, by giving life and voice and awareness to all that exists, so we can listen to what the world around has to tell us and experience the world *from the perspective of each element of the world*...It allows those deepest elements of ourselves to participate in voice and in awareness, articulating our relationship to the world around and its relationship to us, and freeing us from the responsibility of thinking that voice and awareness belong only to that particular identity that I call myself [italics are his]. (Gallegos 1989, pp. 1-2)

This awareness that is cultivated in terms of the elements within and without ourselves is key to balancing the energy work we do.

At the time of this writing (May 2006), my goal was to work through the blockages of the Sound chakra and balance that aspect of my life, just as I had balanced the Water element in my life. I had only been working with my Sound chakra for seven months, but already many changes had manifested in my life. I quit the PhD program I was involved in, finally listening to the dissatisfaction I felt at being involved in something which had increasingly become antithetical to me. At the same time I steadily became more vocal in expressing my needs to my mate instead of repressing them, and I also became much more social with new people, opening up and trusting more than I have for many years. At the same time, negative social experiences and people were weeded out of my life. I found the means to change in order to present myself in a professional environment. Finally, I was able to deconstruct unhealthy communication patterns that I used and created new patterns that were healthier.

In just seven months, my work with the sound chakra brought forth much change in my life. All of the changes were needed and none of them were anticipated. Indeed leaving grad school was probably the biggest surprise to me because of how firmly entrenched I was in the idea that I HAD to get the degree even though I wanted it less and less. But finally listening to myself and what needed to be heard, I recognized my place was no longer in that institution. The work is ongoing, and the changes that I've already gone through as a result of this working have changed how I express myself and indeed how I understand communication in general.

The chakra model meshes nicely with other seven elemental systems. If your model of the astral plane has seven layers, then you can use chakras to work with a particular astral plane as well, with the argument being that each chakra corresponds to an astral level. You can use the chakra to access the corresponding astral/elemental plane. However you perceive it, the important thing to remember is that your chakras are not just energy processors, but also gateways that you can use to travel to the elemental energy you are working with. I'll meditate on a chakra and allow my consciousness to travel to the elemental plane it corresponds to., Here I usually meet a spirit guide who then takes me to wherever I need to go or gives me information. You can use such journeys to work on balancing and healing yourself in regards to that elemental energy, but you can also use it for other purposes. For instance, with practical magic, by balancing the elements, you can work them into other magical workings more smoothly. When I worked with the power spots at Kent, I would sometimes incorporate the element of Fire into the working, especially in the winter, to keep me warmer.

It's also possible to work with the Hermetic tradition of planetary magic and create correspondences between the chakras and the seven planet model of Hermeticism. Tony Mierzwicki's book *Gracco-Egyptian Magick* is an excellent introduction to the planetary energies and the rituals in that book can be incorporated into this working because the focus of those rituals is also to create balance in the life of the person.

The tree of life and/or the Qliphoth is another option. We shouldn't ignore the Qliphoth because it represents "negative" aspects, but instead can use it, by learning to balance it with the energies of the Sephiroth in the tree of life. Probably the best aspect of this kind of ritual is that you can actually adapt it to any and all of these systems at the same time, depending on how you work with your correspondences. For instance my work with water can easily fit into Sephiroth Yesod, as well as the second chakra, and even Blue magic in chaos magic, since learning to be adaptable and flexible also means learning to find opportunities to increase your wealth. The real key to working with external energies and using a correspondence system is learning how the attributes link up to each other and then being able to spot the influence of those attributes in your life and learn from those influences, while using any opportunities to further your work in finding balance. The achievement of balance is not a negation of any of these influences, but rather a means of gaining control of them instead of letting them control you. By working with Water, for instance, I not only managed to get my fire element under control, but also learned to work with what Water could offer me and yet not fall into Water so much that I was drowned by it's emotional currents. Instead I integrated those skills into my Fiery creativity and passion, giving me the best of both worlds, instead of the fallout from either or both.

The eight rayed chaostar of Chaos magic, with a corresponding color for each ray, is a good model to experiment with. You might work with black one year and focus on balancing yourself in regards to death energy. This could involve near death situations, but could also involve learning life saving skills or doing necromantic rituals. A blue year could have you focusing on wealth, specifically learning how to attain it on a physical level, but also doing wealth magic rituals--and of course what you consider wealth might not just be lots of money. I suggest that if you take this approach you integrate Ceilede's model of *Liber Chromatia*, which involves working with the eight selves as a base guide. This article can be found in *Konton*, issue 2.1, available at http://www.chaosmagic.com.

I would advise readers (again) to dedicate yourself to a year of working with whatever energy you choose to balance in your life, regardless of the model. This doesn't mean you can't do other magical rituals or workings. However, once you open yourself up to a particular influence to balance it in your life, you might be experiencing it for a while. For me, Water, as an element, needed a full year of work. There was no way one night could encapsulate the kind of balance I needed to learn with the attributes that Water is usually related to. It took time, and some experiences and continued workings, particularly learning to become adaptable and flexible with situations. But the benefits of a year's work with a particular element have certainly been reaped by allowing that influence into my life and by also learning to use it to balance my other energies, so that they are in sync as opposed to one element dominating the rest.

You're not limited just to the elemental systems I have mentioned here. Any system of symbols, which includes the elements, but can also include a variety of other frequencies, works for this kind of balancing ritual. This includes various forms of light, sound, and energy, and entities such as godforms, angels, and goetic demons. While godforms, angels, and goetic demons in their own right possess a life of their own, they also are representative of different forms of energy in our lives, or if you will, concepts that we associate with them. I've worked with the goetic demon Ronwe, to increase my skills at writing and speaking. My latest work is with Purson, another goetic demon, who is good at manipulating time, and is representative of the element/energy of time.

Learning to work with the external influences in your life is only one side of the coin. The next chapter focuses on fine tuning the balance you've established with intermediate work. The goal is to perform an inner alchemy that creates a true harmony within you, and allows you to integrate the energetic models of magic fully into the physical, emotional, mental, and spiritual aspects of the self.

Exercises

1. Try out the elemental balancing ritual (solo or group). Do the pathworking and ritual and then record over the course of a year the other interactions you have with the element of your choice. Use whatever model I've presented here best works for you or come up with one of your own.
2. Take a look at Bardon's work with elemental accumulation and pore breathing. Are you really breathing in elemental energy? How does the energy feel when it enters your body? What effects do you note? Finally how does Bardon's technique differ from the Taoist breathing techniques I discussed chapter 7?

Chapter Nine:
Advanced Energy Work

By now you know a number of exercises and approaches on how energy can be worked with. Nonetheless these tend to be focused mainly on the surface. Fine tuning what you've learned in previous chapters with the processes in this chapter will help you get the most out of the energy work you do.

As an example, I mentioned in chapter seven the exercise of cycling. The initial exercise is just focused on getting you to experience the feeling of energy as it's directed through your body by someone else, and vice versa. However, cycling can be taken much further. Belanger notes that cycling can be used to improve energy (remove energetic blocks) and can also be used for refining it (2004). This means that cycling can be used to develop and intensify a particular type of energy while siphoning out the rest. Like Belanger, I've found that cycling put toward this particular purpose is highly useful for focusing on a specific type of energy. The act of refinement involves a separation of one kind of energy from another kind. In a case where you are refining energy that goes into you, you are removing elements of that energy that can't be processed by your internal energetic body. These elements would toxify your energy. Naturally the need to refine differs from person to person. Psychic vampires need to refine energy more than the average person, because they can't handle some of the energetic elements that a mundane person can.

I disagree with Belanger about the byproduct energy though, Belanger argues that in the process of working with energy, a byproduct type of energy is produced that can't be worked with (Belanger 2004) If you use the cycled energy for feeding, then the byproduct likely wouldn't be good for you. But even in this context it doesn't mean that the byproduct is waste and can't be used. It really is a matter of perspective. Remember that the very act of refining involves energy you refine for yourself and the "byproduct," which is actually refined energy as well, albeit for a different purpose.

What is that purpose? It depends on what you want to use that energy for. When I refine energy I use the "by-product" as offensive or defensive energy. I'll put that energy into my shields or to deflect people's attention or negative energy. On the other hand such energy is also good for healing people. When healing a person, I cause the byproduct energy to resonate with similar energy in a person's body that is not healthy. Basically I use the byproduct energy as a template, which can guide my to the unhealthy energy in a person's body. Because the byproduct is toxic, it'll have similar qualities to the unhealthy energy in someone else. You can then use that resonance to guide you to the toxic energy and pull it out of the person, and proceed to heal the person.

There is also something to be said for sometimes toxifying your body in order to purge it. As an example, I've used death-rebirth rituals as a way of purposefully using the toxins in my body to poison myself, but also to purge myself of those poisons. Illness is usually the body's way of purging toxins from it. So an evocation of illness or a similar feeling of dis-ease can be used to help you purify yourself before a major ritual. It may seem odd that you would actually call up a feeling that seems to be opposite of purification, but by actually using that feeling to purge yourself of toxins you are effectively purifying yourself. A full recounting of such a ritual can be found in *Space/Time Magic*.

The toxic energy can actually be used a weapon. If someone chooses to feed off of you against your will and you can toxify your energy then you can poison that person. This involves cultivating those elements of energy that would be toxic to other people by learning to work with what can poison your energy. Strong emotions, such as anger and hatred, for instance can flavor your energy, although the emotions are the easiest forms of energy to filter out and, for that matter, feed on. Altered states of consciousness induced by drugs or alcohol can also have toxic energy, but the risks to get that energy are not usually warranted. With that said once you've experienced such a state of mind and body it's easy to use your memory to recall what that state felt like and then imprint that into your energy. The safest way to draw on toxic energy is to simply draw on the memory you have of being ill or hung over. Your body retains its own memory of these events and with some skillful focus on your part you can evoke that memory into life.

To do so, focus on the memory of being sick. You'll probably recall a feeling of dis-ease and tiredness. With that feeling, try and fill in with as much detail as possible a recognition of what it fully felt like. Did your nose run? Were your eyes bleary? Did your skin itch? If you were hung over, did you have a headache or nausea? You'll note as you remember these details that you can actually feel the symptoms again, albeit to a lesser degree. When you've gotten yourself to a point where you can really feel and not just remember the sickness, you've successfully evoked that memory. What I'll usually do at that point, is try and store that feeling away again until I need it, or I happen to need it, let it infest my energy so that if someone tries to draw on it, they'll draw on my illness. They are certainly more than welcome to have it.

Another way to look at the "by-product" is in terms of heat. Heat is a by-product of your body, of cars, and a variety of other things. But heat is also a form of energy and it's relied on to keep people warm. When its winter and I'm walking outdoors, I'll often pull on the heat from passing cars and wrap it around me to keep me warm. In these ways and many others the by-product becomes useful, provided you are willing to consider that it may have a use.

Andrieh Vitimus, an energy worker friend of mine, also uses energy cycling. Instead of refining energy, he uses it to create a vortex that can act as a containment unit for an entity, or can be used to power a sigil or other magical working. I've also used the vortex in my own workings. How this works is that you and/or your partner(s) slowly build up energy and then direct that energy to manifest external to you. You'll feel/see/hear a vortex of energy manifest where you are directing the energy. This vortex will continue to cycle the energy until you direct it toward a specific purpose, such as creating a containment field, sending the energy to heal someone, or amplifying/charging a magical working. Alternatively you don't need to direct the energy toward anything. I've created a cycling vortex that I've used to gently massage energetic blockages between myself and other people (which then opens up communication) and I've also used it to just have a very intimate connection with the person I'm working with. In solo work, the vortex is useful for cleaning blockages and building up a charge for magic you are working.

Cycling, in a vortex, can have some dangers with it, including feedback effects, where the energy is cycled back too quickly for one or more people to effectively process it. Caution should be taken to keep the circulation of energy at a manageable speed for all people involved. To determine this I'll slowly increase the speed of the circulations until a person tells me that it's starting cause feedback. I'll then slow the circulations down just enough that the person can process the energy, but at the same time learn to handle the amount being directed to hir.

I've found the vortex to be most useful in sex magic for the purposes of intimacy, as this technique can get you in touch with the other person's feelings and thoughts. Such a connection should not be made lightly, as it will last after the vortex has dissipated. I reserve such workings only for my mate and suggest that you consider reserving such work for those you are closest to. The benefit of such a deep connection is that it can offer you and your partner a feeling of intimacy and even a form of telepathy. Lupa and I tend to voice what the other person is thinking, and I think it's a result of the energy work we've done together, because we've synched our energy together.

You might not wish for a casual lover to have that kind of connection. Such a connection, with the wrong person, can create problems including stalking, and obsessiveness, as the person or people yearn for that deep of a connection all the time. Even with someone you genuinely love, it's best to reserve such workings for when they are really needed as opposed to all the time. Both Belanger and Kaldera note a similar phenomenon (with similar problems) known as deep feeding, in psychic vampirism, where the vampire draws deeply on the energy of the donor (2004, 2005). Deep connections create a feeling of mergedness, a loss of individuality at times, as one person immerses hirself in the energy of another. Knowing when to back off, to give each other space, and to do such workings only when they are needed is key for using such energy work successfully. For instance, I prefer to use such workings for health issues, as opposed to just energy work.

Another issue with this kind of working involves safety issues with both magic and sex. In general I follow a rule with both that originated in the BDSM community, SSC (Safe, Sane, and Consensual). You want to be safe which means not only having protection against STDs or pregnancy, but also involves trusting your partner(s) both sexually and magically. Sane means that what you're doing is sane, which involves trust but also involves knowing the risks and assessing them accurately. I also think of sane as involving honesty. If you can't be honest with a person or a person isn't honest with you, you need to question the sanity of the person. Consensual is agreement by all participants to do whatever it is that is being done. If "no" or another safe word should be used activity, sexual or magic, should stop. Obviously if that happens in the middle of a ritual it can complicate matters, but in my mind if a person is that uncomfortable I'd rather have them out of the ritual than to disrespect them by continuing.

With energy work it's important to realize that when you share energy with someone you create a connection with hir. That connection can be used for good or for harm. I personally make it a habit that if I break things off with a person I completely remove the connection by pulling any of my residual energy from that person. To leave your energy in someone, when they no longer want it, is unethical and harmful and can create a lot of pain. I know this from personal experience, as in several cases (one of where I was deep fed from) where I shared intimate relationships with people and the relationships ended, they did not take their energy away after that connection was no longer desired. That leftover energy caused a lot of emotional turmoil and made it much harder to get over them.

I've used the cycling exercise to create the vortex with my partner. I place my hands in hers and start sending energy into her. Once she feels that energy she merges her own energy to mine. Both energies begin to mesh even as they continue to cycle between us. We may even kiss and merge our energies through the kissing. As this energy is built up, it can be used to stir the libido. Once the libido is stirred it is possible to use sex to continue creating the vortex. Physical sex greatly enhances the efficacy of the vortex as the connection is maintained not merely through hands or mouth but through the sexual organs and a large area of skin. I have used the vortex during sex to do healing work by focusing on using the meshed energy to tune or vibrate the energetic blockages in my partner. Because the energy patterns of me and my partner are joined together, they resonate together to create a field or vortex of energy which can be vibrated or tuned. I usually imagine strings of energy in my partner's body that I gently pluck, causing them to vibrate. The vibrations shed any energy that is harmful to her. That energy can then be taken and integrated into the vortex and used for other purposes, such as to create wards around our home, for instance. I've also used this kind of working to put myself into an altered state of mind, using the energy to propel my consciousness toward a specific meditative purpose or simply to journey through the far reaches of consciousness.

Still, even examining the cycling work in this context there are questions that remain. For instance, do we really need to use this work for refinement purposes? Couldn't we just cycle the entire spectrum of energy through ourselves? How are we even able to do energy work and what can we learn from knowing that? In other words, is it even useful to understand the underlying dynamics of energy work, or should we just do it and not worry about it?

Fortunately the answers to these questions can be found and, more importantly, they need to be found. Understanding the underlying dynamics is essential to really exploring what energy work can do for you. It's fine and well if you can make an energy ball, but if you don't know what do with it or even how to improve it, its usefulness is rather limited to throwing it at someone (who may not even notice it). The underlying dynamics will show you not only how to work with energy, but also how to refine your workings to maximize on that most wonderful of miracles, your body.

Dynamics of Energy Refinement

Consider first that the majority of people actually don't need to refine energy to feed off of it. Instead they can process energy into vital life force without having to get rid of the extraneous elements. Indeed, these "extraneous" elements are part of the vital energy. The majority of people resonate with energy as it is and have no need to change it. Some of them may have cluttered energetic fields, but through doing daily meditation, exercise, and better health habits they can organize that energy efficiently. But for those people who do need to refine energy, there is a problem. They simply don't resonate with energy as it is. This can take the form of psychic vampirism.

It's important to note that psychic vampirism comes in different forms. Some people don't even know they are vamping someone else, while others are fully conscious of doing it. The ones who are unconscious of it may stop psychically vamping other people as they get more control over their energy. The conscious psychic vampires on the other hand would argue that they are permanently psychic vampires and must feed (Belanger 2004). Kaldera further differentiates psychic vampirism into two forms, primary and secondary vampirism. Primary vampirism seems to be genetic; the vampire is born vampiric, without the means to convert external energy into the energy it needs, so it feeds off of other people (Kaldera 2005). Secondary vampirism isn't genetic,

> Usually it [secondary vampirism] happens to people whose natural energy gets exceptionally low, perhaps through illness, trauma, or addictions...Another way to become a secondary vampire is to have a rotten childhood. Too much draining stress on a child can trigger them into reaching out to replenish it from the people around them. (Kaldera 2005, p. 14)

Kaldera's theory on primary vampirism is similar to the one I mention in chapter 7. It's possible that some forms of vampirism are genetic, or inherited. It could also be due to genetic damage, wherein the person's genes were damaged and consequently the ability to convert various external forms of energy into refined life energy was lost in the genetic code (more on this below).

In regards to secondary psychic vampirism, it is possible to develop a need to feed during times of low energy. However once energy has been recovered, it's also possible to no longer feed. It's a survival instinct used, on the part of the sick person, as a way of keeping hir life energy at a certain level to insure health (Kaldera 2005). The rotten childhood idea is a bit of a stretch, given how dysfunctional the majority of families in the U.S. are. Almost everyone I know has had a rotten childhood, but the majority of them aren't psychic vampires. A bad childhood isn't an automatic candidate for vampirism. I'd suggest that having a rotten childhood could be *one* factor, but there may be others that also contribute to psychic vampirism.

As an example of other possible factors, Kaldera notes that people who ignore their energetic needs in turn develop physical problems such as hypoglycemia, which mirror the energetic needs they are ignoring (2005). It's possible however that the physical health issues are causative of secondary psychic vampirism. In other words, by neglecting physical needs, a need to feed energetically may arise as a way of compensating. In stressful environments, a person neglects needs as a cry for help, but also as an expression of hir own unhappiness with the problem. Neglect enough needs and psychic vampirism may develop as yet another symptom of the problem at hand. The problem though is that psychic vampirism is a symptom of a problem, and only continues the cycle of behavior that first created it,

That need to feed relies on stirring energy up and the easiest way to do that is to create some form of emotional drama (Belanger 2004, Kalera 2005). To be fair though, everyone I know, me included, has at some time or another created drama through actions and words. The problem is when such behavior is continually evoked as a way to feed. The feeding itself doesn't necessarily address the issues that created the secondary vampirism, and in fact may reinforce those issues. "We learn to provoke arguments, stormy scenes, sexual frustrations, tears, fears, or even violence from others, or manipulate everyone else while we look on and feed" (Kaldera 2005, p. 16). That need to feed relies on stirring energy up and the easiest way to do that is to create some form of drama. To be fair though, everyone I know, me included, has at some time or another created drama through actions and words. The problem is when such behavior is continually evoked as a way to feed. The feeding itself doesn't necessarily address the issues that created the secondary vampirism, and in fact may reinforce those issues.

Kaldera does have a very intriguing theory for vampirism: "We are the equivalent of the carrion-eaters, the garbage disposals who get rid of all of the negative filth that wounded people spew every day. In the real ecosystem, there are a number of species whose job it is to eat things that we humans would retch at, and without them, the world would be considerably less comfortable" (Kaldera 2005, p. 29). He equates psychic vampirism with carrion-eaters. It may be that he's right. If we consider that the physical levels of environmental pollution have risen in the world and also accept that this same pollution has an effect on the spiritual environment, it's entirely possible that psychic vampires are needed to get rid of that pollution. Since we do interact with our environments we are affected by environmental pollution. I think such pollution affects us on the spiritual level. Even if that's not the case, the vast amount of psychic pollution generated by the media and also by cultural hang-ups certainly contributes to the psychic well being or lack thereof for a person. Cleaning up such psychic pollution could fit what psychic vampirism does.

On the other hand, psychic vampirism could be caused by the pollution of our environment. The pollution that impacts the physical environment also effects the energetic environment. Energetic pollution could cause a need to feed, due to damage it caused to a person's genetic and/or energetic structure. The result of such damage would be that a person can't process heavily polluted energy. Instead of refining that external energy, a person might turn to someone with energy that is already refined and feed from that person instead. Taking care of our environment would help to undo some of the energetic pollution, but for people who were damaged by the polluted energetic environment another solution would be needed. Kaldera notes the following:

> Some primary vampires...can convert negative energy to clean energy in mere seconds...What primary vampires...do to human energy is snake medicine (convert poison to water) on a psychic level...We take all your horrid stuff off your hands without harm to ourselves, because we are designed to digest it. (2005, p. 31).

On the surface this seems like a good exchange, but there are two potential issues to consider. One issue is a potential cause of psychic vampirism. If a person represses emotions, they hold the emotions in without expressing them. This repression creates energy blockages. These blockages restrict energetic flow. If the blockages are dissolved, the emotional issues will be dealt with and eventually resolving, resulting in a clean energy flow, but if the blockages aren't dissolved, the person may need to go to external sources of energy to get more energy. The problem is that when you pull such energy from people it can actually reinforce the blockages. The other problem is for the donor. While the negative energy may have been pulled away for a time, the cause of that energy hasn't been dealt with and the blockages will return. It's much better to deal with the emotions directly and learn to process them. It can hurt, but relying on someone else to take care of your problems creates co-dependency and doesn't allow you to face the issues and grow from them. If, on the other hand, you work with the psychic vampire to banish the energy from your life, as you process the issues that prompted the energy, then Kaldera's approach may be very useful and a win-win situation for each person.

It is also possible that a person reacts aversely to a specific type of energy (but is still able to process most other types of energy). For example, some people may not be able to handle industrial areas because the type of energy goes against the kind of energy they are used to processing (think of a person from a rural area moving to a city; not only does s/he have to adjust to that city, but also to the energy of that city). In the latter case it is a matter of adjusting to the new environment, learning to effectively process the energy.

The best example I can give to that effect is my own recent move to Seattle. I have been used to living in small college or rural towns. A big city such as Seattle has much different energy than a small town. It was definitely an adjustment for me. At first I felt very disconnected from the energy of the area and even when I made a connection I found that the energy didn't really resonate with me. It felt foreign to who I was and I had trouble processing it. It took me some time and also finding places where I could access energy that wasn't necessarily similar to what I was used to, but which was connected to the environment and could allow me to energetically dip my toes in and get used to the feeling. Eventually I did get used to the energy flow in Seattle and was able to integrate it into my own energy. It took time and a willingness to open myself to it.

Remember to balance yourself in your new environment by visiting other environments. I find a refreshing walk in the woods to be needed sometimes precisely because it gives me different energy and allows me to reconnect with a more embodied form of nature than a city can offer. Another way I've coped with this change is by refining out the environmental toxins. My body tends to purge on a regular basis, and I encourage that purging through a high fiber diet as well as lots of water. This kind of purging can help clean out the physical and energetic toxins from preservatives in food and also the pollution in the water and air.

Energy work, combined with the right diet, can be used to purge such environmental toxins. The internal dissolving of blockages has been very helpful for not only dealing with emotional issues, but also for purging toxic energy. A vortex can be used to gradually siphon the environmental toxins out of a person. I also use Reiki everyday and permeate it through my cells. As my cells resonate with the Reiki, they are cleaned of the environmental toxins, which are merged with the Reiki. Reiki takes the environmental toxins away from me and then refines/recycles them into universal energy.

In a case where it's not an environment change, but an actual need to feed off of people, there are still possibilities toward curing psychic vampirism, despite claims to the contrary that it can't be healed. What needs to be considered are possible causes of psychic vampirism (such as some of the ones I mention above). As an example, though I never identified as a psychic vampire I certainly could and *needed* to feed off of energy from people and often would draw on such energy when I was younger. However, after I started working through the energetic blockages within me I found I needed less and less energy from other people.

Still, it took a long time to get out of the energy addiction entirely. Even recently I had lots of energetic blockages that corresponded to some emotional issues I was dealing with that even affected my physical health. I could do external energy work (i.e. working with energy external to me) just fine, but had trouble drawing on my own energy. It wasn't until I dissolved the blockages that my internal energy began to flow correctly. Beforehand, it seemed to me that if I drew on the energy of other people, especially emotions (energy in motion) I could get a temporary fix or high, but afterwards the internal energy blocks were denser, as if the energy had ended up contributing to those blockages. Yet when they were dissolved, and the emotional issues confronted and put to rest, there was no longer a need to feed. If anything, my internal energy was harmonized with the environment around me so that I could draw on external sources of energy and mesh them with my internal energy.

There's always the possibility that the energetic blockages don't cause psychic vampirism, or that they might only cause psychic vampirism for some people, while other people have a different cause for the need to vamp. To fully get a sense of what that cause could be I need to go on a tangent that will come back to this question.

Resonance Theory

In earlier chapters, I focused on biophotonic energy and mitochondria. Biophotonic energy is emitted from DNA and changes function as the frequency is changed. Mitochondria, as I discovered, are responsible for tuning the biophotonic energy. They process the environmental signals and send that information to the biophotonic energy, which then resonates with the incoming energy and processes it for both the health of the cell and the DNA. Adaptations are made not only physically, but also energetically, so that the person doesn't need to refine energy. This is mostly an automatic function, unless you decide to communicate with the various living consciousnesses that reside in your body.

Mitochondria actually seem to interact with the pineal gland in the brain. As was mentioned earlier, the pineal gland has been associated with astral projection and other forms of magic. I've found that by using the Taoist breathing techniques mentioned in chapter seven and combining them with contacting mitochondria, that the mitochondria use the pineal gland to attune the energetic frequency of the body. The Taoist breathing techniques create a connection of the energetic pathways, particularly when you put the tip of your tongue on the roof of your mouth. Because you are focused, in this type of breathing, on bringing energy into your body, you end up creating an energetic cycle just within yourself. When I contacted the mitochondria while doing this, they traveled along the energetic microcosmic circuit (mentioned in Chia's work) to the pineal gland and showed me how they transmitted information to the pineal gland. Realistically the mitochondria didn't move as they are intrinsic parts of a cell, but they did communicate with each other, a motion in and of itself.

The pineal gland has Melatonin and Serotonin within it. It's also where the neurotransmitter DMT is produced. Melatonin and Serotonin react to the frequency or amount of light that is being processed and are secreted into the brain through the determination of that frequency. In other words, the frequency of energy (which is what light is!) determines the secretion and reception of either of these neurotransmitters throughout the body. Accordingly the tuning the mitochondria use the pineal gland for is a modulation of those frequencies of energy that we receive from the environment, transforming that energy so it can be effectively metabolized by the mitochondria.

The metabolization of energy creates what I call resonance. The environmental energy that we receive is metabolized so that it can resonate with the biophotonic energy found within our cells. The biophotonic energy is flexible enough to take a variety of energy signals and process them so that they can be used to maintain the body and the energetic structures of a person. Another way to conceptualize resonance is that it requires flexibility and tension, similar to a string on a musical instrument. The flexibility is needed so movement can happen, but the tension is needed to direct the movement and create a repeating pattern (Judith 1996). It's the repeating pattern, in energy work, which is particularly important.

A repeating pattern of energy is the energy signature of a person, the energetic "identity." It vibrates throughout your body and overall structure and represents what your energy is. It can resonate with some types of energy more strongly than others; certain types of energy that are processed will have more of an impact on your genetic structure than others. Your body is held together by vibrating particles that consist of the particular frequency that also embodies your energy. It is your energetic signature. The resonance it puts out provides your spirit its fleshy home. Your vibration interacts with other vibrations, but also maintains the cohesion of you by being subtlety different from the vibrations of other people, animals, entities, etc: "Any vibration, be it a sound wave or dancing particle, is in contact with other vibrations, and all vibrations can and do affect each other" (Judith 1999, p. 243).

Although your physical body might mark you as human, your energetic pattern does not strictly adhere to the physical reality of your body. As an example, the phenomenon of Otherkin, people who identify (nonphysically) as other than human, is a case where the physical body is human, but the energetic pattern is not. I have my own thoughts on why Otherkin exist and how that existence is tied directly into a person's energy.

Let us consider that what consists of past life memories is perhaps a person's energetic signature resonating with the energy that is identified as something else. As an example, someone who considers him/herself an elf is likely a person who has high energetic resonance with whatever is considered to be elven energy. Bear in mind that the label elf is a subjective term used to describe a type of entity that may not even use or know the word elf. Regardless of what an elf is, it's a convenient term that can be used to describe a particular energy that is connected to a specific reality where said entities exist. A person who identifies with elves is likely a person whose energetic pattern may have at one time been elven. As such that person's energy pattern still strongly resonates with the elven energy. I've always noticed that people who claim they are Otherkin tend to have energetic signatures that are different from the majority of people and these signatures imprint on the physical body. In other words, the energetic pattern will cause the body to conform toward what it resonates with. Remember that the biophotonic energy is the energetic equivalent of DNA and as such it will be impacted by the energy that is metabolized by the mitochondria. That energy or information will shape the biophotonic energy, which in turn will shape the actual genetics and the genetic information that the human body processes.

I have, as an example, through working with not only elemental energies, but also Other energy, caused my energetic pattern to resonate with different types of energy and accordingly increased the bandwidth of my biophotonic energy. In the case of the Otherkin work, this has involved similar work to invocation. I've invoked a specific entity/energy (dragon in my case) and then integrated it into me afterwards. I did this integration by first offering it part of my essence, and then asking it for some of its essence. The entity agreed. After I integrated the entity's energy into my own, we both found that our energies meshed very well. A further ritual was done where I fully integrated the entity into me (with the entity's permission). This was done to not only maximize the meshing of our energies, but to also give him experiences in a body outside of his own. A deliberate energetic change isn't easily accomplished, as it involves a fairly good understanding of biology and how energy meshes with the body, and some repeated workings with the energy you want to resonate with. It also involves giving something of yourself in return, usually blood or some thing else that represents the human genetic material.

So where does this leave Otherkin? What I'm suggesting is that the type of energy they resonate with is, at least in part, responsible for why they identify as other than human. While reincarnation is the most popular explanation for being Otherkin, the energy signature is important regardless of origin.

Changing/Repairing your Energetic Body via Resonance Theory

What is presented below are possibilities of a cure. Until further experimentation is done these should only be treated as possibilities. Remember as well that each person has a right to be who s/he wants to be and that includes people who identify as psychic vampires.

Returning to the psychic vampirism topic mentioned above, it's possible that instead of energetic blockages causing psychic vampirism, there could instead be genetic damage or mutations at fault. This would mean that the inability to process the full spectrum of energy was inherited either through blood relatives, or possibly through a magical manipulation of the genetic energy information. However even with a cause such as this, it's not impossible to cure. You can alter the energetic pattern and resonance and as such repair any damage to your energetic pattern. If you're a psychic vampire you do this by learning to attune your energy with energy that isn't as refined as what you feed on, but can still be processed. As you open your energetic pattern up to processing other types of energy, the need to feed on other people becomes less and less important as you are able to repair the energetic damage.

The actual repairing work is a slow process. Imagine yourself as a malnourished person, used to a very specific, narrow diet. The enzymes in your stomach will not be able to easily process food that isn't part of that diet. It will take time for the body to readjust and produce the appropriate enzymes that can digest the food. Likewise the energetic body must also gradually be reintroduced to other forms of energy. A sigilization of different types of energy on your DNA may be too direct, but there are other ways to begin the process.

Sigilization, for instance, can be used to draw specific types of energy to you or even used as a way of introducing that energy back into your energetic framework. Instead of overlaying the sigil on your DNA you can use it to make a different kind of working, an introduction to a specific type of energy. As an example, if you want to work with the element of Earth you can use the hermetic gateways to get access to the elemental energy. Once you have accessed that energy, it is possible to get a sigil that you can use to evoke the elemental energy. Now, extend your own energy into it and incorporate some of the elemental energy into yours. Note any experiences and reactions you have as a result of this incorporation and if this process begins to feel uncomfortable, break it off. The benefit of this approach is that you can learn to access, taste, and/or work with a specific type of energy and gradually adapt your energetic signature to it.

Sound work, i.e. mantras, can also be useful. Mantras use sound to establish resonance with specific types of energy. By employing them it is possible to cause your energy to resonate with the energy that the mantras are calling forth. You can vibrate a series of frequencies such as the notes of an octave in conjunction with chakra work or the Lesser Banishing Ritual of the Pentagram (LBRP) to help repair damage and maintain balance. The vibrations alone won't change the energetic resonance a person has, but used in conjunction with the other energetic resources of the body, they become useful tools.

Another technique that is useful is carrying a talisman attuned to the energy you wish to work with. The talisman can be a necklace or other piece of jewelry, or it could be a stone. Any object will do. The talisman can be activated by physical touch so that it's not always on, and when you want to stop working with it, you can simply remove the necklace or put the object down.

Invocation can also be used for repair. When you do an invocation you are establishing a connection from your energy to the energy of another being. You do not need to feed off of that being, but instead can create a mutual exchange of energy and use that exchange for the healing. What happens is that the entity's energy melds with your own energy and can be used wherever there is energetic damage. The entity's energy is introduced to your biophotonic energy and gradually adapted to it, so that it can begin processing that type of energy once again. Healing entities are ideal for repair work, but this technique can also be used to assimilate qualities from entities that allow a person to develop a tougher energetic immune system (i.e. becoming immune to energetic toxins that would be problematic otherwise). This kind of invocation may be required a few times, in order to fully assimilate the entity's energy into your own.

When I was much younger, I used approaches like the ones detailed above to learn how to work with different types of energy. Brennan's system of healing work (referenced in chapter 7) was especially useful for deconstructing how I might be blocking access to certain types of energy with how I had constructed my energetic shields. Shields, by their very nature, are designed to repel energy. But it's important to carefully consider what energy you are keeping out. Lupa, my mate, says that she generally doesn't put up any more shields than what come naturally because, as she says, "I don't like to miss out on anything." Most people unconsciously develop shields that keep out energy which may not be harmful per se, but nonetheless is different from the energy they know. As an example, I was very depressed through most of my childhood and teenage years. This depression definitely had an effect on my energetic shields, in that any energy that wasn't associated with what I considered to be depression was kept out. This wasn't always beneficial, because such energy could have been helpful in balancing my mood. It was only after I started meditating on a daily basis and utilizing some exercises from Brennan's approaches that I began to learn how to deconstruct the energetic shields I'd put up unconsciously. I consequently found I became less depressed and I also found that I didn't need to draw energy from other people, but instead could rely on energy from a wider spectrum. The dissolving practices of Taoist breathing are also useful for dealing with the underlying causes of the energetic shields and you will find that as you dissolve these shields that a lot of energy you kept in those shields will come back to you and re-energize you.

The repair work to your energetic system really occurs on a variety of levels. It occurs on an emotional level in terms of whether or not you've come to terms with your emotional issues from your past and present. Those emotions are energy in motion and even the creation of energetic shields is an application of that energy in motion. But our physiological body's ability to process energy also plays a role in the damage. The diet you eat, the exercises you do, and, most importantly, how well you listen to your body, all have an effect on the energy it can process. Likewise the spiritual practices you choose and how much you experiment with the energetic body affect how well you can process energy. Choosing to modify the energetic body (which can be done) is something which should be done carefully as such modifications can have serious consequences. Removing a part of your energetic body will certainly affect how well you can process energy and indeed whether you can process certain types of energy. Mace notes the following,

> The subtle body we conceive of and reinforce with meditation and magick is the subtle body we get, that except for basic structures…it is mutable…and with work it develops according to the scheme we impose upon it…It is important our conception be open enough to include every center or current we might need. And it is important that our practice not contravene the interaction between psyche and flesh that is necessary for physical health (Mace 1996, p. 61).

The removal of an energetic body part will certainly affect your physical health (and likely your psychological health as well). That alone can cause psychic vampirism, because as you remove energetic structures you also remove the ability to process different types of energy. And though this damage can be undone, it's a long process, and involves a gradual reintegration of different types of energy into your energetic structures.

Instead of removing energetic structures, it's better to change them. Energy is neither created nor destroyed and yet removal does take away from what you have to access. Changing energy does not and is much less potentially harmful. Any changes can be undone as well, if they aren't beneficial. The key is to continually work with your energetic body through magic and meditation, but with an eye toward how it'll affect your overall health.

On a final note about psychic vampirism, there are many people who are vampires who want to stay vampires. Don't offer to "cure" them if they don't want the cure. Each person has a right to be who s/he chooses to be. If you want to know more about psychic vampirism, I highly recommend checking out Belanger's work (*The Psychic Vampire Codex*), Kaldera's work (*The Ethical Psychic Vampire*), and the Atlanta Vampire Alliance's Vampire and Energy Work Research Survey available at http://www.vampiresurvey.com/. All works provide good explanations on what this phenomenon is and how to cope with it if you have it and choose not to try to change it.

Through my work with invocation, I've always noted that a trace amount of energy from the godform or entity worked with is left behind after the invocation ends. That trace amount of energy is a homing beacon for the godform/entity and is used to make the next invocation easier. But that energy can be integrated into your biophotonic energy and to some degree already is. The ability to invoke or evoke is based, in part, off of the ability to process energy that isn't part of the biophotonic frequency, but could be part of it. So when you invoke or evoke an entity, you are actually processing the energetic signal of that being through your own energy. This processing allows it to establish a connection, by which it can then manifest and do whatever it is that needs to be done. Intentional working with the leftover trace energy can be done, integrating it permanently into your biophotonic energy.

The question that arises then is if you are permanently connected to the entity or to the energy that the entity happens to inhabit, and whether you want such a permanent connection. This depends on the entity you are working with and what kind of relationship you have with it. If you integrate the trace energy into your biophotonic energy you are accessing both the entity and the energy it is from. The integration won't give the entity control over your actions, but it will allow easier access. As a personal example, one entity I am bonded to in this way is the Deharan deity Aghama or Thiede. Through a solar meditation/ritual I did a few years back, I integrated his energy into my genetic structure via spit sigils that the sun empowered. While I have since deconstructed the working I did, I haven't gotten rid of the genetic connection to Thiede. It allows me direct access to his energy, which has been highly useful for space/time magic workings. At the same time he is able to connect to my consciousness much easier, without a direct invocation. This has its benefits for me, however, in that I still retain overall control, but he can visit and add his skills to mine and/or occasionally possess my body for a short time. I've never had any problems with this possession, because my consciousness is still aware of what's occurring and can step back in as needed.

Still, this type of energy work may not be your cup of tea. Such a connection can be undone, but it takes a lot of effort and has both drawbacks and benefits. One drawback is that you no longer have direct access to that specific type of energy, but a benefit is that without that energy in your system, you can actually find yourself relying more on what you can do. I favor an integrated approach of learning to meld a specific energy type to my own energy and learning to work with it to the point that it eventually becomes fully part of my energy, as I've discussed earlier in this book. However as will be shown in appendix B it is sometimes beneficial to let go of connections and move on.

What I want to make clear, however, is that it is possible to alter your energetic structure. Much as physical genetics is affected by the environment, and as such adapted toward that environment, so too can the energetic structures of a person be adapted toward specific environments or purposes. The energy signature of Otherkin is an example of this adaptation. The Otherkin may be a holdover of a specific energetic pattern, but it's equally possible that the reason a person is Otherkin is that unconsciously s/he has touched on that energy and allowed it in because of hir identification with a particular form of nonhuman being. In other words, s/he may have tailored hir energy to permanently invoke that particular form of energy into hir. It's a question, in part, of identification and the dynamics of identification. My mate, Lupa, is a wolf therianthrope, meaning that on some level she identifies as a wolf. As she puts it, "Am I Wolf because I imprinted wolfish ways early on, or was I wolflike from an early age because I am Wolf?" Why does one person identify as a wolf, so much so that s/he integrates wolfish behavior into how s/he acts? Modeling a specific behavior on a physical level will call forth that energy into the person. Consequently that energy can be nested into the energetic structures so that a person not only acts a certain way, but in fact has the energy of a wolf within hir.

With intentional magic work such resonance can be used to deliberately manipulate the particular energetic pattern a person has. Someone who is entirely human and then (through whatever rationale) adopts an Otherkin persona not only maintains that human energy signature in order to continue interacting with human society, but also expands it to include the Other energy as well. Your energetic pattern is not set in stone! This is why I've included the DNA sigil workings, because that is how I have altered my energetic patterns. By creating a direct connection to the elemental energies via the DNA I have allowed those energies to interface with the biophotonic energy much more closely. I've incorporated the elemental energy into my genetic energetic pattern. There's no reason why one couldn't experiment with strengthening or even creating a connection with Other energy.

Consider that advanced energy work is really the ability to change your physiology and energetic structures at will. I have been able to induce a state of near death for my body, by simply focusing on the energy of death and letting that energy poison my body to the point that it is on the brink of death. Energy work is really the control of your biophotonic energy and the other types of energy it interacts with. Learning to work on a cellular level with your energy is the first step toward learning to restructure your energy pattern, as it is within the cells that the pattern is created and maintained. In addition, when you do energy work on yourself or another person, applications to that microcosmic level are most effective in terms of healing or, for that matter, disrupting someone else's energy and body.

The ability to restructure your energetic body is highly useful because any damage that is done can be undone by that process. Also restructuring opens you up to more types of energy, provided it's done carefully and with the purpose of sensing other types of energy and then incorporating them into you. Finding this energy depends on how you conceive of the world around you. If, for instance, you don't believe in energy at all, it will be much harder for you to do energy work than for someone who believes it exists. Likewise if you limit yourself to the four traditional elements of fire, earth, air, and water, you are leaving out other forms of energy such as sound (both what you can hear and can't hear) and light (again what you can and can't see). The concept of Otherkin provides yet other forms of and uses for energy to explore. Work with god forms, pop culture archetypes, and other entities in introducing those energies to your system have potential for any person. It really depends on how open you wish to be with what you consider to be energy work and also with how you work with your energetic pattern.

Acquiring other forms of energy has been useful for not only energy pattern purposes, but also the acquisition of skills or benefits that enhance the magic and energy work I already do. The limitations are defined more so by the person than by what exists. What you choose to allow yourself access to is exactly what you will have access to…no more, no less.

Exercises

1. Given everything you've read up to this point, and hopefully all the exercises you've done, see if you can detect the residual energy left over from a successful invocation you did. Focus on working with your biophotonic energy and specifically with the idea of increasing the type of energy you can process. You can use techniques suggested through out the book or come up with your own.
2. Experiment with invocation and evocation, and specifically the trace energies that occur after a successful invocation/evocation. Besides melding those trace energies to yourself, how else could you use them? Think in terms of creating a persona out of the trace energies, a mask if you will…or think of creating a gateway using that energy as the method for triggering the gateway.

Chapter Ten

Textual Alchemy

This particular chapter deals with how multi-media can be used for inner alchemical purposes. My primary focus is on text, but there are other forms of media such as music and art that can be used for healing purposes or have a physiological effect. For example, I've touched on the role sound has on the physiology in an earlier chapter, but have you ever noticed that the music we play at a given instant in our lives is theme music? It represents a specific emotion or value to us and as such can dictate how we're feeling, as well as producing physiological effects, "Listening to (or playing) music is one of the easiest ways for many people of getting into the alpha state...As well as being a great mood-changer, music produces physiological changes: lower blood pressure, slower pulse rate, increased flow of gastric juices" (Proto 1992, p. 59). You might choose music that you associate with being depressed, listen to it when you're happy, and find your mood sinking. The music evokes the depression and so it's worth considering carefully what music you listen to in a given moment. Regardless, what you hear has an effect on you emotionally. It can also be used for physiological therapy, particularly if you consider that sound can affect the overall health of the body, as is most notable through infrasound, which can kill people. A positive example of music therapy is music that's used to induce altered states of mind. For example, the mind machine has music tracks that help a person study better.

In dealing with textual alchemy in general, there are several concepts to consider. One such concept is the meme. A meme isn't limited to text, as I'll explain; text is just one means of replication. Unfortunately the majority of people, occultists included, have an inaccurate idea what a meme is. For instance if you happen to blog, you'll sometimes note that people will post memes—little quizzes or questionnaires that a blogger will answer and then pass on to others to answer as well, which then get passed on—and so forth. It's fair to say that only in the loose sense of the word are those "memes" actually memes, in the same way chain letters only resemble memes. The problem, I find, is that most people aren't aware of the origin of the word or how it's used currently. Instead they vaguely understand that memes can be associated with commercials or blogging "memes", mistaking the example for the actual reality.

So what are memes? Dawkins, who coined the term, is perhaps the best person to start with, "A meme should be regarded as a unit of information residing in a brain (Cloak's i-culture)...The phenotypic effect of a meme may be in the form of words, music, visual images, styles of clothes, facial or hand gestures" (1999, p. 109). In other words, a meme is information that seems to be cultural in origin. It relies on cultural values to exist and might even be said to perpetuate these values. But Dawkins isn't finished, "Imitation, in the broad sense, is how memes *can* replicate. But just as not all genes that can replicate do so successfully, so some memes are more successful in the meme-pool than others [italics are his]" (Dawkins 1989, p. 194). Note that he argues that imitation is *one* possible way to replicate memes, but not the *only* way. Unfortunately he doesn't explain other avenues of replication for memes, which consequently has led other memetic experts to the conclusion that memes *only* replicate through imitation. I'd suggest, however, that if memes are units of information they can replicate through innovation and creativity, which doesn't always involve imitation. The drive to create a painting involves on some level the ability to create something absolutely unique. You'll still rely on acquired skills that involve some imitation, but the ability to conceptualize or create something new isn't imitation.

One of the theorists who argues that memes are solely based on imitation, Blackmore defines memes as the following, "Memes are instructions for carrying out behaviour, stored in brains (or other objects) and passed on by imitation" (1999, p. 17). Both Dawkins and Blackmore are overly focused on placing memes in physical environments, such as the brain, and it's still unclear what a meme exactly is. Instead the focus is on the behavior that involves the replication of it: imitation. Every time you hum or sing your favorite song, you are replicating the meme, i.e. the song or other cultural artifact. Every time you learn a skill, you learn (at the beginning at least) through imitation. But imitation only occurs at the beginning when you are learning a particular skillset. What is not accounted for is innovation, or the ability to personalize those skills and use them for purposes beyond the original usage. I'd suggest, in fact, that memetic replication occurs more through innovation and creativity than imitation, if only because the way a particular skill or concept sticks out in your mind is through how you personalize your understanding of it. Distin has a similar argument. She defines memes as representational content: "A 'representation' is simply some piece of our mental furniture which carries information about the world…So 'representational content' refers to the information that is included in the content of our representations" (Distin 2005, p. 20). In other words the representational content is a mental presentation or conception of the environment we interact with and a personalized understanding. The content is determined by the stimulus, but ironically enough also controls that stimulus and consequently the uses and solutions of the content that a person utilizes (Distin 2005). The meme is spread through communicating that personalized understanding to other people. Those people will also personalize the meme, changing it even as it is replicated. Thus, when one person sings a song and the second person picks up on it, the two versions may have very different inflections, timing, and other details—just look at the many versions of "The Star-Spangled Banner" that have been sung before millions of baseball games! It's the same song, but each person has hir own way of presenting it to the world. This personalization also takes away from the notion that it is the meme that dictates personality, but more on that in a bit.

Dennet defines memes as ideas which are passed on (1991, 1995), while Grant argues they are information patterns that infect the mind (1990). This last approach brings to mind Burroughs who was discussing cultural viral engineering long before Dawkins thought up the concept of the meme (Odier 1969). Another approach to memetics is Packwood's, who argues the following:

> Large potions [sic] of the human mentality are incredibly complex memetic structures, or frameworks, composed of vast numbers of memes, or idealogical structures. This suggests that if memetic structures become complex enough, they can form consciousness out of nothing more than the correct configuration of memes. Spirits are memetic structures which have become so complex they have evolved limited forms of consciousness [italics are his] (Packwood 2004, p. 52).

Packwood's identification of memes with ideology is sound if we consider ideology to be a unit of information. But ideology is usually regarded as much more than just a unit of information. It's a concept, but it's also a philosophy and a motivator of action. It has memetic elements of imitation via slogans, symbols, and other forms of cultural artifacts, but these forms do not encompass the totality of ideology. A meme is useful for transmitting an ideology, but is not an ideology in and of itself. In fact memes cannot exist if there are not similar ideas to support them. Even the counter culture, as a meme, needs the similarity of mainstream culture (specifically the similarity that there is a culture to be counter to) to exist.

The other issue is the identification of spirits as memes. The problem with this approach is mainly a subjective one, dependent on how you define spirits. If you see them as cultural constructs then identifying them as memes is correct. Egregores and other constructed entities are born from successful memes that have made an impact on the consciousness of a culture. If you attribute existence to the spirits outside of cultural, i.e. they have an objective reality, then the memetic definition doesn't work. The reason is that these spirits exist outside of the medium of culture as we know it and are only interpreted through that medium as opposed to relying on culture to exist at all. Another way to look at this is that spirits are artifacts, "Representations, and not artefacts, realize generalized information – and artefacts can persist long after the information that gave rise to them disappeared" (Distin 2005, p. 82). Spirits and entities tend to continue to exist and persist as independent beings long after the original cultures and information that birthed them have disappeared. Indeed, it might be argued that such beings are actually adept at cloaking themselves in the information of new cultures, thus persisting through a multiplication of identity, and yet at the same time existing outside those identities, using them only as a way of interacting with us. The archetype theories of Jung support this idea, with the concept that archetypes reinvent and refresh themselves with the trappings of modern culture, so they are still relevant for people.

Blackmore provides a similar argument to Packwood's, though it directed at the concept of the self,

> Free will is when "I" consciously, freely, and deliberately decide to do something, and do it...But if the memetic view I have been proposing here is right, then this is nonsense, because the self that is supposed to have free will is just a story that forms a vast memeplex, and a false story at that. On this view, all human actions, whether conscious or not, come from complex interactions between memes, genes and all their products, in complicated environments. The self is not the

> initiator of actions, it does not 'have' consciousness, and it does not 'do' the deliberating (1999, p. 237).

The problem with this perspective is that it places all notions of personality and self inside the almighty meme and encourages a lack of responsibility on your part, because it can be argued "the meme made me do it". While I certainly agree that the environment, one's genetics, and memes play a role in the manifestation of you or me, I think something that is missed out on is that we have some degree of choice with all of these factors. Whether we recognize that choice is another matter altogether. Conscious choice involves recognizing that all of these factors have effects on us, but that we also have effects on them and have choices when it comes to whether or not we choose to let some of these factors affect us. Nor can we buy the argument that we have little control over the collective products of our mind. Distin argues that a person can do little about the ideas and responses of other people, but the very use of memes suggests otherwise (2005). Careful planning, use of tactics, and a sense of how a person will react can give another person control of a situation. Advertisement would not be so effective if it could not be used to not only predict human behavior, but steer and control it toward specific desired ends. This kind of control continues until a person consciously chooses to no longer participate or to deconstruct hir reactions.

As an example of such a choice, consider the artifacts that promote memes. This includes music, television, books, but also societal mores and cultural norms, if we accept that memes are cultural units of expression. Suffice it to say, my definition of memes is that they seem to be cultural units of expression that are used to perpetuate particular values and norms of a given culture. You do have a choice in how you interact with these memes and how you choose to let them affect you. I, for instance, have not had cable T.V. (a prime promoter of memes) since 2002. The occasional visit to family inevitably includes a T.V. with cable and when I turn it on, I am amazed at the sheer stupidity of the commercials, which as memes imply that people are dumb and easily distracted. These memes can easily be avoided by shutting off your T.V. and getting rid of the cable. You'll be amazed at how much free time you'll have and how much more productively it can be spent. And if you really have a favorite show you want to see have a friend tape it or get the series on DVD.

We can't escape memes, but we can be choosy about them and that very choice is where the conscious self, the "I" manifests, in that while it is affected by memes, it chooses the memes that are most beneficial for it (or so I would hope). That involves a conscious effort to be aware of the fact that some memes are not healthy, for example the memes that promote cigarette smoking or fast food. This includes not only the advertisements for the bad habits, but also newspaper articles that talk about the success of their stocks and people watching other people put their money toward consuming these things (peer pressure isn't just limited to high school). And the evidence of this lack of health is available for anyone to see, from the movie "Supersize Me" to studies linking smoking and cholesterol to heart disease and other ailments. But sometimes memes are more subtle and insidious, such as the meme that promotes the idea that working all the time is virtuous and we all need to live on someone else's schedule. It's woven into the very fabric of our culture, and anyone who doesn't adhere to it is a "slacker" or "loser". This results in sleep deprivation, low self-esteem and a general feeling of dissatisfaction with life whether the goals of the meme are met or not. You have to make yourself aware of those memes and then decide if you really wish to choose to perpetuate them or choose memes that promote what makes you happy and excited to live.

In *Space/Time Magic*, I discussed at length at how writing could shape space/time possibilities, noting that much of science fiction has come true, at least to an extent (the submarine, the nuclear bomb, and our current dystopian society were all written about many years before those particular realities manifested). Even the lives of authors would often be shaped by their writing. Ernest Hemingway had several near death experiences at Mt. Kilimanjaro, years after he wrote his story about the death of an explorer near it. Franz Kafka wrote endlessly of bureacracy and indeed lived a life of bureacracy and predicted his own death by his drive to write in the short story "The Penal Colony".

My own argument is that writing helps to direct the overall human consciousness toward a specific version of reality. Even the perspective we have on technology and how it's used has been shaped years in advance by the writings of William Gibson and Neal Stephenson, to the point that our cultural conceptions are constrained by the writings that shaped our notions of technology before the technology was even available. The use of virtual reality in both authors' writings has inspired video games, online chat rooms, and even the use of icons for character representation. All of these aspects were used in their books before they were available in computers. The idea that a person's consciousness could also be uploaded into a computer from their works and the fact that so many people already invest so much energy in accomplishing that in virtual reality is a testament to how writing can shape the possibilities of reality. Now some noted occult theorists will disagree with me, "Words *do not equal in space-time* the things or events they denote, yet people react to a choice between words as if making a choice between 'real' things or events in the existential world [italics are the author's]" (Wilson 1990, p. 85). Words do have an effect on reality. The very fact that writing has successfully predicted events and affected the lives of writers suggests that more is going on with the word than Wilson would allow. Words cannot encapsulate an experience that a person has in another media (which can include body experiences, experiences of art, emotion, music, etc.), but words are experiences, in and of themselves, and they shape future experiences by imprinting the probability of those experiences into our minds. Spoken words have resonance—but so do written words, albeit in a different format. Otherwise how could the great works of writing move people so much? How you say something in writing is just as important, and though it cannot convey an experience in its entirety, the written word provides its own experiences. How many times have you read a book and found yourself immersed in the plot or the characters or the concepts? The experience those words give you is no less valid than experiences encounters through other forms of media.

Writing (or any other creative activity) can connect you to your subconscious and open you to probabilities manifesting in your life, including probable versions of yourself. Writing is a tool, a method of expression, and though it's useful for expressing conscious thought, it also conveys and allows manifestation of subconscious thought. In fact, the reason written sigils work when people use them is because they provide a physical manifestation of the thought. Sigils, and writing, in other words, organize the jumble of thoughts and concepts and then provide them material structure from which they can manifest.

Inner Alchemy has shaped my life since the beginning of 2004, bringing forth experiences that were essentially needed to even begin to complete the book project. In January of 2004, I had finished up *Space/Time Magic* and decided it was time to move to my next project. I thought at the time that I already had plenty of material on an alchemy that dealt with the modification of human physiology. I had experience with energy work, breathing techniques, exercise, nutrition, cell and DNA magic, among other relevant topics. I figured it would be easy to write this book. How little I knew.

Over the course of a year a variety of situations occurred in my life that synchronistically tied into the project. I began to undergo an inner alchemy of my own, in part I suspect because of my writing. The need of the writing itself, the words (as living entities of their own right) to be completed necessitated that I have more experiences than I had encountered. What I had already been through wasn't sufficient for writing this book.

So I began breaking through my unhealthy life habits, exploring inner territory that had gone previously untouched by my conscious mind. I fully opened up to a person who came into my life, manifesting some of that new territory in amazing, if sometimes terrifying, ways. And I mutated another love relationship into a friendship, learning more about communication than I'd ever known before. I learned of Taoist breathing techniques (something I never knew about) and ended up incorporating them as a vital part of my inner alchemical works. I had several encounters with a pagan elder who I'd never met and had never heard of, but who helped point the way to work I needed to do to understand myself. And I had all my pettiness exposed to myself, so that I could see the worst sides of myself, but also learn how to alchemically change them by choosing a conscious action over a subconscious reaction. Needless to say all of these occurrences have provided a lot of experiences that are useful for writing about this particular subject, and which happened in an incredibly timely and convenient manner.

And I've noted this phenomenon before. In *Space/Time Magic*, I noted that my personal journals would inevitably focus on a particular theme and bring forth experiences about that theme in my life, until the theme/issue was resolved. Additionally, I ended up being exposed to the work of Brian Shaughnessy, as well as having many space/time related synchronicities (such as meeting other people who were working on similar ideas simultaneously and independently) occur that added to the writing I was doing, so that the book could be brought to completion. Now I can't say that all of this occurred entirely because of the writing, but it did set up the intent and need for more experiences in both cases and also provided an outlet for manifesting those needs into reality so that they could be met and experienced and then added to the project. Basically a cycle was created by the act of writing, so that more writing could be done.

So what am I suggesting? Writing has a life of its own and has a need to be finished. It will bring into your life the experiences you need to have to finish a particular project. Synchronicity abounds with writing, because it is an imprint on your consciousness and subconscious, a calling out to probabilities to manifest into your life in order to give the writing the fuel it needs to complete itself. As such writing will inevitably have an effect on your life that goes beyond just putting words on paper or pixels on the screen. But there is a key component that is necessary for words to have an effect on a writer or a reader, "Only if read with sympathy, with <u>rapport</u>, can it have any effect on anything...Rapport is a mood that allows us to disregard the actual reality we are immersed within, substituting cues from the text for the natural, unscripted stimuli that normally generate our experience. The greater the rapport, the greater the concentration in the text, and the more total one's immersal within the world it represents [underline is his]" (Mace 1996, p. 130). I've experienced this rapport in reading a book to the point that I have actually been invisible to people looking for me in a bookstore. But I've also had rapport as a writer, immersing myself in the text and the demands the text has to continue to be created. And I've found that this process is very much a process of inner alchemy.

It is also hard to deny the effect that words have on a person when put in a situation where s/he are told you that s/he only has a year to live. There have been cases of misdiagnosis by doctors, where a patient was told this, and despite having perfectly good health, the patient ended up dying because s/he believed what the doctor said (Bonewits 1989). Words have power to affect your reality, if you enter into a state of rapport with them. Rapport basically brings words to life, and this is being done through memetics and through the idea of the word as a virus. Another way to view rapport is, "The only way to realize a symbol is by a process of mutual absorption. We must enter it, and it must enter us. We must participate in its essence to an extent of identifying with it at will so that we can project ourselves into it, or externalize it in any manner necessary" (Gray 1980, p. 36). This absorption is done every time a person writes or reads and becomes engaged in the world s/he is entering and sustaining. That world is consequently both internalized and externalized. It is internalized in the mind of the reader/writer via the process of reading and writing by giving voice, in your mind, to the characters, or in the case of non-fiction, to the author. It is also externalized by the belief that you put into the independent reality of the world or experiences you are reading about. We read to experience what it is the writer is telling us about and we write to convey our experiences to other people. Both are externalizations or evocations of the reality we are trying to experience, which is created and sustained by our willingness to believe in it and in the experiences found within it.

Awareness of how writing shapes your personal reality is the first step toward learning to control this textual alchemy, which is essential to fully getting the benefits of it, instead of reaping experiences that could be incredibly undesirable. The awareness you have of the synchronicities of your writing and its relationship to the reality around you allows you to anticipate and change patterns you may have written into your life that are not healthy. These patterns could be specific events or places that continually occur, and because you've associated meaning with them you create a theme that manifests an end result similar to what you wrote about. This can have beneficial or disastrous effects.

I'm not advocating you should suddenly write about happy situations/experiences, particularly if you enjoy writing horror or tragedy, or reporting on world news events. What I'm arguing, however, is that a good banishing after writing has been done may be useful so as to avoid actual manifestation of events in your life that eerily echo what you write. Conversely, writing about positive events could prove useful in terms of manifesting healthier patterns. But what I find more often than not is that what are really being written into existence are patterns in your subconscious mind. The key to changing this kind of creation involves realizing that your subconscious will use writing or other artistic endeavors to push probabilities into your life. You can change these possibilities by recognizing this principle at work and knowing when to let go of rapport with the words and detach yourself from the reality you are creating. So a banishing can help you to let go of the subconscious manifestations that can occur via your writing.

An even better approach is to learn to shape the subconscious patterns via your writing. In other words, although your writing can be an expression of your subconscious, it can also be used to imprint on the subconscious new patterns of thought that are healthier and to deconstruct and dissolve unhealthy conditioning. This is a big reason I believe in personal journaling, as such journals can prove useful for looking back on your life and finding patterns of behavior that may not be healthy for you. Once those patterns are found, you can deconstruct them via writing (or more specifically through reading and noting how often you write about a particular subject, person, or event), exploring why they were created, what event in your life set up the organization of them and then deciding if your reactions to similar events aren't warranted or need to be changed. The change will occur by being aware that you are reacting to a situation and making a conscious choice to not continue indulging that reaction.

Sometimes it is essential to let writing manifest situations in your life. If not for taking on *Inner Alchemy*, I can guarantee I would be at a much unhealthier place in my life. The situations that synchronistically arose as a call to help me fully write about inner alchemy were situations that have also helped me resolve unhealthy issues in my life. The textual alchemy that you engage in can be useful for providing your needed experiences. But maintain conscious awareness of this phenomenon so that even as you are shaped by the process of writing, you also shape that writing's effect. William S. Burroughs did this to good effect, utilizing his writing to insure he lived until his late eighties, as opposed to dying a junkie's death.

Another aspect to explore in textual alchemy is people's attitude toward the word in terms of definition. Part of the power of the word is that people often take a definition as a finite explanation of what something "is." In other words, people think a definition is really explaining the essence of what something is. The problem with this perspective is that it provides an overly literal reading of reality, creating an unquestioning acceptance that what a word means is all that it means. This also creates the notion that words equal the events in space-time they denote, which is the problem Wilson has with words. On one hand, the unthinking acceptance of a meaning of a word is problematic because it creates situations like the example I used with the doctor. A person hears he has so much time to live and doesn't question that diagnosis and consequently conditions his mind to believe that he only has that much time to live. On the other hand, a person's acceptance of the meaning of the word also reveals the power words have over people, to create rapport and consequently alter reality.

Unlike Wilson, I do think that there are beneficial aspects in people carefully choosing words they use. Not only does it make a person more thoughtful (I would hope), but it provides an opportunity for people to engage in critical thinking and conscious creation of reality. Part of being fully aware of what your subconscious is manifesting in your writings involves questioning what those words you use mean and WHY they mean what they do. It also requires being aware of what those words seem to mean to other people. Words have power and to ignore that power is to ignore their potential as well.

The best way to approach this is to recognize first that words have different meanings to different people and will have different usages that accompany those meanings. Let's use you, my audience, as an example. I'm going to make an assumption that the majority of you reading this book are engaged in some form of magical or esoteric lifestyle. This consequently shapes your understanding of what words mean and the effect those words have on you and other people. But if I were to go to my former graduate school program and show my former colleagues this manuscript, chances are they will have different reactions than you will have. This is because they have a different understanding of what the words mean, based on several factors. One factor is the choice of lifestyle. Lifestyle dictates and contextualizes your understanding of the words you read. An occultist who reads this book will be much more likely to accept the ideas as workable and believable because the occultist actively uses the practices described in here. On the other hand, most academics won't have a lifestyle immersed in ritual, energy work, or other aspects of magic and might find many of these ideas to very different from the training s/he has received. Also, it's important to note that there are many subcultures of occultists and academics, with different variant lifestyles. An academic in the sciences will have a different reaction from an academic in the humanities

Another factor is exposure to specific ways of using words, with highly contextual and specialized meanings, "Definitions put into practice a special sort of social knowledge – a shared understanding among people about themselves, the objects of their world, and how they *ought* to use language [italics are mine]" (Schiappa 2003, p. 3). Carefully consider that word ought. It implies something very important about definitions that people often forget, that there are values associated with definitions. Values are different from meanings because values represent specific agencies, or if you will, specific people who have an invested interest in getting you to believe that how they define the word is more important than how you define it and you'd better agree with them over the definition. This focus on how something is defined occurs in academia, where it is expected that grad students will end up defining the terms they use in academic writing (which is the accepted and expected way of phrasing words to signal that you are part of a specific community). But this same approach to definitions and the writing expected from someone occurs in the corporate world, in religious settings, and occultism. There's a reason a lot of occultists put k on the end of magic and it's because they buy into the value that's associated with magick, as opposed to magic. That value determines how the word *ought* to be spelled and defined, and consequently what it *ought* to mean to you and I. And if you don't agree with that spelling or definition there will be certain subcultures in occultism that will eye you askance.

Definitions and words depend on social interaction to exist and to create rapport, and thus manifest reality for people (Schiappa 2003). Without those social interactions words wouldn't even exist. The meanings that are given to a definition are not set in stone and consequently are open to revision and questioning. The problem that occurs is that people don't question and therefore won't necessarily do enough research into how others define words. So you might come up with a definition for the word and concept of meme, but with no research into how other people use it, your definition will not matter. The history that informs a word such as meme will necessarily impact how you use the word and people will know if you aren't using the concept or the word correctly. In essence, it is necessary to contextualize what you mean by doing research and seeking to understand how other people define a word and why they define that word in the way they do. There is benefit to doing this:

> Naming and describing are acts of entitlement. Through such linguistic practices, we give our experiences meaning and make sense of reality. By entitling a given phenomenon, we locate that phenomenon in a set of beliefs about the world that include beliefs about existence-status (what things are real or not) and essence-status (what qualities we may reliably predicate about the phenomenon). Because the range of possible entitlements is theoretically infinite, any given act of entitling should be seen as a persuasive act that encourages language users to understand that-which-is-entitled in particular ways rather than others. (Schiappa 2003, p. 116).

Complicated work, to be sure, but well worth it, if you wish to understand textual alchemy. To change a meaning of word, or just add a new meaning, find out why people are persuaded to believe the definition they believe in. That, after all, is the rapport, or the connection that gives words the ability to affect your reality. Otherwise, if you're the only one who understands you, you have no way to communicate with anyone else; the same goes for if you only understand yourself, and not others.

Definitions act as a way of explaining what words mean, and at the same time orient the person's reality around those meanings. They are persuasive and this persuasiveness is another factor that establishes the rapport necessary for words to have an effect on reality (Schiappa 2003). In sum, the reason words have an effect on and denote reality is because people agree they can do so and participate in this process. You can see this process at work when two people communicate with each other. To some degree those people must agree on the meanings of the words, in order to effectively communicate with each other. The degree of agreement varies in the sense that definitions are bound by situations, but even that can be surmounted by communication and the agreement to participate in creating meaning. This participation is so fundamental to our existence that rather than railing against it, it is better to use words as a magical tool for inner alchemical changes or other changes you wish to work magically.

Textual magic involves a conscious awareness of how you use words and a conscious understanding of the meaning(s) you are investing in words. This allows you to understand the patterns of probability you evoke into reality through your writing. And understanding how you've been influenced by other people's agencies in defining words is equally useful in changing the imprints your subconscious mind may have as a result of those agencies. Think of textual alchemy as a challenge for determining how you feel you ought to define reality via the writing you do. Certainly you may find, as I have, that you call forth a lot more probability by understanding how you're using words, as opposed to just using them and not recognizing the effects they can have on defining your reality.

Exercises

1. As an example of the defining principle, I challenge you to research the word "meme" and try and discover why the word has been defined in the way it has by different people. Do you agree or disagree with the definitions and why or why not? If you disagree how would you define the word? Now try and get others to agree with your definition of this word. Now record how the usage of this definition affects you and other people.
2. If you've been keeping a personal journal, read through it and identify patterns of behavior that occur in the writing. Ask yourself if you would be as aware of these patterns if you didn't write about them and also ask whether or not writing has actually facilitated the creations of these patterns of behavior. Compare entries in your personal journal to other writings you were doing at the time. Are there any similarities in what was written about?
3. Finally, with intent and awareness start a writing project, but keep yourself open to spontaneity. Keep an eye on events in your life and see if they synchronize with your writing. Remember that this, as with many acts of magic, may take time to manifest results.

Chapter Eleven

Learning to be Conscious

When I first started writing this book, I was a person who lived by his reactions. As I write this chapter, it is a year later, and I must admit I only now have even a sense of what real inner alchemy is, at least in terms of learning to be conscious. In fact, most people aren't actually aware that the majority of their actions, words, emotions, etc., may be reactions to events that happened long before they were in whatever situation it is they find themselves in. I am certainly no exception to this, in that it's fair to say I've spent most of my lifetime reacting to subconscious triggers, as opposed to consciously choosing how I want to act. The reactions have lead to a lot of pettiness, drama, and unpleasant situations, but fortunately I have been learning the fine process of becoming consciously aware of how I choose to act in a given situation.

There are some paradigms I will cover in this chapter which, in my opinion, have both advantages and disadvantages present within them. Bear in mind it is my opinion and that what may work for me may not be as useful for you. Each person has to find hir own path to consciousness. The real goal of this chapter, however, is to teach you the importance of becoming consciously aware of how you act and speak, and dealing with your thoughts and emotions in a healthy manner. These thoughts and emotions are, at least in part, reliant on subconscious triggers, which are patterns of behavior that have been imprinted on you by experiences you've had. They can be healthy, but in many cases are not. Fortunately these triggers do not have to rule your life, though it can take a lot of effort to change them, or so it has been in my experience and that of many others. You can learn techniques that can help in making these changes and those techniques are useful, but sustained effort is necessary for changing your behavior patterns.It is important to realize as well that your behavior patterns don't just affect you on an emotional or mental level, but have repercussions energetically and physically. Proto, for example, points out the deadly effect that repressed anger can have on the body; it effectively poisons the immune system and thus lowers its ability to handle disease and stress (1992). I've had my own experiences with anger. I spent years repressing my rage and anger, which lead to depression for me, and also taxed my physical body's capabilities to handle disease. This resulted in more physical sickness and an overall dreary approach to life. In fact, stress of any sort has an impact on your life. We are never without it, and some stress (such as sexual tension) is even beneficial. Nonetheless it has an impact on the physical body and on your behavior patterns, creating subconscious routines, "Everyone follows some routine, and the action becomes, through repetition, deeply rooted in the subconscious mind. Whether you are aware of it or not there is always a 'stress' there (in the subconscious mind) and this is one of the strongest 'stresses' we possess. We have all heard people who 'just must work', because they say they get irritable if they stop or retire. This is because the 'stress' of the routine is there" (Carrington & Muldoon 1973, p. 174). Without questioning where that stress is going or how it's impacting your body and your behavior, you may find yourself in less than ideal situations. By recognizing that stress, even good stress, has an impact on you, you can learn to moderate that effect and moderate your behavior that is impacted by it.

Nor is your subconscious behavior limited to internal stress or emotions. You spend a good portion of your life observing family, friends, acquaintances, and enemies, and from all of those people you learn behavior patterns that become imprinted on your subconscious (Lipton 2005). This imprinting affects you and your body on all levels, but as mentioned above it can be changed. For me, this change started to occur at the beginning of 2005, when I was in a graduate program for the field of composition and rhetoric. For several years I'd felt a deep dissatisfaction with the program and my place in it. This occurred partially through my own behavior and partially because of other people. Instead of being consciously honest with myself about these feelings, I chose instead to act them out through several very unhealthy patterns of behavior.

I began isolating myself from people, including my advisor in the program, my partner at the time, and my friends. I justified this reclusive behavior as a result of my being an author, but that justification was a convenient fallacy that ignored the very real impact that the program had on me. I felt intimidated, humiliated, and unhappy, and I didn't feel like I had an easy way out. I complained a lot about the program and how much I wanted to leave, but never acted on it. The complaining was an obvious symptom of my unhappiness, but I just could not justify leaving, because another imprint I had was that you put up with whatever problems were occurring and worked through the situation, no matter how harmful. There were other patterns of behavior that were destructive and all of them kept me in a cycle of misery and created problems for me professionally and privately.

The problem was that I was reacting subconsciously as opposed to acting consciously. My subconscious tapes (i.e. internal dialogue) continually fed me programmed responses to stimuli and I didn't question those responses, but just accepted them. I hadn't learned that I actually had a choice in my behavior, that I could choose how I wanted to act, as opposed to just blindly reacting to a situation. It was this free will that I was not exercising. I was choosing to be ignorant in my response to the environmental and internal signals. I only began to realize this when I was told of the importance of intent versus impact.

In magical practice intent is focused on sometimes to the exclusion of impact. But this focus on intent isn't limited to the occult; it occurs in everyday life. We all have good intent. We want the best possible outcome for our actions, but instead of factoring that in, we focus only on intent, only on the desire to create, as opposed to questioning what it is we are creating through our intent.

The impact is the result and fallout of your actions, and not always the result you hoped for. I realized that a lot of my actions didn't factor this impact into my intent and so I would create a lot of situations where although my intent had been good, the impact was anything but, and I'd be left with a sense of bewilderment as to what went wrong. I'd acted on my subconscious routines, as opposed to making a conscious choice. I didn't focus on my internal behaviors, but instead focused on reacting to the environment and those reactions shaped a lot of the magic I did, as well as more mundane actions. Needless to say, I think it's a handicap to act without full conscious awareness of your choice, as it can create embarrassing situations, where you speak before thinking through on the words you want to say. How many times have you said something and regretted it later, but wondered why you said it in the first place? Worse yet, you know you are responsible for those situations regardless of your conscious awareness of what motivated your actions.

Having realized this about intent versus impact, I still didn't have much of a sense of what to do about the situations I got into. Oh sure,

I knew the impact wasn't always desired, but I still hadn't caught on to the realization that sometimes I sabotaged myself with my reactions. I hadn't fully realized that I could control those behaviors and I ignored the following principle: "Consciousness, by thinking 'other,' namely, a distinct reality, and by following the law of craving, eventually generates 'other' and becomes other. Matter therefore is the experience and the symbol of self-identification carried to its extreme consequences" (Evola 1992, p. 33). This principle is something which I think is central to magical practice, and life in general, but is not often identified as such. Consciousness generates the experiences you have and seek. It even contributes to self-sabotage and there is usually a *good reason for your choice to subconsciously sabotage yourself*. Certainly this was why I was sabotaging my time in the Ph.D. program (but we'll get to that later). The experiences you create, or respond to, are experiences that you have responsibility for, at least in terms of your choice to participate in them.

I realized this was only an extension of the intent versus impact principle and as such didn't really include an answer to how I could modify the situations I was in. It wasn't until the end of June 2005, when I picked up the book on Taoist breathing practices by B. K. Frantzis that I even began to find a path that would allow more than superficial changes to my psyche. It involved consciously choosing to face my worst inner demons and emotional traumas. It was only in overcoming them that I began to realize that I could consciously control my actions. But even then I found it wasn't easy and I'm not the only person that has observed this,

> As a preprogrammed behavior is unfolding, the observing conscious mind can step in, stop the behavior and create a new response. Thus the conscious mind offers us free will, meaning we are not just victims of our programming. To pull that off however, you have to be fully conscious lest the programming take over, a difficult task, as anyone who's tried willpower can attest. Subconscious programming takes over the moment your conscious mind is not paying attention. (Lipton 2005, p. 169)

There are many schools of thought in occultism that focus on this process of deprogramming. Unfortunately some of these schools, such as chaos magic and NLP/metaprogramming focus on the fake it until you make it phenomenon or the idea that the brain is just a computer to be reprogrammed at will. Unfortunately these changes don't occur at the drop of a hat, and claims are often exaggerated. No occultist I know has yet been able to change hir personality so quickly on more than a superficial level. If anything it has taken a lot of effort, time, and conscious focus to make life changes. The changes I have made have taken over a year to accomplish and I am still focused on changing many of the behaviors I've identified as toxic. The point here is that as occultists we don't have a monopoly on being healthy or otherwise better than people who don't practice magic. If anything we are the same as the majority of people the world over and realizing this might just bring some much needed humility to how we perceive ourselves. We need to realize that genuine behavior change isn't a quick fix solution.

I will admit I have a strong bias toward Taoist alchemical breathing practices. The reason I prefer this paradigm over the others is that, in my opinion, the Taoist techniques don't take an overly mechanistic or psychological approach, but incorporate all levels of a person in the inner alchemical work. I have worked with chaos magic and metaprogramming approaches, as well as NLP, but for me these approaches just didn't provide a sense of resolving issues. Instead it often felt like I was putting a band-aid on a wound, but not discovering the cause of the wound. But not every technique is for every person. NLP may work much better than the Taoist breathing practices for you. Use what works and don't hesitate to try out new paradigms.

The Taoist techniques gave me the necessary introspection I needed in order to discover the root cause of my behaviors. I was finally able to delve into my subconscious and discover what motivated my reactions as well as how to work through the root causes so that I could create new triggers that enabled healthier behavior. Perhaps the most important concept I realized was the need to set boundaries,

> The setting of proper boundaries is the major premise of all psychological methods, and a major point of contention and discussion in all relationships...When people do not have reasonable boundaries, their lives don't flow properly. Their inner lives are usually a jumble of unmet needs and unrealized dreams, while their outer lives are filled with overwork, or desperately important social causes. (McLaren 1998, p. 27)

I'd lived a life where I never really set boundaries for myself or for others and that had created a lot of disorder in my life. I had no real sense of control over myself or my actions. The setting of boundaries occurred by consciously putting effort into changing the reactive triggers I had in my subconscious. I set myself a goal that I would become a fully conscious person, choosing my actions and words consciously as opposed to relying on subconscious triggers.

Because of this choice, I was able to finally examine my life in a critical manner and stop perpetuating unhealthy attitudes and actions. An examination of these actions showed that I only had a hazy idea of what it was I wanted to do with my life, and that I had gotten involved in the Ph.D program for security and because I had no real sense of what options existed for me. Continued frustration with the program helped me realize that my calling wasn't in academia, but instead would be found in the writing I am currently doing. I left the program and soon after found a job that gave me the flexibility I needed to continue my writing, while providing a sense of well being and financial support that I also desired. I am still in the process of working through many of my internal issues, but the previous work has helped me establish a sense of contentment and peace that I long lacked. I am no longer as subject to my reactions or my emotions, but have instead come to a point where I can consciously examine the situation and decide on the best action.

It's important to emphasize that the process is ongoing and not something that ever ends. The situations we have in our lives will inevitably call up subconscious reactions. However, by learning to work through the underlying issues you can have more control and eventually come to a point where you aren't haunted by the traumas of your past, distant or recent. You can even learn to program your subconscious triggers so that they don't put you into unhealthy situations.

I've covered the Taoist practices, in terms of energy work, but while these practices are used to dissolve energy blockages as well as massaging and stimulating the internal organs, they are also useful for psychological work. The dissolving of the energy blockages frees repressed emotions that can then be felt and worked through via meditation. Often I will find myself mentally tracing the pattern of behavior back to its earliest occurrence and then working through that event and changing my reactions to that situation. I have even used retroactive magic to help me in that process, by not only re-living the previous experience, where the behavior first occurred, but also changing the outcome of that experience into a more positive one. Consequently the retroactive workings have made it easier to deal with similar situations in the present as I've already reconditioned my past self to act in a healthier manner.

This work has also unleashed a lot of my deepest fears and personal demons. Because the emotions are no longer repressed they will, at least for a short time, surge through you. I have gone through bouts of depression, sadness, anger, and jealousy since dissolving my energetic blockages. Having a loving partner or best friend that is willing to listen and talk is invaluable for this process as s/he can provide a relatively objective voice to what those personal demons tell you. You are ultimately responsible for how you deal with these emotions and if you aren't ready to face some of the depths they go to, it is advised that you consider psychotherapy. This will allow you to face what you're ready to face, without forcing you to go into depths of yourself that you may not be ready to plumb. Dissolving work is work that occurs every day and if you choose to do it, the emotions will be felt and dealt with for quite some time. The payoff is that you can get to the root of the problem and deal with it conclusively, but it takes effort. As an example, I have been dealing with abandonment and value issues and though these issues seem to be the core issues for me it has taken me six months to come to an awareness of them that allows me to recognize when I'm acting on them as a result of insecurity—and I'm far from banishing them entirely.

The breathing techniques allow you to isolate areas of tension on your body and those areas are indicative of areas of mental tension. The body memory that you have retains traumatic events particularly well. The breathing allows you to feel and isolate the tension and gently massage it so that the physical, mental, and emotional tension is released, felt, and then let go of. Once this occurs you are no longer obstructed by the past situation, but can instead deal with similar situations from a conscious perspective, choosing appropriate actions that allow you to be at peace with yourself and the world around you. The benefit of emotional and mental health is complemented by the rise in physical health and the overall good feeling that arises out of having an awareness of your body. This awareness extends to emotional and mental states of mind and is highly useful for continued dissolving work and an overall feeling of well being.

Another paradigm is that of Chaos magic. This paradigm is primarily psychological and argues that you can fake it until you make it. The idea is to model your behavior off of successful people and incorporate that behavior in yourself (which is similar to NLP premises). It also operates on the ability to change your personality as need be for a given situation. This can include changing your clothes and appearance, as well as behavior aspects (Hine 1993). The problem with this approach is that while it can be useful for pragmatic purposes of finding a job, there are still the underlying tensions that must be dealt with. In other words, changing your personality permanently takes time and sustained effort. You might be able to change clothes and even some personal habits fairly quickly, but chances are that you'll find it easier to maintain the change of clothing as opposed to the change in personal habits. Without understanding the fundamental dynamics that inform the personal habit, i.e., why it is a personal habit, you'll find that your subconscious will prey on you and eventually you'll slide right back to where you started. One reason people have such trouble quitting cigarettes isn't just because of the addictive chemicals, but also because they've likely forgotten why they chose to smoke in the first place. Maybe it was because of parents smoking, or because they were told not to smoke, or because they simply enjoyed smoking. Regardless of what the reason is for that choice, if you don't examine that reason and deconstruct it, you will likely find yourself smoking despite your best efforts to quit. This isn't to say that a person who resolves to change, won't change, but likely s/he will find that it's not a quick journey.

Still, chaos magic has other meditative methods that can help with some of these processes. In chaos magic, there are two types of meditation, excitatory and inhibitory. Excitatory meditation involves lots of actions and activities, which is used to put a person into a meditative state (Carroll 1987). A person might dance until s/he is worn out and use both the dance and the exhaustion to go into a trance or meditation. My partner does this when she dances in drum circles in a wolf pelt. The dancing and wearing the pelt allows her to connect with the spirit of the wolf and go into a trance state where she is that wolf. Excitatory meditation also occurs with sex magic, where the sex is used to raise the energy of the people and create a meditative state of mind that allows the people to focus on a specific goal. Once a person is exhausted s/he is ready for gnosis, which is an altered state of consciousness based on a single focus. In this case it can be best described as a state of knowing and within that state of knowing internal changes can be made to a person's behavior. Likewise external changes can be made for situations that need to be addressed, though as I'll note usually the internal reality you have is inextricably linked to your part in the external situation manifested and so change that occurs within will manifest externally.

Inhibitory meditation is meditation that focuses the person's awareness inward, while ignoring or detaching hirself from the sensations and experiences around hir (Carroll 1987). For this type of meditation I use a technique called *offnung* or open door (note this is not a chaos magic technique per se, but then again no technique is ever limited to a particular system of magic). I described this meditation exercise in chapter five. In this meditation I gradually get my body to relax more and more and as this occurs my consciousness is drawn inward so that eventually I lose awareness of my physical surroundings as I meditate on whatever it is I've chosen to focus on. Sensory deprivation tanks also offer a similar experience for people. The exclusion of senses causes the person to direct hir consciousness inward and the states of consciousness that are experienced can be very enlightening because the body is no longer distracting the mind with external stimuli.

Metaprogramming is another paradigm, which I have already partially covered earlier in this book. What I have liked about metaprogramming is the recognition that any stimulus can be used to set up a negative or positive behavior pattern, "*Anything that is present* in the situation when a person experiences an aversive stimulus, such as intense anxiety of panic, might become paired with that stimulus and thus program the same emotional response [italics are his]" (Lilly 1968, p. 50). This means that you may have to work with a variety of stimuli to fully change your thinking or emotional responses. Traumatic experiences imprint strongly on the person. Surrounding stimuli though unrelated to the trauma can still have an effect on the person, such as music that was playing when the trauma occurred. This is because the person creates associations between the event and the surrounding stimuli, using those associations to explain the actual event that occurred. This is why rituals such as initiations and death-rebirth rituals can be useful for reprogramming behavior. They involve putting a person into an altered state of consciousness and awareness and then imprinting hir through experiences that reinforce the ideology behind the ritual. The external stimuli that a person receives during these rituals imprints the concept of the ritual into the person's consciousness.

Another aspect to consider in metaprogramming (which is closely related to neuro-linguistic programming [NLP]) is the following:

> Programming and metaprogramming language is different for each person depending upon developmental, experiential, genetic, educational, accidental and self-chosen variables and elements and values. Basically the verbal forms for programming are those of the native language of the individual modulated by nonverbal language elements acquired in the same epochs of the development of that individual. (Lilly 1968, p. 153)

All of these elements that Lilly mentions are worth considering in terms of how they may condition your subconscious reactions. The subconscious mind processes far more than the conscious mind, which can only focus on so much information at once. As such the other information still has an effect on you, but it is not overtly acknowledged until you begin to examine its effects. Language is a good example of this. When you learn a different language, you will find yourself thinking differently than how you did in the original language. This will consequently affect the way you process information and experiences in that language. Symbols are also good examples. They are usually layered with a multitude of meanings, but people will generally only comprehend a couple of those meanings consciously. Nonetheless the subconscious will read more into the symbol than you did consciously. Wilson makes an apt point when he explains that, "Whatever the thinker thinks, the prover proves" (1983, p. 25). This simply means that the way we program ourselves to think and understand reality will also involve finding proof that how we understand reality is valid. Wilson calls this phenomenon reality tunnels and argues that a person's reality tunnel will by necessity limit hir perspective, but will still be open to different imprints.

Imprints can be understood as software in the metaprogramming model and such software involves the experiences you have. Lilly's concept of external stimuli being associated with traumas is an example of an imprint. But imprints can be more complicated than that, involving political or religious ideologies. Culture itself is an imprint and it is up to each of us to question those imprints in order to determine if they have any fundamental basis in our realities. We are successful in questioning imprints when we begin to consciously examine our own behaviors and realize where their roots come from, upon which we can begin to change the behaviors. But I must emphasize that it is far more important to discover the root of your behavior than to just go and change it. You may change the behavior for a time, but without understanding it fully there is always the chance that the behavior will be reasserted if the right trigger to a situation comes up. Some behaviors have multiple triggers, so fully exploring the root of your behavior patterns is worth taking time to do.

NLP is a combination of hypnosis, metaprogramming techniques, and pathworking. It is also defined as, "NLP deals with the structure of human subjective experience; how we organize what we see, hear, and feel, and how we edit and filter the outside world through our senses. It also explores how we describe it in language and how we act, both intentionally and unintentionally, to produce results" (O'Connor & Seymour 2002, pp. 3-4). Pathworking is a combination of meditation and NLP, which involves using visualization to imagine a journey or as a way of perceiving yourself from a different perspective (Farrell 2004, O'Connor & Seymour 2002, Andreas & Faulkner 1994). It involves using symbolism, which is how the subconscious mind communicates with you. A pathworking can involve creating an imaginary environment such as a city or home, exploring that place and the symbolism within it, and then relating that symbolism to your psyche (Farrell 2004). It's important to note that a pathworking will change your attitudes and may remove one issue for you, while bring other issues to your attention, much like the Taoist dissolving methods.

As I read through several of the NLP manuals, I realized that I'd been using various NLP techniques for quite some time (such as modeling, pathworking, and anchoring), without even knowing what they were. NLP is very useful for changing external behaviors and learning how other people think. A lot of the focus is on putting you outside of yourself and in another person's space. This allows you to get a sense of that person's particular communication style. While there doesn't seem to be as much focus on the internal dynamics (i.e.

interactions you have with yourself), NLP does provide a few techniques for working on the inner self, including one which I find very useful. When you feel negative ask yourself why you are feeling that way and then listen to the response. The response could be something such as this: "I feel negative about myself because I don't value myself or other people." You'd then ask how yourself could change this tape and continue the inner dialogue (Andreas & Faulkner 1994). NLP does provide some focus on accessing the root of behaviors, but many of the techniques are focused on changing the behavior without seeming to analyze it. For instance, while it's useful to analyze speaking patterns and word choices for how a person processes the external world, such pattern analysis doesn't always indicate the internal processing that's occurring. And while it may be useful to anchor a specific behavior to a gesture, the anchoring doesn't reveal why the behavior is happening and relies more on creating a reaction as opposed to a conscious action. Although I've used both metaprogramming and NLP over the years, it wasn't until I had actually begun an intensive meditative discipline that focused on the internal self that I really began to change my internal and external behaviors. With that being said, I have found NLP to be useful for understanding how other people think and learning to "read" people.

Reading a person is an essential skill in learning how to communicate effectively. It involves listening, but also examining the person's body language, attitude, and even energy. The best way to learn this skill involves going out and spending time observing people. Watch their actions, listen to their words, soak in everything you can about them. Try and determine who approaches who first and how the other person or people react to the approach. Then apply that understanding to your own situations. How do you approach people? How do you interact with the other person throughout the encounter? Do you have a gesture or movement you use when nervous?

Another aspect of NLP that's related to reading people is consciously imitating, or modeling, people. I've done such modeling based on pop culture characters as related in *Pop Culture Magick*. But this modeling can also be applied to people. Do you admire someone? Then watch hir mannerisms and behavior and adopt what you think is successful to your own persona. You can even model actions that you feel will allow you to anchor these changes into yourself. An anchor is a physical gesture that evokes an emotional reaction. When you model yourself on someone else you are essentially evoking emotional states you associate with that person, by imitating or anchoring hir behavior into your own behavior.

Anchoring can be applied to everyday life. Undoubtedly you have a gesture you use whenever you feel worried. It could be thumbing your ear, folding your arms, or some other action. Because this gesture is associated with negative emotions it imprints those emotions further into your psyche. But this can be changed by learning to associate new emotions with the gesture. When you catch yourself doing the gesture think of something you want to achieve, or feel an emotion that better and then use that gesture to anchor the emotion into you. By doing this you free yourself of negative imprints and reinforce positive imprints. I usually like to do this during a commute (as it's a time where you are in between work and home, touching my chin and focusing on feelings of happiness as opposed to worry. What is really occurring is that you are learning to reframe or change experiences by using the gesture to focus your mind on the situation.

In fact, what NLP is really good for is learning flexibility in dealing with external issues. Flexibility in present situations is an excellent inner alchemical skill to learn, because you learn that you do have control over one factor in every situation: yourself. More specifically you have control over how you choose to act in a given situation. That control isn't just emotional, but also includes words, actions, etc. For instance how you choose to word a sentence is essential for how clearly you communicate with someone, as I discussed in the previous chapter.

According to NLP, using negatives in sentences isn't a good idea. The reason is because the brain doesn't process the negative, so if you say "don't slip" to someone, what the person is hearing is actually "slip!", which can consequently produce a negative experience for the person (O'Connor & Seymour 2002, Andreas & Faulkner 1994). Reframing the word choice into a positive message will imprint on a person much better. Likewise explaining to a person why an action is bad as opposed to why s/he is bad is much better in that the person will not associate him/herself as "bad". A mutable approach to reality, then, is essential to claiming responsibility for yourself and what you choose to do and how you choose to do it, without bogging yourself down with needless guilt. But such an approach supplemented with strategy is also useful and NLP teaches people strategy skills that can be used to negotiate situations. It is important to remember that you are dealing with situations and learning to be flexible with those situations as they occur. Thus you don't want to overly associate situations with people. People may be a factor in a given situation, but realize that you may be dealing with the same person in multiple situations, but in a variety of different contexts.

At this point you should have a fairly good idea of some of the different approaches in consciousness modification. In my opinion only using one (even the Taoist model) is limiting yourself, but using two or models in conjunction with each other can be highly useful for helping yourself to become consciously aware of your emotions, actions, and words. I use all of the approaches described above together for specific purposes. NLP is useful for dealing with present situations and learning flexibility. Metaprogramming is excellent as an initial approach to the mind-body connection and as additional support for flexible thinking. Gnosis via inhibitory or excitatory practices can be used for resolving external situations and sometimes for deep introspection. The Taoist dissolving methods are recommended for getting to the root of issues in your subconscious and dissolving the blockages that contain repressed emotions.

There's also something to be said for developing your own approaches toward becoming consciously aware of the dynamics behind your behavior. As an example, in December of 2005, my mate noted that I'd constantly remind her of things I'd done for her. I realized she was right and wondered why. I decided to try an idea out that would involve using my dreams as a method for explaining this behavior to me. I also used magic as a way of starting the process. I had to shave off my dragon whiskers (very long side burns resembling the cheek whiskers of Chinese dragons) because of the (unrelated) need to find a job. I decided to offer the shavings to the five classic Western elements: Earth, Water, Fire, Air, and Spirit. I asked in turn that they provide a gateway to my subconscious through my dreams to help me find the root of this behavior.

That night as I went to sleep I opened a doorway of five colors and was led to a jail cell. My subconscious self was released from this cell and had me sit in a chair, while he held my wrists and whispered in my ear from behind me. He told me the reason for my behavior and said when I woke up I would remember everything. The next morning I did indeed remember everything and over the course of the day voiced to myself deep feelings of dissatisfaction I had with my relationship. This would culminate in a call and late night visit by my mate which led to a resolution to the issues.

Now I could've relied on the methods I described above, but using magic and dreamwork was, I felt, a quicker route to the answer. Sometimes a quicker route is needed and in my case I needed answers for this behavior as it was troubling to everyone involved. The point here, too, is that sometimes the best method of becoming conscious is one you devise on your own. You know yourself better than anyone and you know what you will respond to, but remember to be honest with yourself. Beyond that, consider that your creativity is your greatest ally and skill and employing it to help yourself is useful for opening awareness of why you act the way you do.

One last aspect of consciousness to consider is identification, specifically not only why you identify yourself as a particular person, but also why you might identify yourself by various labels. The labels we have are manifold and often used for convenience. Yet, they come to be associated with a person's consciousness and are often taken for granted. I'm a magician, I'm biologically male, I'm a writer, but do these labels really define my consciousness? And does a person, in choosing the label of self, really claim that consciousness?

Something that always interests me is the number of people in the pagan subculture who identify themselves as something other than human. There's nothing wrong with identifying yourself as elf, if that's something you feel strongly is a part of you on some level of your being, but is it the entirety of your being? Is being human, in and of itself, a bad thing? Questioning the identity of your consciousness and why you choose labels to associate your consciousness with is something that should be cultivated, if only to fully appreciate the mutability of consciousness beyond any defining label. In other words, you label yourself at your own peril...sometimes it's enough to be you and sometimes it's important to embrace the fact that though you may identify yourself as a variety of different things, you can also identify yourself sometimes as human and in doing so appreciate the consciousness of being a human. I only write this, because sometimes exploring the body as it is, is a great way to get in touch with your consciousness and also a great way to ground yourself from some of the other labels you might choose. Sure, you might be an elf, a magician, a vampire, an alien, or something else, but at the end of the day you're also human, a parent or child (or both), a neighbor, an employee (or employer), a gamer, a geek, a business professional, a person who really, really likes chocolate chip cookie dough ice cream, and any of a number of other identities, no matter how small or seemingly insignificant.

Focus on conscious awareness is essential to inner alchemy. With conscious awareness we take full responsibility for our choices. We learn that identity is a conscious choice. Intent is measured against impact and an action is considered carefully. Undoubtedly you will backslide into reactions, as I have done, but you can pull yourself up and try again. In doing so you free yourself of your past and embrace the present moment for all the opportunity it can offer.

Exercises

1. In this chapter, I've referenced a number of different books. Pick up at least one book on each paradigm, read it, and try out the exercises. Note the results you achieve and which systems work for you and in what contexts they work. Then mix and match these systems so that you use them in conjunction with each other. Note the result. You should put at least six months into this project as measurable results will take some time.
2. Try out my subconscious dream technique that I developed for a particular situation and note the results. I suggest using it for a particular troublesome behavior pattern that you or another person have noted about you, such as my habit of apologizing more than I need to. Remember to give an offering of hair or some other personal effect, to open the gateway to your subconscious. Try this technique out to figure out why you are doing so.
3. Finally, devise a technique of conscious working utilizing elements from these systems, or systems of magic you are familiar with, but nonetheless make sure it's an original, personalized approach. Again, note results. Ask yourself, in regards to all of these exercises, what worked really well for you and what didn't. Continue exploring along this vein as you see fit.

Epilogue:
Tying all of this together

We've come now to the end of this book (beyond a few appendices with additional approaches). But the end of a book is not the end of a journey. It is, in fact, just the beginning, for you, but also for me. There will be another book on inner alchemy and space/time magic, a blending of the two approaches, because there are a lot of tie-ins, both microcosmic and macrocosmic (see *Space/Time Magic* for the macrocosmic implications of DNA magic). Combine the two together and you have an intriguing variety of approaches for dealing with consciousness raising as it manifests both within you and in the environment around you.

I argued, in this book, that you can't divide the body from the mind or the emotions or the spirit, but by the same extension you can't divide your identity from that of the environment. Or rather, you can, but doing so leads to a very detached approach to life that consequently produces a society that squanders the natural resources it has and focuses more on material than on achieving a harmony with all of life. This detached society should sound rather familiar to you, as it is likely a society you live in. And while some people could try and escape said society and live a hunter/gather lifestyle devoid of money or many of the other materials that a contemporary society has, they will find in the end that they really can't escape. The need to socialize, medical necessities, and the simple fact the majority of places on Earth are becoming more and more "civilized" makes such a choice impossible. So what can you do?

The answer involves not in escaping from society, but in cultivating a variety of perspectives that allow you to do what you can to not only change yourself, but work for positive change in this culture. Even more important are changes in the environment at large, not just the few wild places left, but also your home, your workplace, the city you live in or near. It is the people around you and, as this book demonstrates, the life that exists within you. And what you put into that environment, how you choose to live in that environment, has its effect on you, even as you affect it. So what kind of perspectives do we need to cultivate in order to have a healthier environment, society, and culture?

The first perspective to cultivate is an awareness that you are connected to your environment: "Taoists see themselves as conscious individual cells interconnected to other conscious cells in the vast body of the universe" (Frantzis 2001b, p. 31). This approach of seeing yourself as a cell in the body of the universe is a humbling realization. No longer are you alone, adrift, but instead you are connected to the universe and *every* living being in it. Consider on a different level that your moods are affected by the weather, at least in terms of the mood it sets for you, "Now, notice the weather. Think about the ways in which the weather reflects your moods, how it changes like you do throughout the day" (Perry 2003, p. 190). In other words, realize that your perceptions of the environment also have an affect on your internal reality. You are in a connected cycle with everything. In fact, let's narrow it down further to people. If someone frowns at you, how does that affect you? Try, next time you're in a convenience store, to sincerely thank the clerk for what s/he is doing and watch hir reaction. Note the results and then ask yourself how you contribute consciously or subconsciously to how other people feel and think and act in a situation, and of course apply it to yourself as well.

My goal with this book has been to show you that you can connect with yourself, with all of your being, in a meaningful manner that unveils the universe within you. It's my thought that you can't really connect with the external environment until you learn the value of connecting with the environment within yourself--until you recognize the miracle of you, you won't recognize the miracle of what you have around you. Western culture emphasizes a detachment and dissection of everything to the point that people seemingly have no appreciation of what they have around them. But this detachment occurs first with the body and undoing that detachment will lead the way to reconnecting with the environment around you.

I speak from personal experience, because the process of writing this book was very life-changing for me. I had always felt very detached from the rest of the world, and this often resulted in an inability to fully relate to people, places, and events around me. When I originally began writing this book, I had no idea that my life would change so much, or that the writing would play a large role in that change. Over the course of 2005 I found myself facing situations and parts of myself that I needed to examine to truly understand what inner alchemy is. The refining of myself, the dissolving of issues and the unleashing of repressed emotions was and is the path to realization of my connection not only to the miraculous universe within myself, but also to the people around me and the larger universe I inhabit.

With that thought I want to finish this book off with a couple of suggestions on how you can tie the work in the previous chapters together. For example, some of the neurotransmitter workings I've been doing have involved working with multiple neurotransmitters while also doing Taoist dissolving work. Taoist breathing techniques are primarily used to work through energetic blockages in the body, but also are useful because when done properly they stimulate the deeper blood veins and massage the internal organs. I've used the meditation to work with the blood veins and called on the neurotransmitters Arginine, Corticotropin, Adrenalin, and Testosterone via the symbols I'd obtained for them. Work with them has proven most useful, accelerating the healing process of reawakening the libido. I've also found neurotransmitters to be useful in other healing magic. I learned from Tyrosine (which is concerned with the transmission and moderation of frequencies) how to vibrate pollution out of energy. My latest work has been with amino acids such as Tryptophan, Phenylalanine, Histidine, and Arginine, which I've been using to regenerate connective tissue in my mate's legs, when healing her. Combining them with other techniques in this book has proven fruitful for a variety of healing and other work and undoubtedly this will continue to be the case.

There is the possibility of relating a lot of this work to the macrocosmic level. Certain patterns replicate on both a micro- and macrocosmic scale; whether it's the electrons circling atoms or planets circling the sun, the spiral of chakras or the spiral of galaxies, there is a connection on many levels that can be explored. In the end it is up to you to make the most of what you get out of this book. It is only a guide, and the real adventure is just beginning.

My next solo project is the *Multimedia Magic,* and my next co-written project (with my mate Lupa) is *Kink Magic: Sex Magic Beyond Vanilla*. Until then keep experimenting, keep adventuring, and above all keep questioning the stagnant and insist on the innovative.

Appendix A:

Entheogens & Drugs: Should you use them or not?

In the mainstream culture, there is an over-reliance on legal drugs. People have a pill (i.e. legal drug) to pop for every problem. While the pill may take the edge off of what you feel, the issue that occurs isn't fully dealt with. Thus you have people who can't handle emotions and rely on pills to solve the problem. In addition, the side effects that occur make these drugs bad for the body, and more drugs need to be taken to get rid of the side effects. When you add in physiological treatment for the pains of the body, people forget that drugs are not cure-alls. They're just meant to help the body utilize its own resources. Overuse causes a decrease in the production of the natural chemicals of the body. The drugs take over the receptor sites and the body starts to rely on them instead of the natural chemicals (Restak 1992).

I'll admit I've resisted taking pills. I used to have manic depression; however, I knew the answer was not in taking pills, but instead could be found through a regime of meditation and pathworking with the natural chemicals in the body. That said, I've also taken the occasional Tylenol for a headache and I think any inner alchemical work does depend on a lot of willingness to be patient with yourself and your body as you do the work. It took me five years of continuous meditation to regulate my moods effectively so I was no longer depressed; the work is still ongoing in terms of mood regulation and likely will be until the end of my life. I can certainly say that on a day I don't meditate my moods tend to swing a bit more.

Now if you're in a serious accident, taking those pills may be helpful for dealing with the pain. But with that understanding I also think it's important to utilize the natural resources of your body. There's no reason you couldn't work with Norepinephrine, the neurotransmitter that is a painkiller, to help you with your pain. Likewise, other neurotransmitters can be worked with to aid in the healing of the body. Additionally, you can use energy work to stimulate damaged nerves and tissue and repair the damage to them. Mind you, all of this work is something which requires time and patience. Healing doesn't occur overnight and the body could not handle an overnight healing, which would shock the system too much.

But using the natural resources of your body over time will not only allow you to connect with your body, but also allow you to heal it and grow from the experience. Just relying on artificial drugs will not insure that your body will heal. But as always consult a physician for your condition. Magic is not a replacement for professional medical treatment, but can certainly be used in tandem with it. It's one thing to use energy to get rid of a normal headache; it's another to use it to cure cancer without any medical treatment.

In some areas of modern occult culture the over-reliance is on entheogens, magically and recreationally. Recreational use of drugs is highly problematic. There is a lack of knowledge about how such entheogens were used by native cultures. Unless you are trained by a shaman from such a culture, the use of the entheogen for magical purposes can be somewhat risky (Bonewits 1989). At the very least research into proper dosage and settings is necessary to avoid potential harm to yourself or other people. I have used recreational drugs before, but the majority of my experiences have been negative. These negative experiences prompted me to develop work with neurotransmitters as an effective alternate to reaching the same states of altered consciousness.

There have been positive experiences that occurred with the help of knowledgeable people. In those experiences I found that the states of mind I achieved were comparable to states achieved via meditation. The difference, however, was that in order to stay at those states more entheogens need to be ingested, whereas with meditation it's more a matter of choosing when you want to stop.

I suspect that the reason some occultists get into entheogens is because they aren't willing to take the time to develop the discipline involved in meditation. The idea that you may have to spend years reaching some of the deeper altered states isn't appealing to everyone. Some people want results now and the entheogens will get results. The irony is that the use of entheogens actually lowers the effectiveness of meditation: "The prolonged use of recreational drugs does indeed retard progress in meditation on many fronts....They [Taoists] found that these substances damage the kidneys and liver and lodge resin residues in the bones of the forehead, residues that slowly leach into the brain, with undesirable results. These side effects distort the energy of the body, slowing the energetic interactions of the body, chi, and spirit" (Frantzis 2001a, p. 188). The energetic connections have to be unclogged, which can involve a lot of work. I have noted, when healing people who've done lots of drugs, that the energy is much more sluggish.

You don't necessarily have to have the drug physically in your system in order to get the effects. My partner, Lupa, has been known on more than one occasion to pick up a decent buzz from the ambient energy of drunk or stoned people in the same room as she is. Also, once you've done an entheogen, your body maintains a memory of it which can be called upon. Phil Farber is currently releasing a DVD series on entheogenic magic, including how to evoke a previously experienced altered state of mind via entheogens, by remembering in as much detail as possible the various sensations the entheogen caused. This recreates the altered state of mind, though not to the degree that it's experienced when actually using an entheogen. Even so the effectiveness of the altered state isn't diminished by using memory. In addition, using the memory allows you more control over your state of mind.

Recreational drugs can be useful for the occasional purification through toxification as well, i.e. the path of poison. I've used a similar approach to Farber's for this. I've basically called on every feeling of pain, depression, etc., as well as the use (and overdose) of drugs I've taken, to put my body into a state of toxic shock. This has been useful for creating near death experiences and also useful for purification purposes as the body will start to clear the toxins out. I've gone into more detail on the path of poison in *Space/Time Magic,* and so will not elaborate further here.

You may wonder then if working with the neurotransmitters produces the same effects. I've found that they don't, as they are part of your body and as such part of the energetic system you have within you. The side effects you'd experience with drugs are avoided in this kind of work. This means the neurotransmitters won't clog up your system, though you should still maintain balanced workings with them. You can overdose on anything, even water. In addition, if you aren't careful in regulating your work with neurotransmitters, you can end up accidentally throwing off your own balance of these chemicals.

In the end I urge anyone who does choose to use such substances to be mindful of the law and be responsible in your use—consider legal (at least at the time of this writing) drugs such as salvia divinorum or kava kava[3]. Personally, I feel that entheogens are not necessary to achieve an altered state of mind; the natural miracle of your body is sufficient for that. But again, everything I've said here about entheogens and drugs is just my opinion, and yours may vary.

[3] http://www.iamshaman.com is an excellent site for legal entheogens.

Appendix B:
The Detachment Ritual

Readers familiar with my previous books will recall an ongoing experiment working with the power spots of Kent, Ohio. I had essentially bonded myself to the land, with the concept that in doing so I could draw easily on the natural resources to power my workings. I had some success with this working, and also found that by having my energy in the land, I could tap on the land's energy for my magic. However, as with anything else such connections can cut both ways. Because I'd bound my energy to the land I was very much "stuck" in that area. The power spots were basically containing a lot of my own energy and environmental energy that hadn't been released and were acting to keep me in the area. This was evidenced by the overall feeling of stagnation I felt in my life and specifically in the lack of progress I was experiencing in the graduate program I was in at the time. So I decided to do a detachment ritual from the land with several goals in mind.

The first goal was to see some form of progress in my graduate studies, in order to move on from Kent State. The second goal was to free myself of the energetic attachment to the land so I could move on with my life somewhere else. I based the detachment ritual on the principle of Taoist dissolving. The connection I had with the land was no longer beneficial, but instead had become a blockage that needed to be dissolved so that the energy, and I, could move on.

Before I continue with the description of the ritual, a brief examination of power spots is necessary. Power spots are physical spaces where a lot of energy has been invested into a particular location. Some obvious places include Stonehenge, the pyramids in Egypt, and Native American sacred sites (Keith 2005). But you needn't limit yourself to these (and many of them are off-limits anyway). Any place that is invested with meaning can be a place of power. When I was in Kent, I picked out a number of places that had power associated with them, because people spent time and invested meaning in them. A statue of a brain, the site of the May 1st 1971 shootings, and even some department buildings on the university were all places that I chose as power spots because of the activity and meaning associated with them. I created the power spots using spit sigils and the sun. The idea was that the sun would charge the spits sigils and imprint them into the Earth energy so that it connected with me. This worked very well for quite a while and the experimentation with altering some of the physical laws did seem to work, but because I had invested my energy into the land, I was attached to it and needed to become detached to move on.

I consider the detachment ritual to be inner alchemical, both for releasing my energetic connection to the land, and for pushing me out of a rut and into some much needed changes. I needed to revisit every site of power and undo the original working. I did this by making a new spit sigil that would dissolve the connection when the sun imprinted it in the land. I revisited every spot, walking the entire time, and remembering the original working and why I had done it. And every time I put a new spit sigil on the power spot, I felt as if a connection had been undone. This was in part psychological, as the dissolving wouldn't occur until the next day, but I did feel as if a burden had come off of my shoulders. My energy felt much freer and I also noted that the energy held in the power spots was released. I did this working in September of 2005 and the results I wanted manifested gradually over the next few months, albeit in a manner that was a bit unexpected, but not exactly undesirable. I ended up leaving graduate school due to a lack of forward movement within the program and a realization that my writing and ideas did not fit into academia. I moved out of Kent shortly thereafter and eventually went to Seattle.

The key aspect of the detachment ritual is that it detaches you and your energy from the environment you are in. Even if you haven't done a power spot ritual, you will usually find that your energy is invested to some degree in the job you do or the home you live in. This is a natural result of inhabiting those environments and investing yourself in them. Your detachment ritual need not be as elaborate as mine was. As an example, a friend of mine did his own variation of the detachment ritual. He went into his job and studied the environment there, specifically how people reacted to his presence and how he reacted to them, but also looking at the placement of the office he was in, the objects in it, and so on. He then visualized detaching his energy from the office and from the people he worked with, in such a manner that he no longer needed to be there. The very next day, on a spur of the moment decision from his bosses, his department was dissolved and he was let go of. His desire to detach from his job and find new work was granted.

It's up to you as to how elaborate you wish to make your detachment. If you want include physical objects from the environment because it will aid in the process then do so. Or you can do what I did, which is walk all over the place, remembering what occurred and letting your memories then fade away while using some other form of magic to aide in the process. Or you can use a candle of whatever color represents detachment to you and some work with a godform such as Ganesha (remover of obstacles) to get out of a bad situation. What matters is that you use a method that fulfills the principles of the detachment ritual and allows you to move on with your life.

It's intriguing to note that any connection is only as permanent as you make it. Your actions and choices affect that connection and as such it is entirely possible to detach yourself from connections with people. I've covered some ideas on that process in *Space/Time Magic,* as well as in the basic energy work chapter in this book. Regardless, remember as well that while detaching yourself from a place or person is an option it's not always the best option. If you detach yourself from a job without having another one lined up you may end up job searching for a while, which is not a fun process. Likewise you may come to regret detaching yourself from a person. But the decision is yours to make...choose wisely, choose well, and be willing to live with your choice.

Appendix C:
Neuro Sorcery

by Zachary Walters

A neurotransmitter acts as a chemical relay, modulator, and/or amplifier of signals between neurons and other cells. The variety of neurotransmitter effects on the human body/mind far exceed the complexity of any mythology. Neurochemically speaking, our brains house a pantheon of deities that can and do affect us every moment we live. Understanding the neurotransmitters' roles within our body/minds can unlock the very secrets of consciousness itself.

I first became interested in neurotransmitters early in my occult life. The myths of the Norse berserkers and my own preference for the Nordic magickal traditions led me to begin working with Adrenaline. My theory at the time stated that the Viking berserkers had managed to develop a reliable means of Adrenaline overload, and that this condition gave them their reputed ferocity and stamina in battle. After some experimenting, I developed a method of increasing my Adrenaline levels almost at will. Many years and reality shifts later, I conversed with Taylor about this subject after I read about his experiments with the neurotransmitters as spirit guides. We both seemed eager to explore this new angle, and I began researching the neurotransmitters. I worked at a hospital at that time, and would sneak into the psychiatrist's offices at night to do research from the impressive library therein; and of course the haphazard groping through the internet for reliable data. After a few weeks of study, I began to experiment in earnest. A few of the approaches I took to working with the NT's included direct contact via invocation, anthropomorphizing them as godforms, inner bioalchemical experiments, and the creation of a new paradigm for myself incorperating the NT's and other biochemicals into traditional mythology and magickal practices.

Experiment: Serotonin and the Body of Light

During a conversation with a fairly traditional Hermetic friend of mine named Thomas about evocation, he mentioned that some of his most intense experiences on the astral plane occurred when he visualized his body, especially his head, full of a brilliant white light. He claims that this visualization propelled him to higher states of consciousness. I agree with him, and I think Serotonin elevation produced the effects.

Many traditional occult practices utilize a visualization of lights during a ritual. The Lesser Banishing Ritual of the Pentagram, the Middle Pillar, Chakra meditation, etc., all contain a visualization of bright light in the region of the head. This visualization may contain more than symbolism It seems to produce the very stuff of dreams.

Serotonin production occurs as a result of bright light exposure. It also seems that the brain cannot distinguish what it imagines or remembers from what it experiences. Therefore, if one were to visualize a bright light intensely enough, the production of Serotonin should increase as if one were in bright light. Also, a light meditative state normally accompanies such visualizations, which would put the brain in the Alpha frequency range. Serotonin, and its child DMT, seem to affect the body more intensely while in this state due to a lower demand on the brain and the subconscious observation of the body/mind that occurs when one expects a magical effect to take place. So Thomas and I set up an experiment to test this hypothesis, and to our good fortune, Taylor and another friend joined in shortly after we began.

The setup for the experiment took this form:

Each participant was to monitor the amount of bright light and Tryptophan heavy food (the best indicators we had of presently available Serotonin in the system) they were exposed to during the day of the visualization. The visualization itself consisted of white light centered on the head, especially the pineal gland, with a duration of 15 minutes to an hour. The participant was to attain an Alpha level brainwave frequency through meditation, biaural beats, or whatever method suited their personal preference. The participant was to record and report whatever effects were had. The participant was to do the exercise in a low light environment as to not be producing Serotonin naturally.

Results:

Round one

Control: Participant 1 (Thomas) did the visualization after a day of what he considered "normal" light exposure and Tryptophan consumption. He achieved Alpha state through rhythmic breathing and backwards counting from 100. He maintained the visualization for one hour. He reported the effects as having a "vibration" all over his body, and very vivid dreams that night.

High light/ Medium Tryptophan:

Participant 2 (Taylor) did the visualization using the Audio Strobe mind machine for attainment of the Alpha level. He reported "extremely vivid dreams" as well.

Low light/ High Tryptophan:

Participant 3 (Zac) achieved Alpha level through a brainwave entrainment CD and backwards counting from 100. He reported a "floating in warm water" feeling and intense "tingling" in the limbs. He also reported some vivid visuals during the meditation, but no exceptional dreams that night.

Participant 4 (Jerry) achieved Alpha state through highway driving. He reported an open eyed visual of an orange spot in his vision. He also nearly ran off the road. He later reported vivid dreams.

Round 2

Low Tryptophan/ Low light

Participant 1 achieved Alpha level though meditation. Reported no noticeable results inconsistent with normal meditation. No exceptional dreams.

Participant 2 also participated in this one. He achieved Alpha level through massage. Reported nothing inconsistent.

Low light/ High Tryptophan

Participant 2 achieved Alpha level through meditation. Reported an intense vibration throughout the body and very vivid dreams

High Light/ High Tryptophan

Participant 3 Achieved Alpha level through mental exhaustion and maintained with pranayamic breathing. Subject reported:

> "The white light came much easier during this one. It took it a little while, but the pineal opened. I had a floating feeling… and my "body" kept pivoting on an axis roughly located in my naval region. I constantly felt to on the verge of motion. I noticed very vivid visualizations start to form. I opened my eyes. The room was dark, but not totally dark. Maintaining Alpha level, I am happy to report open eyed random visualizations that gave way to constructed

visualizations. Upon concentrating on an image, the image formed. including the Egyptian god Set, Srodin and Melatai, and the Tattwas. Color was good. No audio that I remember."

Further Hypotheses: Biaural Neuroalchemy

The experiment demonstrated that Serotonin production may indeed occur in larger amounts when white light is visualized. However, the other effects remained unexplained. For instance, the two most commonly occurring effects of this experiment were a "vibration" within the body and vivid dreams. This led me to believe that more was at work here than Serotonin.

Serotonin production occurs during bright light exposure. Melatonin production occurs with a removal of that exposure. Serotonin keeps us alert, energized, and for the most part in an elevated mood. Melatonin, on the other hand, works to prepare our body/ minds for sleep by reducing the brainwave frequency and acting as a slight depressant.

So, when we produced Serotonin by visualizing light, while our body produced Melatonin due to the darkness, we created a biaural rhythm within ourselves. In this state, something unexpected happens. Both Serotonin and Melatonin belong to the neurotransmitter family Tryptophan. Another distant relative and derivative of Tryptophan is Dimethyltryptamine, or DMT. Called the "spiritual molecule" by some, DMT acts on the brain as a powerful hallucinogen. DMT also occurs naturally in the human body. DMT synthesis and release also happens to occur in the pineal gland.

My conclusion: by visualizing bright light (producing Serotonin) while in darkness (producing Melatonin) the dual stimulation of the nervous system forced the synthesis and release of DMT by fooling the body into thinking that it was dreaming. "Mind awake, Body Asleep." Taylor later followed up on this theory with stunning results detailed in chapter five of this book.

Entis Mythology

When I began working with the Neurotransmitters, I decided to write a mythology for the pantheon as if it were widespread and worshipped long after people forgot that they were "just" biochemicals. I decided to use consonant mutation for most of the names. For example, the gods will be called the Entis, a slight mutation of NTs, and individual NTs will be called Enshai. An example of this follows. This is the myth of the births of Srodin and Melatai, Serotonin and Melatonin respectively, from their mother Trypova.

Character Key

Trypova:	*Tryptophan*
Aych Twow:	*H2O, or water*
Garbom:	*Carbon*
Fenlane:	*Phenylalanine*
Trozin:	*Tyrosine*
Adralin and Nadralin:	*Adrenaline and Noradrenaline*
Dohbamahny:	*Dopamine*
the Shalz:	*The cells*
Srodin:	*Serotonin*
Melatai:	*Melatonin*

Places / Landmarks:

The Kingdoms of Ryeb and Lev: the right and left hemispheres of the brain

The River Songwum: blood and the entire vascular system Bimahl: The pineal gland

The Nexus of Lightning: the neurons

The Great Valley: the divide between the hemispheres of the brain.

The Great Dam of the Two Worlds: the blood/ brain barrier

Trypova traveled on her splendorous boat that floated upon the sacred river Songwum. Before her loomed the great valley that separated the Kingdom of the Gods into the lands of Ryeb and Lev. Trypova was heavy with child, her smooth stomach bulging with what was divined to be twins. She thought back to the time of conception. She was traveling on her boat, and she drank deeply from the waters of the Songwum. A form arose, Aych Twow, the lord of the primal sea himself. He moved gracefully onto her boat, his hair flowing into his shoulders. He, if one must call it a he, was old before Trypova was born. He and his brother Garbom are said to have created the entire world when they swirled around one another in their endless dance.

Aych Twow seduced Trypova, and she let him penetrate her every pore. Within minutes, she was left alone with thoughts of the sea foaming between her legs. Trypova knew that she carried his child, and returned to her Kingdom. Her rival, Fenlane and his grandchildren Adralin and Nadralin were hard at work. The people, the Shalz, were suffering. Fenlane's wayward child, who had long ago conspired to join Trypova's house was waiting for her. Dohbamahny, the temptress and Goddess of Desire, stood in her flowing robes of scintillating purple. Trypova was overjoyed to see her. The two embraced as sisters and conversed. Upon hearing her friend was heavy with child, Dohbamahny revealed a secret that she had heard in her travels through the valley.

"Sister, you are heavy with children, and no ordinary children at that. These shall end the suffering wrought by the terrible Lord Fenlane and his berserkers. I warn you, there will be dangers that face them, but the children of Aych Twow are destined to be reborn again and again. You must birth them each time, however." Dohbamahny said.

"Where shall I go? If Fenlane hears of this, he will no doubt slaughter them before they are born but once."

"You must return to Bimahl, the sacred pod which is destined to open. Your children will arise from Bimahl and none but you and yours will shall have domain there."

Bimahl, the sacred pod. Trypova embraced her friend, and departed upon her boat. Bimahl resides in the center of the Great Valley. A faint glow radiated from it that guides travelers along the way. Trypova was nervous, as the Great Dam of the Two Worlds stood before her. The River Songwum could not flow passed this Dam, and travelers had to venture through the realms of Trozin and Fenlane once on the other side. She girded herself with her love for Aych Twow, and entered the Nexus of Lightning. The sky stormed constantly in this kingdom. Trozin's song of creation echoed throughout the land as his mighty thunder shook the very sky. Trypova ventured for many days, and finally, she found Bimahl. It pulsed and hummed with energy. She knew at once that this was the birthplace of Gods. Bravely, she strode up to it, and placed a silken hand upon it's smooth, egg shaped surface. Her eyes rolled in the back of her head, and she fell into Bimahl.

Trozin heard a new sound, one that he didn't make. He turned his mighty brow to gaze into the valley. From Bimahl, which only he and those he trusted knew about, a vibration swept over the entire universe. He gazed in awe as Bimahl opened, and a form rose out. So radiant was this form, that even Trozin's lightning paled in comparison. With flowing robes of purest white, and skin of purest white, and eyes of purest white the figure rose into the air. Throughout the entire universe, the Shalz turned to gaze upon the Sun, and their hearts were filled with a joy that they never knew before.

"Srodin is the name you may call me, my True Name shall be known only to my Mother and Father. My mother still lays pregnant, but I have much to do."

Srodin, the Sun itself, rose from Bimahl and lifted the entire world off of his father's aching shoulders. The Shalz beheld visions of wondrous glory that only the Gods had seen before. So powerful was he that even mighty Adralin bent a knee. For half a day did he hold sway over the Universe.

Back at Bimahl, a second form rose. Trozin turned his mighty brow and beheld a sight that only he could withstand in it's full glory. A figure of purest black, with robes of purest black, and eyes of purest black rose from Bimahl. So dark it was around her, even Trozin's lightning barely illuminated her form.
The figure rose, and said:

"I am Melatai, sister of Srodin. Though my mother lays exhausted from birth, I have much to do."

She rose up to her brother, and laid a hand upon his shoulder. She whispered in his ear, and he embraced her. She kissed his radiant forehead, and let him fall. The Shalz were bewildered. The Sun, the glorious Sun, had ceased to shine. In it's place, his sister stood. The Shalz soon forgot the Sun, as Melatai's silken fingers worked the pain and suffering from their tired forms. Her subtle whispers sent them to sleep, something which they hadn't experienced before. She smiled softly upon the sleeping land, and that smile can be seen as the Crescent Moon.

Neuropaganism: Neurotransmitters and other Biochemicals as the Divine

Biochemical Anthropomorphism is the theory that postulates observation of human behavior during stages of biochemical intoxication gives rise to the behaviors, abilities, and attitudes of so-called Gods and Goddesses. For example, the worship of the Sun God is carried out in such a way as to bring about Serotonin overload; and the resulting behavior is then attributed to the God or Goddess being "invoked". With this theory, I was able to get past Archetypal thinking and deal more directly with the apparent biological origins of magical entities. Avoiding archetypes allowed me to approach working with these chemicals in a much more personal way than with the Jungian or pseudo-Jungian concepts permitted.

Once I had formulated this theory, I needed a pantheon to test it out on. Luckily for me, the Egyptian pantheon provided a fertile garden from which to feast. Not only have some recordings of their festival and ritual practices survived, but the mythological tales lend themselves to an easy interpretation into the biochemical anthropomorphic paradigm.

Ra, and the plethora of solar gods that are cognate with him, obviously represent Serotonin. High levels of Serotonin are found in the Alpha personality type. High Serotonin levels have also been linked to a great deal of self control, elevated moods, and critical thinking. This certainly paints the picture of a King. Visualizations, mantras, and meditations on the sun fires associative neurons that trigger Serotonin production, not to mention direct exposure to sunlight which was certainly part of his cult. One cannot help but feel powerful when surrounded by Solar energy because of the Serotonin flooding our bodies.

Horus and Set, the warring family members, are Noradrenaline and Adrenaline respectively. Both dieties are associated with war and rage. Both deities are boisterous and strong. Horus the Avenger and Set the Defender represent the Adrenal flood that washes through us when we are wronged. Set, as slayer of Apep and defender of Ra, is the Rage that tells us to turn around and slay the monster that is chasing us. Horus is the Avenger that tells us when we have been wronged, and to confront those who have wronged us. These are all reactions of the Noradrenaline and Adrenaline overload. One does not have to be conscious to be in this state. The body reacts, and the mind (Solar Barge) is protected. The description of Set is also of note. He is said to have pale skin and the strongest of the Gods. High levels of Adrenaline cause blood to be redirected away from the skin and into skeletal muscles. Breath deepens, the eyes dilate, and you make start shaking. Stories of mothers flipping cars, people ripping doors off of their hinges, or tearing arms off during fights while under Adrenaline intoxication lend themselves to supporting Set, the mightiest of the Gods, as Adrenaline.

The worship of Bast lends itself to producing high levels of Dopamine. Herodotus, *Histories Book II* provides an excellent description of the Her festivities.

When the people are on their way to Bubastis, they go by river, a great number in every boat, men and women together. Some of the women make a noise with rattles, others play flutes all the way, while the rest of the women, and the men, sing and clap their hands. As they travel by river to Bubastis, whenever they come near any other town they bring their boat near the bank; then some of the women do as I have said, while some shout mockery of the women of the town; others dance, and others stand up and lift their skirts. They do this whenever they come alongside any riverside town. But when they have reached Bubastis, they make a festival with great sacrifices, and more wine is drunk at this feast than in the whole year besides. It is customary for men and women (but not children) to assemble there to the number of seven hundred thousand, as the people of the place say. (2000, p. 60)

Orgies, music, intoxication, etc all lend themselves to producing an obviously high amount of desire and pleasure; and these are the trademarks of Dopamine. Other considerations are Thoth/ Aceytlcholine, Apep/ Cortisol, and Isis/ Tryptophan.

Utilization

There are a few ways to utilze the this particular paradigm in conjunction with existing ones. You may want to use it as a stand alone system. If you primarily work from the Sprit model (i.e, Gods, Goddesses, Fae, etc) then adopting the idea that biochemicals are the interfaces in which the divine communicates to and through us may yield more powerful invocations / pathworkings. Knowing which mundane chemical reactions are going to occur during an invocation may allow you to better construct the working. If you work from the Energy model (chi, prana, etc.), then the metabolic process these chemicals trigger in the body can be viewed as the transfer of “energy” from one place to the other. The biochemicals could also be viewed as the organic interface of "energy" that allows the physical body to change along with the Energetic body. Also, the production and uptake sites of these chemicals within the body can be viewed as a system of Chakras that can be stimulated for their unique effects.

Everyone's biochemical makeup is different, and accordingly their biosorcery be different. Some may encounter Serotonin as a brilliant white ball of light, others as a radiant youth. Invocations, likewise, are highly personalized in this paradigm. What triggers Dopamine in some will trigger Adrenaline in others. Personal experimentation will yield entire Pantheons, each unique to you, for you to interface with and explore.

Appendix C Bibliography

Herodotus. (2000). *The histories of Herodotus of Hallicarnassus*. George Rawlinson (trans.). Ames: Omphalokepsis

Appendix D:
Kink Magic

By Taylor Ellwood and Lupa

Recently kink magic has become a new field of magical practice, wherein the concepts of shamanic journeying and BDSM are merged so that the pain and pleasure, dominance and submission of BDSM are used to create an altered state of mind. In this trance, a person's psychological issues can be explored and the energetic blockages worked through. A brief explanation of the theory behind kink magic is as follows,

> In the realm of theory this is manifest in the two poles of the sources of power in Sado-Shamanism: the physiological and semiotic or symbolic. The physiological pole is focused on the actual physical, somatic (body-centered), chemical processes, alterations and manipulations which are caused to occur in the participants. This pole of the theory underscores somatic mechanism as the production of endorphins through painful stimuli, the physiological effects of prolonged physical stress and so on...In this world [the semiotic pole], quite to the contrary of the physiological world, every individual system is in some way different and unique. (Dawn & Flowers 2001, p. 27-28).

It is our experience that while the physiological pole can be predictable to some degree, the semiotic pole, which deals with symbolic reality, will change and shift as the person undergoes different experiences. If the opener (top/dominant/master) is attuned to the initiate this is not an issue, but if not, then the opener may not have such an easy time leading the initiate (bottom/submissive/slave) into altered states of consciousness

Many magicians spend years working on their psychological flaws and issues, digging deep into their pasts and dredging up frightening beings from their own personal Abyss. Often this involves a solitary trek into the layers of consciousness, braving the inner trials and tribulations of self-evolution. Sometimes, though, this journey cannot be undertaken alone; a guide is needed.

Guided meditation is a popular method of journeying inward in magical practice today. One person (or more) speaks, drums, acts or otherwise creates an environment conducive to another person(s)

being able to visualize an entryway into the Self in order to make appropriate changes through symbolism and rite. It can be a very calm affair involving soothing music and soft words, or it can be a wild orgiastic trance-dance that violently throws all participants into a frenzied spiral down the tunnel to the personal Otherworld. It all depends on whether the participants prefer inhibitory or excitatory forms of trance.

BDSM (bondage/discipline/sadism/masochism) is a dynamic between two or more people that involves any/or/each of the following: bondage and restriction, application of pain, psychological humiliation, controlled exchanges of power, roleplaying, and fetishes. It may or may not be sexual, depending on the nature of the relationships of all participants involved. While it is generally limited to certain environments—the bedroom, for example—some people do extend the BDSM dynamic to everyday life to a mutually-agreed-upon boundary.

Generally speaking the BDSM relationship is divided into two primary roles. The dominant/top/master is the person who symbolically takes control of the situation. The submissive/bottom/slave is the one who symbolically sacrifices hir control. The method by which the power exchange takes place varies widely. It may be a mild as teasing the other person to a level of slight discomfort, or it may involve an all-out, drag-down wrestling match in which the dominant sooner or later gains the upper hand. In some cases the initiate automatically surrenders hir power without a struggle. While some people prefer one role or the other, many are switches—those able to switch back and forth between roles. In a relationship between two switches the balance of power during a single scene may change hands very quickly, fluidly and, to all appearances, almost undetectably. In order to keep the dynamic within the agreed-upon boundaries, a safe word is employed. If spoken by either participant the play ends and both/all stop and discuss the situation before going on or stopping for good.

Both magic and BDSM are ideally safe, sane and consensual, to borrow a term from the latter community. Safe is obvious—the physical forms of the participants must not be harmed. This is not the same as hurting someone in BDSM play. Hurt is before the safe word is used; harm is after. Sane involves the safety of the mind; it is incredibly easy for either participant to negatively mindfuck the other to the point where long-term psychological damage is done. Consent is a another no-brainer; if all parties do not willingly consent to all actions then someone's going to be liable for legal and other repercussions of assault, sexual and otherwise. Because of these three elements in both magic and BDSM, it is required that all participants trust each other implicitly.

Any tool can be used for constructive or destructive purposes. Humans have long misused pain and punishment to further their own bad conditioning by turning them on other humans for purposes of destruction. Our purpose here is to explore the constructive rather than destructive uses.

For example, let's look at the overlying dogma of the Catholic church. For centuries this religious body has threatened bad behavior with hellfire and damnation in the afterlife and often retribution in this life. The Inquisition was a primary example; those caught in its web were often no more than political prisoners who had done no true wrong, and they were subjected to horrific tortures in order to expiate their sins (and capture other sinners.) This was often justified by the excuse that the flames of Hell would be much, much worse than the burning at the stake of this life.

Of course, there were probably few Inquisitors who truly believed they were helping to purify their fellow human beings. No doubt there was no shortage of extreme sadists among that lot; given the frequency with which female (and sometimes male) prisoners were raped as a means of torture, the Inquisitors were not immune to the temptations of the flesh no matter how vile a manifestation thereof.

This attitude continues today. Children and adults alike cruelly taunt others of their kind supposedly to teach them a lesson about being socially abnormal in some way. It's obvious that the tormentors get a lot more pleasure than is warranted out of this, and very little rehabilitation occurs on the part of the target. The inhumane treatment of prisoners, too, is testament to our perception of punishment as being worthy only of "bad people" who are "beneath" their captors.

Yet in true rehabilitation the root cause is not to further destroy someone who is obviously already broken, but to raise them up to the level of their healthier peers. When punishment is applied in order to truly help the sufferer the goal is not to break hir and leave hir broken so that s/he is no longer functional enough to cause further problems, but instead to break and hir them in a healthier manner by their will.

Consent is exceptionally important in kink magic, as well as its base components BDSM and magic. If a person is forced into an altered state of reality that s/he is not ready for, the results will be counterproductive. In kink magic the initiate must indicate hir willingness to participate in the ritual and to have hir limits pushed. This is why there is also the safe word, a key that opens all locks no matter how deeply into the ritual the participants are. In our own dynamic we have taken each other to the very edges of our comfort zones, even further than we thought we could go, and the results were incredible. But much of this was due to the deep trust we have in each other, that we will protect each other in our journeys together.

In some indigenous cultures pain is used as a controlled method of altering the consciousness in order to create change within. This can be as mild as dancing the self into exhaustion, or may involve such ordeals as hanging the body from hooks imbedded in the pectoral muscles. The Sun Dance of certain American indigenous tribes, for example, combines long periods of dancing with mortification of the flesh. (Anonymous, August 22, 2005) In these cases the initiate is a fully willing and consenting participant who enters the ritual arena with the intent to grow.

In kink magic, the submissive is the penitent, the supplicant, the aware sinner seeking absolution—the initiate. The dominant is the hierophant, the confessor, the source of punishment and thereby redemption—the opener. The opener does not thrust any guilt upon the initiate except for that which is already there. The goal is to expiate the guilt along with the bad programming and leave the initiate free of those burdens. The opener is the keeper of pathways and gates, acting as a spirit guide and leading the initiate into new experiences and states of mind that can be used to overcome psychological programming and energetic blocks that otherwise hinder the person, "The magician makes a change in his or her internal universe and a corresponding change occurs in the outside world – with no logical or objective connection between the two events. This technique is also useful in making permanent changes in the mind or psyche of the magician – which is not as way as it would first appear to be" (Dawn & Flowers 2001, p. 2). BDSM is particularly useful for making these kinds of internal changes, because of the altered state of mind that the initiate is put into, wherein s/he is able to face long suppressed memories, emotions, or other issues that may need to be resolved. The sub space may be the only place where the initiate feels able to face such issues and because of that such a space is ideal for the work that is engaged by the opener and initiate.

In combining the two paradigms the central practical focus is attaining that altered states of consciousness necessary for the opener to guide the initiate into the personal Underworld. One way this is done is by using a form of drumming, as is commonly used in Shamanic workings, that helps to create a state of mind where the person's mind descends into hir psyche. This drumming can be done on a separate drum or even done on the initiate, using the body as an instrument. Usually the opener will create a steady rhythm that can be used to induce the altered state of mind. Lupa, for instance, has been able to reach a moderate state of relaxation through a massage (light application) with a deerskin flogger.

But this is just one method for doing this. We will admit we've not really worked with the above method as a couple, preferring a more spontaneous approach that nonetheless involves doing not only a lot of energy work and psychological play, but also knowing when and where to challenge a person's conventions of reality through just the right word or action, or even inaction. Also it is our thought that if you do take this approach you plan on working with your partner or partners for an extended period of time. One weekend will not do it. The reason is because you are entering into sacred territory and also a very intimate space, whether you are the opener or the initiate. In addition you must have a thorough understanding of each others' needs, wants and flaws. This provides material for the partnership to work with.

One of the primary uses for kink magic is healing. This is not contradictory. While gentleness and kindness can go a long way in correcting internal flaws and bad conditioning, there are times when a more violent method is chosen by the initiate in order to exorcise particularly stubborn demons. After all, a broken bone that has healed incorrectly must be re-broken to be properly set. In this way a poor circuit in the brain must be uprooted and rewired when simply cleaning the circuit board does no good. When the initiate gives hirself over to the opener(s), s/he is saying "Heal me. I consent to give my control over to you so that you may observe me, read me, tear me open and fix what's wrong. I may struggle as my fear prevails over my surrender, but be aware that I want your aid in fighting that fear and all it hides."

The role of the opener is to insure that this healing occurs in a manner that is beneficial for the initiate. At the same time, the act of entering sacred space does put the opener in a similar altered state of mind. S/he must maintain awareness of this state of mind while leading the initiate deeper and deeper into hir consciousness. Perhaps the best way to even start this kind of relationship is to go with what we call a soft top approach. A soft topping is the use of sensuality, the exploration of the initiate's body, in a manner that is designed to get to know the initiate. The goal of the first meeting isn't to do any overt pathworking or energy work (though this can happen). Rather it is meant to get to know the person intimately on not just the physical or emotional levels, but also the energetic levels. Soft topping will involve some power exchange and maybe a bit of roughness, but will more or less be an energetic meshing of the two people through sensuality, as well as learning the physical and mental triggers of both participants.

In our case, the first meeting did end up involving some pathworking along totemic lines. For Lupa, her primary totem, Wolf, tended to resist complete surrender into sub space. Taylor intuitively sensed that this energy was getting in the way of what he was trying to do. He switched from a wrestling, painful, hard topping, to a sudden massage, gentle, relaxing and at the same time putting Lupa's Wolf to rest, and calling up Fox, a more subtle, playful energy. As it would turn out, this proved to be very useful, as she became much more receptive.

At this point, it is important to note that while the common stereotype about BDSM is about inflicting pain, this is far from the full potential of what the scene can be about. Even a gentle touch, when applied at the right time and place, can be useful for topping a person. What is often misunderstood is the focus on pain, using pain to get a person to say hir safe word, as if that was the objective. In reality the goal should be to stretch hir boundaries and limits in a manner that still does feel safe to hir. Particularly for the healing work this is essential, because the goal is to help the initiate heal, not drive hir past hir limits and possibly cause more harm than good. Another point to consider is creativity in stretching the mind of the initiate. The same stimuli can become less provoking over time; we have found that variety not only keeps us from getting bored, but also keeps all the senses aware and on edge. Even we, the kinky, can get caught up in routines.

As with any ritual, ceremonial accoutrement can help support the illusion necessary to transport the participant into the necessary altered state. Some people in both magic and BDSM are fond of lavish environments, complete with stimuli for all the senses. Others need only a few items to trigger the start of the journey. For example, we use almost no physical tools whatsoever. Our bodies are the primary tools in our practice. If we do bring in extraneous items it's for a specific purpose and a rare occurrence at that.

The tools don't necessarily have to focus solely on the initiate, either. If the initiate has an emotional connection to the opener, the opener can bind the initiate and force the initiate to watch as s/he uses the tool on hirself. As an example, when Taylor introduced Lupa to knife play, one of the things he did involved using his knives on himself and making her watch. This forced Lupa into a state of helplessness and vulnerability because she could not even stop the opener from hurting himself. Needless to say it was not a physical pain that was inflicted on her, but a psychological pain.

Often the most effective scenes don't involve tools at all. At one point Lupa, while preparing to train to be an opener, asked for a break as an initiate (but did not use her safe word which would have meant stopping the play). Taylor agreed, only to pretend to leave. This put Lupa, already deep in sub space, into a state of near paralysis due to an unexpected welling-up of her own abandonment issues. Taylor only stepped out the door for a moment and ended up coming back. Gently through energy work and talk he led her back to a state of mind where she was able to process what had happened. Undergoing that experience fully gave her an idea of what it would be like to have someone walk out on her and leave her helpless, an exploration of a fear that had hindered her for years. It also served as a reminder to us both of where certain boundaries were being stretched close to the breaking point. Needless to say such a deep experience was not only an initiation into BDSM and the potential dangers that can occur, but was also an initiation into the responsibility of the opener to the initiate, something we feel every potential opener needs to go through before topping someone.

The important thing to remember for magical purposes is that creativity and spontaneity in kink magic are far more important than just tying someone up and flogging hir to a bloody mess. By using the knife on himself, Taylor got a far more powerful reaction out of Lupa than if he'd used the knife on her. And by pretending to leave, he was able to bind her with no physical restraints whatsoever. The power dynamic was in place that he was the top, but he didn't need to physically hurt or restrain her to make her feel helpless and consequently put her into a state of mind she'd never experienced before.

Another important aspect of kink magic is the energy work. This energy work occurs partially through the arousal that is generated in each partner, "The higher the level of arousal or excitement, the more sexual energy the magician will have to work with…The build-up and release of energy, in sexual orgasm for example, is a powerful and magically useful phenomenon. But on another more subtle level this sensation is interpreted *symbolically* by the psyche – and it is thought of as a magical substance as malleable as the link in the formation of magical sigils" (Dawn & Flowers 2001, p. 3). The arousal of energy is one part of the equation involving, as it does, what pleases the person not only physically, but also emotionally, mentally, and even spiritually. When a person feels a delightful tingle on the body, it's not a just a physical sensation, but also an energetic surge, with the energy reacting and responding to the touch of the opener. When the opener opens an initiate, s/he opens the energetic gate and pathways of that person. At the same time an empathic bond can be formed between the opener and the initiate: "If the magically forged empathetic bond has been formed by the dominants and they are guided by that link in the application of every technique, they will be able to work successfully and safely with almost all techniques. *Stay in touch with your submissive*" (Dawn & Flowers 2001, p. 49). This empathic bond goes both ways and if the people involved are switches, it can be used by all involved depending on how the power dynamic shifts. As an example, through our play and pathworking, we came to share an empathic bond. We could read each other like open books. While the majority of the time Taylor is the opener of the relationship, sometimes Lupa takes that role and as such can also read Taylor and is guided intuitively toward using whatever is needed to bring him to a state of mind that can be used for healing work or sexual alchemy. However, the initiate should also be able to maintain enough of a connection to the opener to tell if there's something wrong with hir; after all, top space can be quite vulnerable as well and lead the opener into uncharted territory in hir own self.

But there is another key to this dynamic of energy work beyond the arousal and even beyond the empathic bond. This other key is the skill the opener has with energy work at peeling open the initiate. Energy work is essentially the ability to use one's chi, prana, or energy in a variety of methods that can heal or hurt. A very gifted opener can even use the initiate's energy or other frequencies of energy such as elemental or deity's energies. These forms of energy can be used to apply a variety of sensations to a person.

As an example, Taylor concentrated on accumulated fire elemental energy at the tip of his finger, using Franz Bardon's elemental accumulation theories found in *Initiation into Hermetics*. He then burned Lupa with this energy, causing her to feel a hot searing pain with just the touch of his finger on her arm. But energy work can be more subtle than that, right down to even psychically drawing energy from the initiate and then putting that energy back in or cutting through a person's defenses to the energetic core. At one point, Lupa in the role of opener cut Taylor open symbolically, freeing up a large mass of energy that can be best described as the essence of his pain. The result was an altered state of mind for Taylor, where he was able to re-experience memories that he'd suppressed as well as giving grief to those emotions. The experience was so intense that he almost threw up. When energy work is added to the mix, it makes the reactions that much stronger.

Again, we cannot stress enough that in working with kink magic, all of the precautions standard to both magic and BDSM must be taken. In addition, all participants MUST know each other well—this is not an experiment to be done with strangers. Give each other some time to learn about each other in all ways before embarking on this journey. If you cannot trust your partner(s) 100%, regardless of whether you are the opener or the initiate, DO NOT put yourself into a potentially unsafe situation!

Caution aside, kink magic is a method of magic and personal exploration that shifts the self on many levels at once. It is a powerful tool, and the results of its application are by far some of the most effective we've encountered. (It's quite a bit of fun, too, we might add!)

Appendix E:
Energy Work from the Other Side

by Lupa

There's plenty of information about being on the giving end of energy work, but what's it like on the other end? How does it feel to be the target of all this magic?

Well, it's kinda tingly and warm…but there's a lot more to it.

Taylor has been doing regular healing work on me since Autumn 2005. At the time I was employed reading utility meters. I walked four to ten miles a day, five to six days a week. It was hell on my body, especially my legs. In addition, I was malnourished from a bout with anorexia, and my body was cannibalizing my connective tissues, which added to my pain. In short, I was a mess.

Once Taylor and I started seeing each other on a regular basis, he convinced me to let him try healing my injuries as I had to stay in the job until the end of February. I'd never really had much work done to me, and so I was a little hesitant. Still, I was willing to give it a try at that point. Half a year later and I'm feeling 110% better.

It amazes me how I perceive what's going on every time he heals me. The energy surrounding the injuries is always stagnant when he starts his work; it simply doesn't flow. That's a large part of the problem right there. Energy is similar to blood in that it needs to flow to be able to heal the body, to cycle the impurities out of the system and introduce fresh, healthy energy. So the first step is to break up that stagnation.

He always starts by massaging my legs and feet (which, of course, feels wonderful, unless he hits a bad knot in the muscles). This begins to break down the clogged energy on the surface, at which point he's able to reach down deeper. This part always hurts like a motherfucker. Yes, healing energy can feel all tingly and warm—but sometimes it doesn't. That's especially true with healing below the surface. Putting a bandage on a wound feels a lot different from pouring antiseptic on it and stitching it shut. It helps some if I relax, but the healing is deep enough that it always hurts to a degree.

Part of it is because of what's going on. The stress injuries to my tendons and ligaments in particular appears in my mind's eye as black, rubbery cords wrapped tightly around the tissues. I've tried removing them myself before—whatever tiny piece I can grasp may break off, but the rest just snaps back into place. Taylor has a lot more practice with energy work than I do, so it seems effortless when he draws the cords up out of my body with a spiraling motion of his hand, wrapping them around his fingers, then pulling them out. That's the part that hurts. Not physically, of course, but there's still a part of the brain that registers pain at having these things removed from such a deep part of my flesh, even if it is strictly energetic. Energy affects people a lot more than most folks realize.

It amazes me to no ends that my legs actually feel looser and not as cramped after this point, like there's more space between the fibers. Then comes the nice part, when Taylor introduces healthy energy to my system. It always feels like cool water flowing into my own energy—which, incidentally enough is very similar to how I envision Reiki energy when I'm using it.

These days my legs aren't so much the problem as my hands and wrists because of the typing. I can always tell the difference between days with and without healing. The days without are a lot less comfortable. Perhaps it's psychosomatic, but if our ritual helps me to feel better, then that's all that matters.

Healing isn't the only way Taylor's used energy. We've used it in our bedroom as well. There are times when he tops me that he'll pull energy from me to weaken me—a more subtle form of bondage. It's not unlike psychic vampirism, only he's not feeding on me so much as simply taking the energy away. He doesn't need it—it's just part of the play.

That in and of itself is a peculiar experience, though not an unpleasant one. There's something alluring, when I bottom, about being made utterly helpless. Energy drainage is a particularly intimate way of doing so. It's also psychologically effective—there are no visible bonds holding me, and yet I'm noticeably weakened. It's not just suggestion, either. He never warns me beforehand. One minute I'll be putting up a fierce fight, and the next, for no apparent reason, I'll be limp and complacent. I don't normally play that way. I take a lot of....shall we say...convincing, before I'll even stop fighting physically—and then there's even more work to do before I'll give in entirely. Going from (consensual) resistance to complete surrender in 60 seconds is not my style.

And yet that's what happens with energy work. It's not just a physical drain, but also psychological/ emotional/etc. After a certain point, there's just no resistance left. Again, it's not psychic vampirism in the traditional sense, but it's reminiscent of vampiric lore equating vampirism with seduction. Draining the victim to make hir more willing and complacent.

It's a bit amusing to look back on the early days of our relationship. I'd been entirely stuck in the "Magic is psychology" viewpoint I came across so much in Chaos magic. Being able to experience energy as its own force in a number of ways showed me that it's not just all in my head. There's something there, and the energy model is as good as any other to explain it.

Appendix F:
Environment Friendly Products

by Taylor and Lupa

In this Appendix we're going to offer a list of environmentally friendly products and companies you might want to shop with. In our opinion, internal alchemy is facilitated by what you put into your body, and into the environment around you. The more we practice sustainable and environmentally friendly processes the better off we are, in terms of taking care of ourselves and the miraculous being we inhabit, Earth.

Depending on where you live, these may be easy to find, especially if you live in more progressive cities. Whole Foods and other stores marketed towards progressive consumerism are good places to start, as are independent co-ops. Type "recycled paper products" and similar phrases into any search engine and you will find a plethora of websites that sell Earth-friendly products.

These are just a few suggestions; type in "earth-friendly products" in your search engine and you'll be rewarded with numerous links to businesses providing just about anything you can think of—clothing, office products, food—that are all environmentally responsible.

Cleaning Products:

- Bon Ami: For sinks and tubs, leaves a soapy residue, biodegradable.
- Simple Green: Effective for cleaning anything and usually only requires a small amount. It's biodegradable, so it won't harm the environment.
- Vinegar and water: any type of cooking vinegar will work, mixed 50-50 with water.
- Baking soda: An excellent abrasive for tougher cleaning.
- Boiling water: Pour down clogged drains to help clear them out, or for periodic cleaning.

Paper Products and Other Disposables:

- Seventh Generation toilet paper and paper towels or Earth First paper towels and toilet papers. The paper is 100% recycled,

80% post consumer content. Check your local grocery store for this or other brands of recycled items.

- http://www.treecycle.com/ has everything from printer paper and envelopes to gift bags and boxes to cups and trays, all made of recycled paper, along with other Earth-friendly products.
- If you need to print out something informal that will just get discarded later, such as directions to a place, use the back side of a used sheet of paper.
- Recycle any paper you throw out, even if it's just a receipt. The same goes for plastics, aluminum, and cardboard.
- Reduce your consumption of disposables. Use regular hand towels instead of paper towels, and carry your groceries in canvas bags. If you have to get plastic grocery bags, use them as small trash can liners.

Food Products:

Even if you see the label organic on food, make sure you check the ingredients. Occasionally a product will say organic but have ingredients that aren't organic.

- Free range meat is meat that was not raised in a stock yard, and specific to poultry, birds not raised in cages. Free range meat is also often hormone free and the animals are fed a vegetarian diet, as opposed to having meat mixed into their meals.
- Organic vegetables and fruit aren't sprayed with chemical pesticides. In addition, the fertilizer used doesn't contain chemicals. Organic farmers must maintain certain standards of growth and maintenance of their lands for a number of years before being certified organic, and must stay at that level to keep the certification.

Bibliography

Andreas Steve, & Faulkner Charles.
(1994). *NLP: The New Technology of Achievement*. New York: Harpercollins Publisher.

Andrews, Ted.
(2000). *How to See and Read the Aura*. St. Paul: Llewellyn Publications, Inc.

Andrews, Ted.
(1993). *Enchantments of the Faerie Realm: Communicate with Nature Spirits & Elementals*. St. Paul: Llewellyn Publications, Inc.

Anonymous.
(2005, August 22) Sun dance.Wikipedia. Retrieved on September 19, 2005 From: http://en.wikipedia.org/wiki/Sun_Dance

Anonymous.
Created August 3, 2000 *How is Snake antivenom made?* Accessed August 17, 2006. From: http://ask.yahoo.com/ask/20000803.html.

Anonymous.
Last updated August 14 2006 Mitochondrian. Accessed August 21, 2006 From: http://en.wikipedia.org/wiki/Mitochondria

Anonymous.
(1996).*Thee psychick youth manifesto*. New York: Sine Nomine.

Albertus, Frater.
(1974). *Alchemists Handbook.* York Beach: Weiser Books.

Bardon, Franz.
(2001). *Initiation into Hermetics*. Salt Lake City: Merkur Publishing, Inc.

Belanger, Michelle.
(2004). *The psychic vampire codex: A manual of magick and energy work*. York Beach: Red Wheel/Weiser LLC.

Blackmore, Susan
(1999). *The meme machine*. New York: Oxford University Press.

Bonewits, Isaac.
(1989). *Real magic*. York Beach: Red Wheel/Weiser LLC.

Brame, William and Gloria Brame
(1993). *Different Loving: A Complete Exploration of the World of Sexual Dominance and Submission.* New York: Villard.

Brennan, Barbara Ann.
(1988). *Hands of light: A guide to healing through the human energy body*. New York: Bantam Books.
Brennan, Barbara Ann.
(1993). *Light emerging: The journey of personal healing*. New York: Bantam Books.
Bruce, Robert.
(1999). *Astral dynamics: A new approach to out-of-body experience*. Charlotteville: Hampton Roads Publishing Co., Inc.
Carrington, Hereward & Muldoon, Sylvan.
(1973)*The projection of the astral body*. York Beach: Samuel Weiser, Inc.
Carroll, Peter.
(1987). *Liber null & psychonaut: An introduction to chaos magic*. York Beach: Samuel Weiser, Inc.
Ceilede.
(2005). Liber chromatia: An exploration of the eight selves. Pp. 20-22. *Konton 2.1*.
Chia, Mantak.
(1983). *Awaken healing energy through the Tao*. Santa Fe: Aurora Press.
Chia, Mantak & Winn, Michael.
(1984). *Taoist secrets of love: Cultivating male sexual energy*. Santa Fe: Aurora Press.
Chia, Mantak, & Abrams, Douglas.
(1996). *The multi-orgasmic man*. San Francisco, Harper Collins Publishers.
Cleary, Thomas.
(1996). Introduction. In Thomas Cleary (trans.). pp. 9-32. *The Taoist classics, V. 2*. Boston: Shambala.
Davis, Susan.
(2003). *Mom's Musings: Energy and Balance: the chakras*. Unpublished.
Dawkins, Richard.
(1989). *The selfish gene*. New York: Oxford University Press.
Dawkins, Richard.
(1999). *The extended phenotype: The long reach of the gene*. New York: Oxford University Press.

Dawn, Crystal, & Flowers, Stephen.
(2001). *Carnal alchemy: A Sado-magical Exploration of Pleasure, Pain, and Self-transformation*. Smithville: Runa-Raven Press.
Dennett, D.
(1991). *Consciousness explained*. Boston: Little Brown.
Dennett, D.
(1995). *Darwin's dangerous idea*. Boston: Little Brown.
Distin, Kate.
(2005). *The selfish meme*. Cambridge: Cambridge University Press.
Dunn, Patrick.
(2005). *Postmodern magic: The art of magic in the information age*. St. Paul: Llewellyn Publications, Inc.
Evola, Julius.
(1992). *The Yoga of Power: Tantra, shakti, and the secret way*. Rochester: Inner Traditions International.
Farrell, Nick
(2004). *Magical pathworking: Techniques of active imagination*. St. Paul: Llewellyn Publications.
Frantzis, B. K.
(2001a). *Relaxing into your being: Breathing, chi, & dissolving the ego*. Berkeley: North Atlantic Books.
Frantzis, B. K.
(2001b). *The great stillness: Body awareness, moving meditation & sexual chi gung*. Berkeley: North Atlantic Books.
Gallegos, Eligio Stephen.
(1987). *The personal totem pole: Animal imagery, the chakras and psychotherapy*. Santa Fe: Moon Bear Press.
Garbie, Scott.
(2005). *Learning to wiggle your ears: A golden road to health magick*. Pp. 30-31.Konton 2.1.
Grant, G.
(1990). *Memetic lexicon*. Retrieved from http://pespmcl.vub.ac.be/memes.html.
Gray, William G.
(1980). *Magical ritual methods*. York Beach: Samuel Weiser, Inc.
Hine, Phil.
(1993). *Prime chaos: Adventures in chaos magic*. Tempe: New Falcon Press.

Judith, Anodea.
(1996). *Eastern body western mind: Psychology and the chakra system as a path to the self.* Berkeley: Celestial Arts.
Judith, Anodea.
(1999) *Wheels of life: A user's guide to the chakras*. St. Paul: Llewellyn Publishing, Inc.
Junius, Manfred M.
(1993). *The practical handbook of plant alchemy*. Rochester: Healing Arts Press.
Kaldera, Raven
(2005). *The ethical psychic vampire*. New York: Xlibris corporation.
Keith, William H.
(2005). *The science of the craft: Modern realities in the ancient art of witchcraft*. New York: Citadel Press.
Kress, Gunther.
(2003). *Literacy in the media age*. New York: Routledge, Taylor, & Francis Group.
Leyborn, Su.
(2006). Have mind, will change. *Magick on the Edge: An Anthology of Experimental Magick.* Taylor Ellwood, Stafford: Immanion Press.
Louv, Jason.
(2006). A mutagenesis. In Jason Louv (ed.). Pp. 259-280. *Generation hex*. New York: The Disinformation Company, Ltd.
Lilly, John C.
(1968). *Programming the human Biocomputer*. Berkeley: Ronin
Lipton, Bruce.
(2005). *The biology of belief: Unleashing the power of consciousness, matter, and miracles.* Santa Rosa: Mountain of Love/Elite Books.
Lisiewski, Joseph C.
(2002). The alchemical teachings of Frater Albertus. Pp. 278-296. Undoing yourself with energized meditation and other devices. Tempe: New Falcon.
Lupa. (2005).
Riding the red tide: Menstrual magic and treasure of our women's blood. (pp. 17-19). *Sagewoman, 67.*
Lysebeth, Andre Van.
(1995). *Tantra: the cult of the feminine*. York Beach: Samuel Weiser, Inc.

Mace, Stephen.
(1984). *Stealing the fire from heaven*. Milford: Self-published.
Mace, Stephen.
(1996). *The subtle body*. *Addressing power:* Pp. 60-68;. Pp. 130-147 *Sixteen essays on magick and the politics it implies*. Milford: Self-published.
Mace, Stephen.
(1998). *The magick of Julian, Emperor of Rome*. Pp. 20-39. *Nemesis & other essays*. Milford: Self-published.
McLaren, Karla.
(1998). *Your aura and chakras: The owner's manual*. York Beach: Red Wheel/Weiser LLC
McTaggart, Lynne.
(2002). *The field: The quest for the secret force of the universe.* New York: Harper Collins Publisher.
Nan, Huai-Chin.
(1984).*Tao & longevity: Mind-body transformation. Trans. Wen Kuan Chu*. Boston: Weiser Books.
O'Connor, Joseph, & Seymour, John.
(2002). *Introducing NLP: Psychological skills for understanding and influencing people*. London: HarperCollins Publisher.
Odier, Daniel.
(1969). *The job: Interviews with William S. Burroughs*. New York: Penguin Books.
Packwood, R. Kirk.
(2004). *Memetic magic: Manipulation of the root social matrix and the fabric of reality*. Seattle: Jaguar Temple Press.
Penczak, Christopher.
(2004). *Magick of Reiki*. St. Paul: Llewellyn Publications, Inc.
Perry, Laura.
(2003). *The Wiccan wellness book: Natural healthcare for mind, body, and spirit*. Franklin Lakes: New Page Books.
Pickands, Marcia L.
(1997). *The psychic self-defense personal training manual.* York Beach: Samuel Weiser, Inc.
Po-Tuan, Chang.
(1996). *Understanding reality*. In Thomas Cleary (trans.). pp. 33-210. *The Taoist classics, V. 2*. Boston: Shambala.

Proto, Louis.
(1992). *Increase your energy: The science of smart living*. York Beach: Samuel Weiser, Inc.
Rabbit, Black.
(2005). Chaos chakras, symbiotes, neo-ki. Pp. 4-6. *Konton Magazine 2.3.*
Randolph, Pascal Beverly.
(1988). *Sexual Magic*. New York: Magickal Childe Publishing, Inc.
Restak, Richard M.
(1994). *Receptors*. New York: Bantam Books.
Schiappa, Edward.
(2003). *Defining reality: Definitions and the politics of meaning*. Carbondale: Southern Illinois University Press.
Seth.
(2005). *Blood magic*. New York: Universe, Inc.
Takeda M. Kobayashi M. Takayama M. Suzuki S.
Ishida T. Ohnuki K. Moriya T. Ohuchi N.
(2004). *Biophoton detection as a novel technique for cancer imaging*. Pp. 656-661. *Cancer Science. 95(8).*
Talbot, Michael.
(1991). *The holographic universe*. New York: HarperCollins Publishers Inc.
The Anti-Group Collective.
Meontological Research Recordings Teste Tones. Liner notes.
The Anti-Group Collective.
Psychophysicist. Liner notes.
Vitimus, Andrieh.
(2005) Pentilian versus bacteria X. (pp. 22-25). *Konton Magazine, 2.4.*
Willis, Jack.
(2002). *And other devices.* Pp. 260-277. *Undoing yourself with energized meditation and other devices.* Tempe: New Falcon.
Wilson, Robert Anton.
(1983). *Prometheus rising*. Tempe: New Falcon.
Wilson, Robert Anton.
(1990). *Quantum psychology: How brain software programs you and your world*. Tempe: New Falcon.

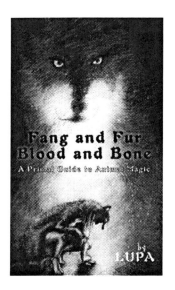

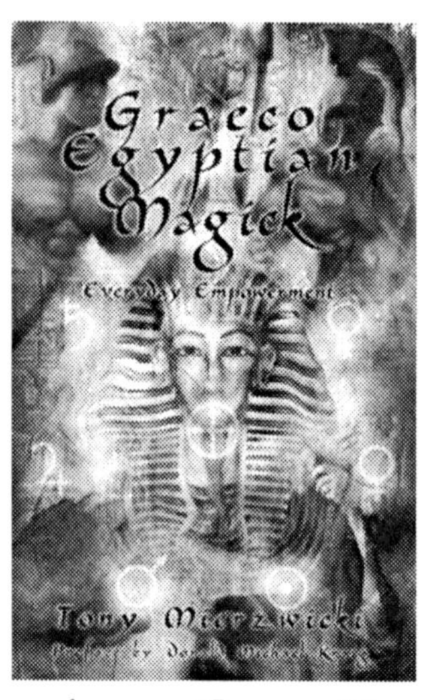

Tony Mierzwicki & Megalithica bring Ancient Magick of Alexandria Egypt to todays world

A recreation of a planetary system of self-initiation using authentic Graeco-Egyptian Magick, as practiced in Egypt during the first five centuries C.E. Including results of six years of workshops in the USA and Australia, this is a practical intermediate level text aimed at those who are serious about their spiritual development and already have grounding in basic spirituality, but beginners who carefully follow the instructions sequentialy should not be deterred

Megalithica books

Megalithica Books
An Imprint of Immanion Press
8 Rowley Grove,
Stafford, Staffordshire, ST17 9BJ
United Kingdom

orders@immanion-press com
http://www.immanion-press.com

£12.99UK/$21.99 USD
ISBN 1-9057-1303-7

CPSIA information can be obtained at www.ICGtesting.com
Printed in the USA
LVOW11s1526070815

449239LV00001B/9/P

9 781905 713066